CLARA Z[illegible]

Rosa Luxemburg's Views on the Russian Revolution

1922

First published by the Communist International

Republished in the United States
in 2017 by Red Star Publishers
www.RedStarPublishers

The cover picture shows Clara Zetkin (left)
and Rosa Luxemburg in 1910

Contents

Introduction to U.S. Edition

Rosa Luxemburg was one of the most important leaders of the revolutionary movement in Germany. From the beginning of World War I, she, Karl Liebknecht, Clara Zetkin and others in the Social Democratic Party (SPD), denounced it as an imperialist war, fought to overthrow the German imperial government and to withdraw the country from the war. Liebknecht, who was a member of the German Parliament, was the only member who voted against war credits. His slogan, later taken up by the German Communist Party (KPD), was: "Not a penny, not a man" for the imperialist war. The revolutionaries, including Luxemburg and Liebknecht, split from the social-democrats, forming the Spartacus League. Most were arrested for their opposition to the war and were only freed in the November Revolution in Germany in 1918 that put an end to the war and the monarchy. Luxemburg and Liebknecht led in the formation of the Communist Party of Germany (KPD) in late December, 1918.

The social-democratic leadership supported the war, although they later split into the Majority and the Independents (including Karl Kautsky). The Independents opposed the war in word, while refusing to break with the right-wing Majority. Luxemburg and Liebknecht were murdered on January 15, 1919, by soldiers in the army of the social-democratic government led by Chancellor Friedrich Ebert.

Many revolutionaries, who were bitterly attacked by the bourgeoisie and their reformist hangers-on during their lifetime, were praised by these same forces after their death. This is also true with Rosa Luxemburg. The modern social democrats, in Germany and elsewhere, have tried to uphold her as a "good revolutionary," although from the beginning of World War I she strongly opposed the main positions of German social democracy, which she called a "stinking corpse." Today there is even an organization called the "Rosa Luxemburg Stiftung [Foundation]", which functions in Germany affiliated to the social-democratic Left Party and also has an office in New York. Why do these forces claim to uphold Rosa Luxemburg?

Luxemburg's difference with Lenin and the Bolsheviks

In September, 1918, Luxemburg wrote a short pamphlet called: "The Russian Revolution" on the basis of partial accounts that she was able to receive in jail. The pamphlet contained a critical but friendly view of some tactics of the Bolshevik Revolution. The pamphlet was first printed in 1922 by Paul Levi, who had deserted the KPD and later returned to the SPD. He printed the pamphlet, against the specific request of other comrades of Luxemburg, in order to use her views against the Bolsheviks.* It was in response to the printing of her pamphlet that Clara Zetkin wrote this book. It is the continued misuse of Rosa Luxemburg's views on the Bolshevik Revolution that makes this book, written 95 years ago, still relevant today. It was published in German and Russian, but this is the first time it has been translated into English.

Zetkin was called the Grand Dame of German socialism. She was a good comrade-in-arms of both Luxemburg and Lenin, and a member of the KPD from its founding until her death in 1933. One of her best-known writings is "Reminiscences of Lenin."†

One of the main criticisms of the tactics of the Bolsheviks that Luxemburg made in her pamphlet concerned the question of democracy, and particularly the dispersal of the Russian Constituent Assembly shortly after the October Socialist Revolution in Russia in 1917. To understand this, we need to remind readers of what took place.

Before the overthrow of the Tsar in March of 1917, Lenin and the Bolsheviks put forward a program for a democratic revolution in Russia as the first stage toward socialist revolution. One demand during this stage was for a Constituent Assembly, basically a single-chamber parliament with representatives chosen by all adult citizens. After the overthrow of the Tsar, the bourgeois Provisional Government delayed in holding elections for the Assembly. By the

---

* Other renegades, including in the U.S., have also tried to use Luxemburg against the Bolsheviks. Bertram D. Wolfe, a one-time leader of the Communist Party USA, later became an open anti-communist who worked for the U.S. State Department. He republished Luxemburg's "The Russian Revolution" together with a 1904 pamphlet, "Organizational Questions of the Russian Social Democracy" (which he re-titled "Leninism or Marxism") with his own reactionary introduction.

† This is available in the Archive section of the Revolutionary Democracy web-site at:
www.revolutionarydemocracy.org/archive/zetlen.htm

time of the socialist revolution in November of 1917, a system of workers', peasants' and soldiers' soviets ("soviet" is the Russian word for "council") had been established throughout the country. The revolution had come to power under the slogans of "Peace, Bread and Land" and "All Power to the Soviets."

The Bolsheviks fulfilled their promise to organize elections for the Constituent Assembly, which were held in November of 1917. At that time, the revolutionary forces were concentrated in the major cities, particularly Petrograd and Moscow. The Bolsheviks received about 25% of the vote, exceeding by far the votes for the opportunist Menshevik party, which got just over 3%. This showed that the Bolsheviks had the support of the majority of the workers. The largest share of votes, 41%, went to the peasant-based Socialist-Revolutionaries (SRs). The Bolsheviks had taken over the agrarian program of the SRs, calling for and implementing the policy of "land to the tiller."

When the Constituent Assembly met in January of 1918, armed Bolshevik workers surrounded it. The Assembly was asked to recognize the transfer of power to the Soviets, and the measures of peace and confiscation of the land of the landlords that the Congress of Soviets had proclaimed. When the Assembly refused, the troops dispersed it. That is how, in Soviet Russia, bourgeois democracy was succeeded by proletarian democracy. (For further discussion of this, see Lenin's article: "The Constituent Assembly Elections and the Dictatorship of the Proletariat," *Collected Works*, Vol. 30, written in December of 1919.)*

Let us return to Rosa Luxemburg. After her release from prison, she, together with her comrades, immediately threw herself heart and soul into the fight for a working class revolution in Germany. The German workers and soldiers were solidly in favor of social-

---

* While this is not the place to discuss this in detail, it is important to distinguish Lenin's position from that of the modern-day opportunists and revisionists. Since Khrushchev's time, most revisionist forces have said that the working class could only take power when it has won over the majority of the population (under capitalism), as reflected by a majority in parliament. Lenin said that the working class could take power when it had won over the majority of the class-conscious proletariat, which would seize power and then use its position to win over the majority of the working people through struggle.

ism, but they were divided on how to bring it about. They had formed their own councils, mainly in Berlin but also in other cities and states in Germany. However, these councils were still under the leadership of the two social-democratic parties (as the Russian Soviets had been under the leadership of the opportunist Mensheviks and Social-Revolutionaries in the months after the February Revolution). The social-democrats, while giving some verbal support to the councils, spent most of their energy calling for elections to the National Assembly, the German equivalent of the Russian Constituent Assembly.

The Spartacus League, and later the KPD, clearly criticized this view in their newspaper, *Rote Fahne* (*Red Flag*). Clara Zetkin refers extensively to articles written by Luxemburg herself that pointed out that the National Assembly would only lead the revolution back along the path of bourgeois democracy, and that what was needed was "All Power to the Workers' and Soldiers; Councils."

Zetkin quotes from Luxemburg's article in *Rote Fahne* titled "They Even Threaten":

"Either one wants the National Assembly as a means to cheat the proletariat of its power by paralyzing its class energy and dissolving its ultimate socialist goals in a blue haze. Or one wants to put all the power in the hands of the proletariat, to develop the revolution that had already begun into a powerful class struggle for a socialist society and for that purpose to establish the political rule of the great mass of the working people, the dictatorship of the workers' and soldiers' councils. For or against socialism, against or for the National Assembly, there is no third choice."

Zetkin thus makes clear that, in the two months between Luxemburg's release from jail and her murder, her practice and her articles in *Rote Fahne* show that she had taken essentially the same position as Lenin and the Bolsheviks, in favor of the dictatorship of the proletariat and power to the workers' councils, as against bourgeois democracy and the National Assembly. She also states that Leo Jogiches, Luxemburg's comrade-in-arms and personal companion who was murdered in March of 1918, also stated that Luxemburg had changed her position on these questions and he was therefore against the posthumous publication of her pamphlet on the Russian Revolution.

On a similar question, Luxemburg had criticized the Bolsheviks' suppression of the press of the bourgeois and opportunist parties when they were clearly working to overthrow Soviet power. But once again Zetkin shows that Luxemburg supported similar actions by the German workers. In December of 1918, workers in Berlin had dispersed a counter-revolutionary demonstration and confiscated anti-Bolshevik leaflets. *Rote Fahne* commented on this:

"...the privilege of the ruling class to dissolve meetings of the proletariat by armed gendarmes, the privilege of Ebert and Wels to order protesters shot down, was interfered with by armed soldiers; the soldiers believed that freedom of the press did not include freedom to print slanders and they stopped the lies of the bourgeois press that had continued for four years."

There are other, secondary points that are brought out in this book. One concerns the agrarian question. In her September 1918 pamphlet, Luxemburg had criticized the Bolshevik policy of "land to the tiller," the breaking up of the estates of the landlords and distributing them among the peasants. She thought that this was a step away from socialism and would turn the peasants into small-property owners who would no longer defend the revolution.

Also, Luxemburg had long criticized the Bolshevik policy of Lenin and Stalin on the right of nations to self-determination. She thought that this would lead to the dismemberment of Russia, since what was needed was the strictest centralization.

The period of the Civil War and foreign intervention, after Luxemburg's death, showed that she was wrong on both these questions. During the Civil War, the whiteguard forces, wherever they seized power, took the land away from the peasants and returned it to the landlords. Furthermore, the imperialist powers, wherever they occupied the territories of the oppressed nationalities, made them into puppet states. In most of these territories the imperialist forces were overthrown by the revolutionary forces of these nationalities with the help of the Red Army. Thus, this period actually solidified the support of the peasants and the oppressed nationalities behind the Bolsheviks. This showed the correctness of Lenin's view that the working class must first seize power, and then win over the majority of the working people through its positions.

In his 1922 article "Notes of a Publicist" (*Collected Works*, Vol. 33), Lenin wrote: "Paul Levi now wants to get into the good graces of the bourgeoisie – and, *consequently*, of its agents, the Second and the Two-and-a-Half Internationals – by republishing precisely those writings of Rosa Luxemburg in which she was wrong.

We shall reply to this by quoting two lines from a good old Russian fable: 'Eagles may at times fly lower than hens, but hens can never rise to the height of eagles.' Rosa Luxemburg was mistaken... in what she wrote in prison in 1918 (she corrected most of these mistakes at the end of 1918 and the beginning of 1919 after she was released). But in spite of her mistakes she was – and remains for us – an eagle. And not only will Communists all over the world cherish her memory, but her biography and her *complete* works... will serve as useful manuals for training many generations of Communists all over the world."

This volume is the joint product of the efforts of Red Star, USA, and Revolutionary Democracy, India. As will be seen most of the translations have been carried out by colleagues in India. This shows the continued interest of scholars in the heritage of both Clara Zetkin and Rosa Luxemburg as well as their commitment to non-profit ventures. While individual translators are given at the end of each chapter, we are particularly grateful to Pranjali Bandhu who assisted us at every critical juncture in the translation of the book. Ms. Bandhu is also responsible for all the footnotes, except the ones marked C.Z. It is a great source of pleasure that this book is being published as part of the commemoration of the centenary of the Great October Socialist Revolution.

George Gruenthal
New York City
April, 2017

Foreword

The following work was already completed at the beginning of this year. It was written in profound indignation over Paul Levi's attempt to conceal the desertion that had begun from the camp of the proletarian revolution into the camp of reformism using the name of Rosa Luxemburg, reformism's persistent adversary and antagonist. A concurrence of unfavourable circumstances prevented me from immediately publishing my repudiation of such calumny.

Since then things have turned out just as anticipated at that time. Paul Levi has gone his own 'Way': from the Communist Party—which learning from bitter experiences is gradually day-by-day developing into a mass party in work and struggle—via the Independent Social Democratic Party and together with it back to Majority Social Democracy. Even before Gera and Nuremberg Paul Levi was all ready for the 'unification', just as Hilferding and Crispien were long prepared for it. Despite Gorlitz. In a very short historical period the social state of affairs has come to such a state of crisis that no kind of hybridization in the structures and relationship of revolution and reformism are possible. The time to make a choice has come.

The publisher of Rosa Luxemburg's 'posthumous pamphlet,' has made his choice. He has done himself in and continues to irrevocably do so with each clash of weapons in the historical battlefield of the class struggle between the proletariat and the bourgeoisie. Today he has ceased to be one, whose voice friends and foes alike await and take note of, in the same way as the orienting blare of a trumpet. Therefore, does it matter that he continues to vilify the Bolshevik party, without whose leadership the Russian Revolution would not be the "most powerful factor of the World War"! Does it make any sense then, to argue against his actions and his tendency?

I have asked myself this question and answered in the affirmative. The paper bullets that the midgets have shot at the giantess Russian Revolution on the occasion of the publication of the 'posthumous pamphlet' have fallen flat to the ground and got trampled upon. Extant are, however, the great historical problems broached by the revolution itself with each passing day. Rosa Luxemburg had grappled with them earnestly; others have only toyed with them literally.

These problems are not merely problems of the Russian Revolution, but also the proletarian revolution, whose thunder is approaching closer to us slowly but surely with each passing day. Who dares to predict how long it will take for them to stand before the proletariat of the not yet soviet States in their significance as burning practical questions of the day? Just as they stood for a short while before the working class in Germany until the German bourgeoisie with the help of reformist leaders was successful in strangling the immature, uncertainly advancing proletarian revolution. This will inevitably be different for different countries and will depend on the specific historically given circumstances, but the essence of the problems will remain the same. Because even if it grows and develops within 'national walls,' it cannot deny its origin: the bourgeois class society with its irreconcilable antagonisms and this is international.

Problems of the proletarian revolution constitute the content of my observations. I have not changed the polemical manner in which they were written months ago. In my opinion they contribute to bring out sharply the fundamental differences in historical standpoint between petty bourgeois democratic-reformist socialists and revolutionary communists. By no means do I make the claim to have 'settled' the controversial issues through this work. At the least, I hope it contributes to the understanding of the proletarian revolution in Russia and the politics of its leading party.

This work appears on the eve of the fifth anniversary of the establishment of Soviet Russia. I lay it down at the grave of Rosa Luxemburg, the unforgettable and irreplaceable one, who jubilantly welcomed the conquest of state authority by the Russian proletariat. A soul yearning for the light who finally sees the morning dawn after a long, dark night; an inquiring mind that strives to conquer the great, creative new; a strong will, which irresistibly urges forward. I dedicate this work to the heroic Russian proletariat and its faithful leaders. To that proletariat who covered with wounds, threatened by enemies, abandoned by the world proletariat, has to this day retained the inviolate courage to believe in its great historical task and in full awareness of international solidarity work and fight for its fulfilment. And to those leaders who measure up to the greatness of this proletariat.

Clara Zetkin
24 October, 1922

I

Rosa Luxemburg's Life Work

Its meaning and coherence / Its vilification by the reformist opponents due to Levi's 'posthumously published pamphlet' / History of the 'posthumously published pamphlet'

Far more than Rosa Luxemburg's tragic denouement alone, the reason why she, who was murdered by an officers' conspiracy—as brutal as it was cowardly—shall forever "remain enshrined in the great heart" of the liberation-yearning world proletariat of today, and the liberated humanity of tomorrow, is: the treasure of her lifetime's work dedicated to the liberation struggle of the exploited. It is a treasure of rare wealth; a lifetime's work of exceptional consistency, coherence and greatness. A heart glowing with revolutionary fervour meant concentrating an iron will and rich talents into a powerful force, focused at the one titanic goal, which the young Marx striving for knowledge had with a Faustian urge set for himself: to change the social world.

In the service of this goal Rosa Luxemburg remained throughout her life a devoted believer and visionary, a mediating high priestess, a questioning, researching and deliberating scholar, and a bold adventurous fighter who stormed forward, undaunted by obstacles, mocking dangers. Her exceptionally keen potent mind analysed social matters and proceedings not only with relentless logic, but also always comprehended them dialectically, in the course of their development. Drawing from a thorough and comprehensive knowledge of society past and present, stimulated and nourished by the most diverse fields of knowledge, she crystallized knowledge into path-breaking insights about the motivating forces, the direction and the conditions of social evolution of our times. Marx's historical materialism was not for Rosa Luxemburg the final prescript to gauge historical life, but it certainly did equip her with a sure-fire method to understand the history of life in its surging and descending variability, its strict laws, its colourful aura replete with meaning and meaninglessness.

The focal point of her endeavour to penetrate and master the colossal and ever growing body of knowledge, what was paramount in her ardent desire, her all-consuming activity, was the revolution: the revolution as the supreme expression of societal creative power; as the proud, highly visible summit of a rising and ebbing wave of new historical life. The truth-seeker wanted to be a shaper of reality. In her personality and in her life knowledge, will and action were so conjoined as to form an unbreakable whole.

Thus, in the pre-war period, undeterred by the revolutionary phraseology of German social democracy, Rosa Luxemburg could be the leader of the Opposition against the opportunistic practice of this party, and at the same time be one of the towering figures of the Second International, well-armed, proficient and well-versed in the fight against Bernsteinian reformism and revisionism of every variety and every nationality, as well as against all anarchist and pretentious anarchist whims and infantilism of the petty bourgeoisie professing to be revolutionary. The tenacious struggle for the realization of her childhood dream to awaken the Polish proletariat and lead it along with the workers of Russia, Germany and of all capitalist states to a revolutionary assault against the bourgeois order on the basis of a targeted class struggle in a firmly directed front allowed her to gain an early and clear appreciation of the problem of the international character of the fate of the proletarian classes in all its overriding importance. While carrying out the ideological and organisational groundwork of establishing Social Democracy in Poland and Lithuania she encountered relentless hostility from the nationalism and social patriotism of the PPS (Polish Socialist Party). In a series of brilliant confrontations she grappled with it, revealing it to be a dangerous form of opportunism.

Thus Rosa Luxemburg stood unrivalled, as the one called upon and chosen to reveal the imperialist character of the World War from its very beginning; to shred critically the glitteringly spun web of legends and historical distortions, with which the Scheidemanns and Davids of different nationalities, but with the same maxims of betrayal, had veiled it; to urge the masses of the exploited to set an example of their international solidarity by making the revolution into the supreme law of their actions. She was more than the nucleus of the initially tiny but then gradually growing comradeship in ideology and struggle that comprehended the World War as a prelude to the world revolution and fearlessly set out to mobilize the proletariat for it. She was its sacred glowing heart, its coherent brain, and its diamond-hard will. She acted upon her ideas unhesitatingly and without procrastination, undue vacillation or flurry. With steadfast devotion to the world revolution, Rosa Luxemburg fought in theory and practice relentlessly and mightily both the open traitors of the proletariat, who in the name of 'defence of the homeland' and other lies delivered the workers to the slaughterhouse of imperialism as well as the cowardly social patriotic impostors, who invoking party discipline and other 'realities,' tolerated the mass fraud and fled from the battle scene.

And again, Rosa Luxemburg, leading in the midst of the densest hail of bullets, sees as within reach, what had been historical perspective. The revolution was kindled with the conquest of political power by the workers and peasants in Russia under the determined leadership of the Bolsheviks and with the establishment of the dictatorship of the working people in a Soviet system. It seemed as though its blaze would tear across the globe at a roaring speed. Did not its fire signal flare up more and more? Military collapse of the Central Powers; evident breakdown of the capitalist economy in all countries; upheaval in the Austro-Hungarian Dual Monarchy; overthrow of the Imperial German Empire. Going by the level of economic development of Germany, and the significance, the political training and organisation, the sufferings of its proletariat, the assumption that the overthrow would result in a full-scale proletarian revolution, and that this would urge the workers of Western Europe to join in the struggle for liberation, was not an audacious fantasy.

Once again Rosa Luxemburg experiences that the proletarian masses of Germany did not measure up to the maturity of knowledge, will, and self-sacrifice expected in a revolutionary situation. They can be fooled afresh by leaders who are historically accustomed to bank upon bourgeois reforms, and whose fear of the power of the bourgeoisie is greater than their confidence in the revolutionary forces of the proletariat that need to be unleashed. The Ebert-Scheidemanns openly betray the proletariat, which is driven back from the battlefields of the revolution to the 'peace' of capitalist exploitation. The Haase-Dittmanns build the bulwark for these remarkably disgraceful deeds by retreating before the struggle for continuing the revolution. One fraud has thereby replaced another. Instead of the 'duty to defend the country' the masses are being preached the hope of 'democracy'. Of such a democracy as that of the bourgeois state, which exposed itself on 6 December 1918 as being a bloody class dictatorship of the bourgeoisie, when Wels, Berlin's social democratic city commandant, gave the order to open fire on the unarmed war cripples and unemployed demonstrators.

Liberated by the revolution from protective custody Rosa Luxemburg immediately takes on the fight against betrayal, confusion, weakness, indecision. She contends for the souls of the proletarians, for their revolutionary awakening and action against all the powers of the bourgeois world, all the influences of the social democratic parties that are hostile to the revolution or apprehensive of it. With a keen eye for the needs and conditions of the German Revolution—as the now next most important step of the world revolution—she tracks the non-revolutionary and counter-revolutionary aberrations and infidelities of the Ebert-Haase 'Council of People's Representatives' and later the brutal lackey services rendered by the Majority Social Democratic government purged of the Independents for the bourgeoisie. All such ringing slogans, all the glittering falsifications of concepts, by means of which the revolutionary will of the workers to act is emasculated, are relentlessly torn to pieces by Rosa Luxemburg. Her passionate conviction pulsates in the daily feverish struggle animated by her brilliant, versatile talents and her thorough knowledge. And just as the revolutions of the past were always a treasure trove of knowledge for her, so now her historical, political understanding and action are stimulated, empowered and encouraged by the achievements and influence of the proletarian revolution in Soviet Russia.

At the peak of her endeavour to forge ahead with the revolution Rosa Luxemburg falls, the victim of monarchist militarist murderers and their moral, political accomplices: the Ebert-Scheidemann government. She falls, stalked and surrounded by the hatred and the fear, the defamation and the insults of the bourgeoisie who were trembling for their safe-deposit vaults and violent rule, but also on the part of those leaders of the labour movement who were forcing the revolution into the straitjacket of a purely bourgeois-democratic upheaval or wanted to see it "in the non-threatening garb of a girl's school". Rosa Luxemburg's fine frame may have disappeared from the fray of the colliding classes, but her bold, insightful clear mind takes the lead in promoting the cause of the exploited and dispossessed of all countries so long as they have to fight against capitalism. For the splendid entity of that, what Rosa created and what she was, stands in front of the masses, like a huge block of Carrara marble. Not throughout smoothened and carved, but with edges, corners and bumps, shimmering white, continuously glowing, and with the strength for braving the rigours of the weather. This imperishable monument set by Rosa Luxemburg herself shows the masses where the rough, steep paths of the proletarian revolution differ from the gentle, flowery paths of bourgeois reform.

But what did we witness even before the third anniversary of the smashing of "the most brilliant brain among Marx's disciples"? The people of the *Vorwärts* walk all over the pure marble block of Rosa's life work, and write on it with hands stained with the blood of the Great War and of German revolutionaries: "How foolish of the officers of the Eden Hotel, that they murdered Rosa Luxemburg. If she had continued to live, she would have become ours, ready for choking the revolution and for the Stinnes coalition." Then the men of *Freiheit* show up and paint ruffled, blurred strokes on the block with trembling fingers, "Had Rosa Luxemburg not been intoxicated by the revolution, had she not carried an inverted image of the present social world and had she not unsteadily vacillated in her thinking, had she stayed on the ground of Marxism as theoretically constructed by Kautsky and Hilferding and as practised by Haase and Dittmann, she would have been ours."

Just think of it! The people of the same *Vorwärts*, which just a day before the murder of Rosa Luxemburg, had downright incited to such ignominy through the notorious verses of Zickler, whose poetic worthlessness was in concert with the worthlessness of sentiment. The men of the same *Freiheit* that in November and December 1918, in January 1919, exasperated by Rosa Luxemburg's sharp but objective reckoning with the USP shield-bearers of the counterrevolutionary Ebert-Scheidemann policy did not know to how reply to her convincing reasoning other than with distortions and insinuations, and furthermore by maligning the murdered woman with the calumny that she had fought her party opponents with 'poisoned weapons'. Now suddenly they all discover their admiration for the "woman with a high intellectual calibre", for the "sharpness of her mind," the "scientific character" of her historical thinking, and they appreciate "the legacy" she has left behind for the proletariat. They want to persuade the masses forcing their way up out of darkness and distress – and perhaps persuade themselves sincerely – that Rosa Luxemburg was one with them in the evaluation of the greatest, most significant event of our time: the Russian Revolution, or more specifically: in the assessment of the Bolshevik Party, the thinking brain, the daring will, the very well equipped arm of the

Russian Soviet Republic. Must it still be emphasized that this assessment has been translated into a one-sided, hateful condemnation of the policy, of the methods and means of the revolutionary struggle of the Party, under whose leadership the revolution in Russia has clearly and distinctly manifested its proletarian nature? Sickening, and leaving a bitter aftertaste! The bitterest fact, however, is that the impetus and appearance of justice for the frivolous game of the Stampfers und Hilferdings was given by the action of a man who was a close comrade of Rosa Luxemburg in the recent decisive years. The reformist leaders rely on the pamphlet that Paul Levi has published and introduced from the literary estate of Rosa Luxemburg: "The Russian Revolution: A Critical Appraisal."[*]

In a deeper sense, compared to many corpulent works, Rosa Luxemburg's brief and sometimes only sketchy piece of writing, illustrates a history of its own. Its gray background is her protective custody in Wroclaw sealing off the tempestuous stream of events and the means and possibilities to arrive at an understanding on the broadest possible objective basis. At its core is the concern about the Russian Revolution, of whose ramifications the far-sighted historical thinker was cognizant from the very beginning; it bears the ardent desire of the passionate revolutionary to actively intervene with brilliant criticism. In his "Foreword" the publisher has given an account about the emergence of the treatise. Rosa Luxemburg wrote it after a visit from Paul Levi in September 1918, to convince him— contrary to the opinion he held in those days— that a critical discussion by international communism about the policy of the Bolsheviks was necessary.

The publisher of the posthumous pamphlet is reticent about other matters of equal importance and interest: namely, whether Rosa Luxemburg had intended getting her work published later. Although she wrote to me in the summer of 1918 twice that she proposed to work with Franz Mehring on a scientific and critical attitude to the Bolshevik policy, although she informed me of her own then intended larger work, in her further correspondence about this matter she mentioned it as "accomplished", and later never returned to it. The whys and wherefores would be obvious to all who are familiar with Rosa Luxemburg's activities after the outbreak of the German revolution. This activity is characterized by positions

[*] Gesellschaft und Erziehung publishers, Berlin. [CZ]

on the problems of the Constituent Assembly, democracy, dictatorship, etc. which stand in contradiction to her earlier criticism of Bolshevik policy. Rosa Luxemburg had grappled her way to a changed historical evaluation.

That was the only reason—and in my opinion one to be respected—why Leo Jogiches was resolutely against the posthumous publication of the critique. Leo Jogiches was the critical conscience of Rosa Luxemburg all through his life, her closest and, above all, in every respect an equal-ranking comrade. He is the only person who had the right, morally and politically, so to speak, to decide as Rosa's executor. And whoever has had the good fortune of having known this rare man, known him in his generous, wonderful friendship and struggle alliance with Rosa Luxemburg, would well know that he would have never expressed an opinion in this matter, if he had not been convinced about acting in the spirit and according to the will of his friend. This was all known to Paul Levi; but with a negligent flick of the hand he has trampled over the will of the two illustrious deceased. The praise of bourgeois and even the social democratic 'anti-Bolsheviks' and their brazen demagogic exploitation of the posthumous pamphlet are unambiguous pointers to the fact that he cannot appeal to the 'superior right' of the revolution, of the international proletariat.

Paul Levi asserts point-blank: "Certain parties intended a fiery death for the pamphlet." These idle tales for good children, who should learn how to shudder, of course made the rounds of the papers, whose editorial staff dreamed of delivering a "devastating blow" to the "rigidly dogmatic and criminal" Bolsheviks. The frightened fantasy there certainly saw, next to the burning pyre of 'heretical' writings, Zinoviev as the red Grand Inquisitor and Bela Kun together with Radek as his plodding and rabble-rousing henchmen. May fine and truth-thirsty souls calm down! Actually what lies behind the 'fiery death' story is basically nothing but this:

Leo Jogiches – how astonished he would be that he has been conjured up as a "certain party"! – had entrusted me with the task of looking through Rosa's desk and some boxes for manuscripts, letters, etc. The yield was low. The Noskides had ransacked the apartment of this 'hounding Bolshevik' like vandals, a routine matter for these protectors of order and property. I conscientiously carried each rummaged leaflet as a holy relic to Leo, and we reviewed and discussed the findings. Among them were some pages with keywords, notes, disjointed sentences of Rosa's critique of the Bolshevik policy in the agrarian and nationality question. Leo handed me these papers back with the remark: "Burn them. It is all too fragmentary, and Rosa has written more about this and other issues of the Bolshevik tactics. But those are not to be published either."

I must have looked at Leo then, probably in wonder and amazement, for he continued: "This is not for our Russian friends. They can still tolerate further criticism. No, no! This is for Rosa. She had significantly modified her preliminary analysis of Bolshevik methods and tactics in important ways. What she wrote about it during her detention in Wroclaw was an initial, tentative and unfinished attempt to come to grips with the Russian Revolution scientifically and critically. Rosa had no access to sufficiently documented material in Wroclaw. She could also have no live contact with leaders of the Russian Revolution, who had their own perspective on issues. When she arrived in Berlin and entered the fight for the German Revolution, she went zealously forth, orienting herself thoroughly about the revolutionary developments in Russia. The German Revolution itself demanded this. She familiarised the masses with the questions of dictatorship, democracy, the Soviet system etc. Rosa no longer wanted to come out with her old criticism. She intended to write a new, larger treatise on the Russian Revolution."

Leo then spoke in great detail to me about Rosa's estate, in particular about her literary estate, which was for the international proletariat to inherit and own. He and I were 'naturally' administrator and executor, and we would, of course, enlist Adolf Warski's and Julian Marchlewski-Karski's services for ordering and publishing them. I could not bring myself to burn the sheets that bore Rosa's clear, distinctive handwriting. I also thought that the notes could later be of interest and value. It never came to my attention that someone had intended a "fiery death" for Rosa's criticism. How could that have ever been possible! The manuscript was, moreover, with Paul Levi, or rather in the hands of those who are obedient and faithful to him.

The press of the social democratic coalition politicians and opportunists in Germany acted as if Paul Levi was the first to bring to the world the revelation of the knowledge "of Rosa Luxemburg's true opinion of the Bolsheviks". In reality, it had been known for a long time that Rosa was initially critical of and rejected isolated views and actions of Bolshevik politics. In the brochure: "Rosa Luxemburg, Karl Liebknecht, Leo Jogiches" Karl Radek wrote last year: "Cut off from the world, relying on very little information about the situation in Russia, she was full of anxiety about the fate of the Russian Revolution. She dreaded that the German imperialism would succeed in strangling the Russian revolution and from this point of view she was critical of Bolshevik tactics on the peace issue. But while the Kautskys, who now want to take cover behind the wings of Luxemburgian criticism of Bolshevism, did not lift a finger to move the German working class to undertake the real revolutionary struggle, the lack of which created the dangerous situation in which the Russian Revolution found itself in its foreign affairs, the Luxemburgian criticism always ended in an appeal to the German workers, whom the criticism held responsible for all the dangers faced by the Russian Revolution. And so we always knew when we read Rosa Luxemburg's articles in *Spartacus* that we, despite her criticism of us, in fact, agreed with her because she sought to fulfil the very same responsibility in Germany that we had fulfilled in Russia. As the November Revolution opened the prison gates for her, the disagreements between her and us came to an end, which is the best assurance of the fact that they were anyway not of a fundamental nature. "

As Radek stated this, not only did he know well his Kautskys wishing to escape under "the wings of Luxemburgian criticism", but he had also anticipated Paul Levi, who followed this sublime example of 'true Marxists'. For those, whom Radek's testimony in this matter is not fully valid enough may want to read about it in the *Freiheit*. On 20 January, 1919, five days after Rosa Luxemburg's murder, Luise Kautsky wrote in a "commemorative sheet", which, unfortunately, I cannot quote literally but only try to remain true to the sense: "When I spoke in March 1918 with Rosa, she was still very critical of Bolshevism." It is clear that even in this connection promoting oneself is part of the job.

(Translated by Tina Gopal)

II

Rosa Luxemburg's Views on the Russian Revolution in September 1918

"The Russian Revolution, the mightiest event of the World War" / The Russian Revolution, an issue of the international proletariat / "The elementary duty of socialists to unearth the treasures of experiences and lessons of the Russian Revolution" / The utopian and anti-revolutionary core of the Menshevik and Kautskyan view of the Russian Revolution / The historical merit of the Bolsheviks / Critique of the Bolshevik agrarian policy / Critique of the Bolshevik nationality policy / Critique of the Bolshevik attitude to the Constituent Assembly / Critique of the electoral franchise in relation to the Soviets / Criticism of the Bolshevik policy of the proletarian dictatorship in its relation to 'terror' and 'democracy'

Are then the character, the content and the value judgments of Rosa Luxemburg's criticisms really meant to make the Bolsheviks tremble just as they would before the trumpet of the Last Judgment? Absolutely not! 'Destructive' for the policy of the leading Russian Revolutionary Party is not what Rosa Luxemburg has written. 'Destructive' is rather the poison that the enemies and opponents distil out of it. And not merely for the 'Bolsheviks' and the communist parties of the Third International that are so vehemently hated by them, but ultimately also for the Russian Revolution, the proletarian revolution in general, – whether the Wannabe-Beneficiaries of the posthumous pamphlet are aware of this or not. Therefore, the proletarians have a two-fold right to hear what Rosa Luxemburg tells them.

Her remarks begin with the central theme recurring throughout the essay: "The Russian Revolution is the mightiest event of the World War". It states further—the otherwise pro-citation and pro-revelation *Vorwärts*, just like others, wisely concealed the following—"Its outbreak, its unprecedented radicalism, its enduring impact, refute the lying phrase which official German Social Democracy so zealously churned out at the beginning of the war to give an ideological cover to German imperialism's campaign of conquest. This was the phrase concerning the mission of German bayonets, which were to overthrow Russian tsarism and free its oppressed peoples. The mighty sweep of the revolution in Russia has had a deep-going impact which has transformed all class relationships and brought to the fore all social and economic problems. With the fatality of its own inner logic it consistently moved forward from the first stage of the bourgeois republic to ever more advanced stages, finally reducing the fall of tsarism to the status of a brief and trifling minor episode – all these things show as plain as day that the freeing of Russia was not an achievement of the war and the military defeat of tsarism, not some service of "German bayonets in German fists," as the *Neue Zeit* under Kautsky's editorship once promised in an editorial. They show, on the contrary, that the freeing of Russia had its roots deep in the soil of its own land and was fully matured internally. The military adventure of German imperialism under the ideological blessing of German Social Democracy did not bring about the revolution in Russia but only served to interrupt it at first, to postpone it for a while after its first stormy rising tide in the years 1911-13, and then, after its outbreak, created for it the most difficult and abnormal conditions."

Rosa Luxemburg thereby repudiates "the doctrinaire theory", "that Kautsky shares with the party of the official Social Democrats, according to which an economically backward and predominantly agrarian country like Russia was not yet ripe for social revolution and a dictatorship of the proletariat." Similarly, she repudiates the conclusions derived thereby, that in Russia only a bourgeois revolution was feasible and that a coalition of Social Democrats and liberalism was a historical commandment. Rosa Luxemburg notes that the "Mensheviks" in Russia, "the German opportunists" and "the official German Socialists" are harmoniously united "on this fundamental conception of the Russian revolution, from which follow their detailed positions on questions of tactics": "If the Russian Revolution has gone beyond that point and has set as its task the dictatorship of the proletariat, this is simply a mistake of the radical wing of the Russian labour movement, the Bolsheviks, and all the trials and tribulations encountered by the revolution in its further course, all the turmoil, which it has fallen victim to, present themselves purely as a result of this fatal error."

Rosa Luxemburg questions the outcome of "this doctrine, which is endorsed as the fruit of 'Marxist thinking' by Friedrich Stampfer's *Vorwärts* and Kautsky alike". Theoretically, it follows "the original" Marxist "discovery, that the socialist revolution is a national, so to speak, the domestic affair of each modern country by itself." Practically, there is this tendency of denying "any responsibility of the international, primarily the German proletariat, in the fate of the Russian Revolution, the tendency of denying the revolution any international connection whatsoever. The course of the war and that of the Russian Revolution did not establish Russia's lack of ripeness, but that of the German proletariat in fulfilling its historical tasks, and the first task of a critical analysis of the Russian Revolution is to emphasize this very clearly. The fate of the revolution in Russia was totally dependent upon international events. That the Bolsheviks based their policy entirely on the world proletarian revolution is the clearest proof of their political foresight and firmness of principle, and of the bold scope of their policies."

Subsequently, Rosa Luxemburg emphasizes "penetrating and thoughtful criticism" of the Russian Revolution to be the "elementary duty" of socialists of all countries, in order to "harvest its treasures of experiences and teachings". "Dealing as we are with the very first experiment in proletarian dictatorship in world history, specifically under the hardest conceivable conditions: amidst global conflagration and chaos of the imperialist mass slaughter, embroiled in the iron trap of the most reactionary military power in Europe, accompanied by the complete failure of the international proletariat, it would indeed be crazy to conceive that in an experiment with the dictatorship of the proletariat under such abnormal conditions just everything that was done or left undone in Russia represented the acme of perfection." Under such historically 'fatal conditions' engulfing the Russian revolution, even immense idealism and the most storm-resistant revolutionary energy are incapable of realising democracy and socialism, "but only impotent and distorted attempts at either.... Only in the background of this bitter knowledge can we gauge the enormous magnitude of the responsibility of the international proletariat for the fate of the Russian Revolution. Furthermore, only on this basis the crucial importance of the united international action of the proletarian revolution makes itself felt... Engaging critically with the Russian Revolution in all its historical connections is the best training for the German and the international working class for the tasks that emerge from the current situation."

The first period of the Russian Revolution, from March to October 1917 is—like the great English and French Revolutions—"the typical development of every first great general confrontation of the revolutionary forces generated in the womb of bourgeois society with the shackles of the old society. Its development moves naturally in an ascending line: from moderate beginnings to ever greater radicalization of the aims and, parallel with that, from a coalition of classes and parties to the sole rule of the radical party."

On the very day after the first victories of the revolution—the establishment of a democratic republic—"an internal struggle within it over the two burning questions – peace and land" – was kindled. Because: "From the very first moment, the driving force of the revolution was the mass of the urban proletariat. Its demands, however, did not limit themselves to attaining political democracy, but also focused on the burning question of international politics: immediate peace. Simultaneously, the revolution was based on the mass of the army, which raised the same demand for immediate peace, and on the mass of the peasantry, who pushed the agrarian question—this axis of the Revolution since 1905—to the forefront." The fate of political democracy, of the Republic, was linked with the questions of peace and land. The bourgeois classes, overwhelmed and swept away at first, retreated to silently organize a counter-revolution. The Kaledin Cossack campaign against Petersburg clearly expresses this disposition. After a few months this developed into an either-or situation: "Victory of the counter-revolution or dictatorship of the proletariat."

"In this the Russian Revolution has but confirmed the basic lesson of every great revolution, whose law of life it is: It must either advance very rapidly and resolutely, demolishing all obstructions with an iron fist and always placing its goals ever farther ahead, or else it will very soon be hurled backward behind its feeble point of departure and suppressed by counter-revolution." Rosa Luxemburg substantiated this judgment by the example of the great English and the French Revolutions. She derides "Kautsky and his associates" with biting mockery for "wanting to see the Russian Revolution preserve the 'bourgeois character' of its first phase." In the identified situation "we can judge the utopian and reactionary core of the tactics by which the Russian Kautskyan socialists or the Mensheviks allowed themselves to be guided.... They clung desperately to the coalition with the bourgeois liberals. This means to the forced union of those elements which had been split by the natural internal development of the revolution and had fallen into the sharpest conflict with one another."

"In this situation, the Bolshevik tendency performed the historic service of proclaiming from the very beginning, and pursuing with iron consistency, the tactics which alone could save democracy and drive the revolution ahead. All power exclusively in the hands of the workers and peasant masses, in the hands of the soviets – this was in fact the only way out of the difficulty in which the revolution was caught. This was the sword stroke, which slashing through the Gordian knot led the revolution out of a tight spot and opened up for it the free field of uninhibited further development.

"The party of Lenin was thus the only one in Russia to truly grasp the real interest of the revolution in that first period. It was the element driving the revolution forward and, as such, the only party carrying out a socialist policy. . .

"The party of Lenin was the only one which grasped the mandate and duty of a truly revolutionary party and which by the slogan, "All power in the hands of the proletariat and the peasantry," ensured the continued progress of the revolution.

"Moreover, the Bolsheviks immediately set as the aim of this seizure of power a complete, far-reaching revolutionary programme: not the conservation of bourgeois democracy, but dictatorship of the proletariat for the purpose of realising socialism. They have thus acquired the permanent historic merit of having proclaimed for the first time the ultimate goals of socialism as the direct programme of practical politics.

"Lenin, Trotsky and comrades have given in full measure all that, which a party in a historic hour could muster by way of courage, energy, revolutionary far-sightedness and consistency. All the revolutionary honour and capacity which Western social democracy lacked was represented by the Bolsheviks. Their October Uprising not only salvaged the Russian revolution, it also redeemed the honour of international socialism."

The party of the Bolsheviks was able to seize leadership and power only because it had the courage to issue the appropriate slogan for advancing the revolution and to follow it with all its consequences. As with the 'Levellers' in England and the 'Jacobins' in France it was the 'excessiveness' of their claims that ensured the achievements of the revolution and constituted the driving force of the entire movement. "But the concrete task facing the Bolsheviks in the Russian revolution after the seizure of power was incomparably more difficult than that of their historical predecessors."

Rosa Luxemburg examines the way the Bolshevik policy has

attempted to solve the concrete difficult tasks. First, with relation to the agrarian question, whose paramount importance and complicated nature she briefly refers to. "The slogan of the direct, immediate seizure and distribution of the land by the peasants was certainly the shortest, simplest and most succinct formula to achieve two things: to crush landlordism and to immediately bind the peasants to the revolutionary government. As a political measure to secure the proletarian-socialist government, this was an excellent tactic. Unfortunately, however, it had two sides to it, and the reverse side consisted in the fact that the direct seizure of land by peasants has usually nothing in common with a socialist economy."

This keen judgment is justified as follows. The socialist transformation of the economy with respect to the agrarian conditions presupposes two things: "In the first place, the nationalisation of large estates precisely as the technically most advanced concentration of agrarian means and methods of production, which alone can serve as the starting point of the socialist mode of production in the countryside... Of course, one need not take away from the small peasants their parcels of land. We can with confidence leave them to be won over voluntarily by the superior advantages of socialised enterprises first for a union in co-operatives and then finally for complete inclusion in the general socialised economy....But every socialist economic reform on the land must obviously begin with large and medium land-ownership. Here the property right must above all be transferred to the nation, or to the state, which, in the case of a socialist government, amounts to the same thing, if one wants it to be so." The second prerequisite is: "The separation between the rural economy and industry which is so characteristic of bourgeois society, should be ended in such a way as to facilitate a mutual interpenetration and fusion of both, to clear the way for the planning of both agrarian and industrial production according to a unified point of view..."

"That the Soviet government in Russia has not carried through these mighty reforms – who can reproach them for that! It would be a sorry jest indeed to demand or expect of Lenin and his comrades that, in the brief period of their rule, amidst the raging maelstrom of domestic and foreign battles, surrounded by countless foes and opponents, to expect that under such circumstances they should already have solved, or even tackled, one of the most difficult tasks, indeed we can safely say, the most difficult task of the socialist transformation of society..." But: "A socialist government that has come to power must in any event do one thing: it must take measures which lead in the direction of those fundamental prerequisites for a later socialist reform of agriculture; it must at least avoid everything which may bar the way to those measures."

Rosa Luxemburg is convinced that the agrarian slogan of the Bolsheviks "necessarily tended in the opposite direction." It led "to the sudden, chaotic conversion of large landownership into peasant landownership. What was created is not socialised ownership, but a new form of private property, the destruction... of the relatively advanced large-scale units into primitive small businesses that operate with technical means from the time of the pharaohs." Due to the indiscriminate nature of the division the ownership differences and class antagonisms on the land were not eliminated, but only exacerbated. "This shift of power, however, has taken place to the disadvantage of the interests of the proletariat and of socialism. In the past, at the most only a small caste of noble and capitalist landed proprietors and a small minority of rich village bourgeoisie stood in opposition to a socialist reform in the rural areas. And their expropriation by revolutionary masses is just a child's play. But now, after 'seizing ownership,' an enormously expanded and strong mass of owning peasants stands as an opponent of any attempt at the socialisation of agriculture, who will defend tooth and nail their newly acquired property against all socialist designs. Now the question of the future socialisation of the agrarian economy, that is, of the socialisation of production in general in Russia, has become a question of the opposition and struggle between the urban proletariat and the peasant masses." The French small peasant created by the Revolution became its boldest defender. "However, the Russian peasant after having seized the land with his own fist did not in the slightest dream of defending Russia and the revolution to which he owed the land. He sunk his teeth into his new possession and abandoned the revolution to its enemies, left the state to decay, and the urban population to hunger."

Rosa Luxemburg is further of the opinion that the Bolsheviks were in part to be blamed for the aggravation of the objective difficulties of the situation, and that the military defeat was transformed into the collapse and disintegration of Russia. All this because of "a slogan which they have placed in the foreground of their policies: the so-called right of self-determination of nations, or—that which was really implicit in this slogan—the disintegration of the Russian state." The slogan "was a special battle cry" of the Bolsheviks against the imperialism of the Miliukov and Kerensky government; "it formed the axis of their internal policy subsequent to the October Revolution and it constituted the entire platform of the Bolsheviks at Brest-Litovsk; it was their sole weapon to counter German imperialism's political power."

The ‘tenacity and inflexible consistency’ with which Lenin and his comrades adhered to this slogan—as Rosa Luxemburg explains, "blatantly contradicts their otherwise outspoken centralism in politics and is wholly inconsistent with the attitude they have assumed towards other democratic principles... The contradiction that is so obvious here is all the more incomprehensible, since the democratic forms of political life in each country, as we shall further see, actually involve the extremely valuable and most indispensable foundations of socialist policy, while the famous ‘self-determination of nations’ is nothing but hollow, petty bourgeois phraseology and humbug. Indeed, what is this right supposed to signify? It belongs to the ABC of socialist policy that it opposes every kind of oppression, including that of one nation by another."

"A kind of opportunistic policy" Rosa Luxemburg assumes is the reason why the Bolsheviks made "a hollow phrase ... downright into their hobby horse... they clearly reckoned that there was no surer method of binding the many foreign peoples within the Russian Empire to the cause of the revolution, to the cause of the socialist proletariat, than that of offering them, in the name of the revolution and of socialism, the most extreme and most unlimited freedom to determine their own destiny." The Ukrainian interlude at the Brest-Litovsk peace negotiations and the behaviour of Finland were soon to teach the Bolsheviks that their calculation was wrong. The bourgeois and petty bourgeois classes of the various nations and nationalities, incorporated within the old Russia, used the slogan of "national self-determination" as an instrument of their counter-revolutionary class politics. This was done both against Soviet Russia, as against their own proletarian masses. “In the midst of the harsh reality of class society, the nationalist phrase is simply converted into a means of bourgeois class rule." In countries that had broken away from Russia it carried confusion and paralysis into the proletarian masses, who till then had fought with the Russian workers in a united front.

"How is it that suddenly the counter-revolution triumphed in all these countries? The nationalist movement has torn the proletariat away from Russia, consequently paralysing it, and delivered it into the hands of the national bourgeoisie in the peripheral countries... To be sure, without the help of German imperialism, without "the German rifle butts in German fists," as Kautsky's *Neue Zeit* wrote, the Lubinskys and other petty scoundrels of the Ukraine, the Erichs and Mannerheims of Finland, and the Baltic barons, could never have bulldozed the socialist masses of the workers in their respective lands. But the Bolsheviks provided the ideology that masked this campaign of counter-revolution." The object of the Bolsheviks should have been, "to work for the most compact union of the revolutionary forces throughout the Empire, to defend tooth and nail its integrity as a revolutionary territory, to oppose all specifically nationalistic aspirations by championing the unity and indivisibility of the proletarians of all nations in the area of the Russian Revolution as the highest command of its politics. We have every reason to thoroughly look into the policies of the Bolsheviks in this regard. The 'right of self-determination of nations,' associated with the League of Nations and disarmament by Wilson's grace, is the battle cry under which the coming reckoning of international socialism with the bourgeois world will play itself out."

Rosa Luxemburg indicates in a few words to the fact that from the characterised Bolshevik policy, which she considers to be defective, the dictatorship of Germany followed. "From the time of the Brest-Litovsk treaty to the time of the supplementary treaty there is terror and the suppression of democracy." She wants to examine this on the basis of "a few examples"; on the basis of the position of the Bolsheviks on the Constituent Assembly, on universal suffrage, on democracy in general, the type of dictatorship, and the nature and extent of terror.

In her view, the resolution of the Constituent Assembly in November 1917 marks "a turning point" in the Bolshevik strategy. The party had stormily demanded the Constituent Assembly before its victory and vehemently fought the Kerensky government because it postponed the convocation of the Constituent Assembly. Trotsky had declared the seizure of power by the Soviets as "the salvation of the Constituent Assembly," and as the "entry point" to it. The first step after the victory of the Soviets was the dissolution of the Constituent Assembly. It was justified on the grounds that the Constituent Assembly was elected long before the decisive turning point and its composition reflected a picture of the outdated past and not of the current situation.

Rosa Luxemburg finds "quite excellent and convincing" what Trotsky, based on indisputable facts, says in this respect in his pamphlet "From the October Revolution to the Brest-Litovsk." The "outgrown and therefore still-born Constituent Assembly" had to be annulled. The Bolsheviks "did not want to, nor should they have entrusted, the fate of the revolution to an assembly which reflected the Kerensky Russia of yesterday, a period of vacillations and of coalition. Hence the only thing that then remained to be done was to convene immediately an Assembly in its place that would emerge from the renewed Russia that had made further progress." However, "the special inadequacy of the Constituent Assembly which came together in October, led to the general conclusion of the redundancy of any Constituent Assembly whatsoever" and was taken still further. From the special inadequacy one drew a general conclusion "concerning the unsuitability of any popular representation whatsoever emerging from universal popular elections during the revolution."

Rosa Luxemburg challenges Trotsky's view that "the cumbersome mechanism of democratic institutions" cannot keep pace with the experience and maturity which the masses gain from the direct struggle for governmental power. They might derive much less, "the bigger the country and the more incompetent its technical apparatus is." She is of the opinion that "in this assessment of representative institutions a somewhat schematic, rigid view is expressed that contradicts the historical experience of all revolutionary epochs most emphatically... Any living spiritual connection between the representatives once elected and the electorate, any permanent interaction between the two is denied here. Yet all historical experience contradicts this! It demonstrates the contrary, namely, that the living fluid of the popular mood constantly flows around the representative bodies, penetrates them, and directs them."

Rosa Luxemburg refers to the changes in the 'Long Parliament' in England, in the Estates-General in France, to the fact that "in every bourgeois parliament at times ... the various little Scheidemanns suddenly find in their breast revolutionary tones – whenever there is rumbling in factories, in workshops and on the streets. And should this constant, vibrant influence of the mood and the political maturity of the masses upon the elected bodies be renounced for the sake of the rigid scheme of party emblems and electoral lists in the very midst of a revolution? Quite the contrary! It is precisely the revolution that by its glowing heat creates the delicate, vibrant, receptive political atmosphere in which the waves of popular feeling, the pulse of popular life instantaneously influence the representative bodies in a wonderful way ... The "cumbersome mechanism of democratic institutions" possesses a powerful corrective – namely in the living movement of the masses, in their incessant pressure. And the more democratic the institution, the livelier and stronger the pulse-beat of the political life of the mass, the more direct and accurate is the effect. Every democratic institution has its limits and shortcomings, but the Bolshevik remedy of "the elimination of democracy in general," is worse than the evil it is supposed to control: for it stops up the very living source itself from which alone all the innate shortcomings of social institutions can be corrected: the active, uninhibited, energetic political life of the general public at large."

Rosa Luxemburg characterises suffrage as developed by the Soviet government as "a very remarkable product of the Bolshevik dictatorship theory". In her opinion, it is "not entirely clear what practical significance is attributed to it...." It contradicts the fundamental rejection of popular representative bodies elected through general elections. "We are not even aware whether suffrage was put into practice anywhere... More likely is the assumption that it is only a theoretical product, so to say, a bureaucratically designed leftover... Suffrage, as indeed every political right, is not to be evaluated by some practical schemes of justice or in terms of similar bourgeois democratic phraseology, but by the social and economic conditions for which it is designed. Suffrage as worked out by the Soviet government is designed for the period of transition from the bourgeois-capitalist to a socialist form of society, that is, for the period of the proletarian dictatorship." Labour is the rationale behind it, the right to vote is to be made available only to those who live by their own labour.

According to Rosa Luxemburg such suffrage "has meaning only in a society, which is economically in a position to ensure an adequate civilized life to all those who want to work on the basis of their labour." But this does not appear to her to be the case in Russia at present. Under the given circumstances "it is clear that countless existences are suddenly uprooted and thrown out of their orbit without any objective possibility of finding employment for their labour power in the economy. This applies not only to the capitalist and landlord classes, but also to the broad layer of the lower middle class and even to the working class itself."

A mass return of urban proletarians into the rural areas is taking place. Increasing sections of the population have to be maintained as Red Guards by the state out of public funds. On the other hand, the Soviet government was forced to 'lease', so to speak, the national industries to their former owners, to make a pact with the bourgeois consumer co-operatives, and similarly was forced to consult the bourgeois specialists etc. Rosa Luxemburg concludes: "In such circumstances, a political right to vote based on the general obligation to work is quite an incomprehensible measure... In reality, large and growing sections of the petty bourgeoisie and the proletariat are rendered without any rights, because the economy does not provide them the means to exercise their obligation to work. This is an absurdity making the right to vote into a utopian product of fantasy dissociated from social reality. And precisely for this reason it is not a serious tool of the proletarian dictatorship. It is an anachronism, an anticipation of a juridical situation appropriate in an already realized socialist economy but not in the transition period of the proletarian dictatorship."

As a means of proletarian dictatorship Rosa Luxemburg envisages political disenfranchisement subject to certain circumstances. She writes: "When the entire middle class, bourgeois and petty bourgeois intelligentsia boycotted the Soviet government for months after the October Revolution, paralyzed the railway, post and telegraph services, the schools and administration and thus rebelled against the Labour government, naturally all kinds of coercive measures were applied, such as deprivation of political rights and economic means of subsistence etc. in order to break the resistance with an iron fist. This was a simple expression of the socialist dictatorship which did not shrink from using force when enforcing or thwarting specific measures in the interests of all. But when it comes to an electoral franchise that decrees the general disfranchisement of quite broad sections of society and places them politically outside the framework of society, while simultaneously it is not even in a position to provide a space for them economically within that framework, when it involves a deprivation of rights not as concrete measures for a concrete purpose, but as a general rule of long-standing effect, then it is not a necessity of dictatorship but a makeshift improvisation. The same applies to the Soviets as the backbone, to the Constituent Assembly and to universal suffrage."

Furthermore, in Rosa Luxemburg's opinion, what should not be considered is "the abolition of the most important guarantees of a healthy public life, the political activity of the working masses: the freedom of the press, rights of association and assembly, which have been outlawed for all opponents of the Soviet government... It is an obvious, indisputable fact that without a free and untrammelled press, without the unrestrained right to association and assembly, the rule of broad masses of the people is entirely inconceivable."

"Especially the enormous tasks, which the Bolsheviks approached with courage and determination, required intensive political education of the masses and accumulation of experience which is never possible without political freedom. Freedom only for the supporters of the government, only for members of one party—however numerous they may be—is no freedom. Freedom is always and exclusively the freedom for the one who thinks differently. Not because of any fanatical concept of 'justice' but because all that is instructive, beneficial and purifying in political freedom depends entirely on this essential characteristic, and by becoming a special privilege 'freedom' becomes ineffective. Far from being a sum of ready-made prescriptions which have only to be applied, the practical realization of socialism as an economic, social and juridical system is something which lies completely hidden in the mists of the future. What we possess in our programme are nothing but a few major signposts indicating the general direction in which to look for the necessary measures, but these indications are mainly negative in character at that. Thus, we more or less know what must be eliminated at the outset in order to free the road for a socialist economy. But when it comes to the nature of the thousand concrete, practical measures, large and small, necessary to introduce socialist principles into economy, law and all social relationships, there is neither a socialist party programme nor a socialist textbook. This is not a shortcoming but rather the very thing that makes scientific socialism superior to the utopian varieties. The socialist system of society should and can only then be a historical product when it arises out of the school of its own experiences and its realization is the result of the development of living history, which has the fine habit of always producing along with any real social need the means to its satisfaction, of simultaneously producing the solution together with the task, exactly in the manner of organic nature, whose part it ultimately is."

"However, if such is the case," Rosa Luxemburg continues, "then it is clear that socialism by its very nature cannot be decreed, or introduced by *ukase*. It presupposes a number of repressive measures – against property, etc. The negative, the dismantling, can be decreed; the positive, the building up, cannot." This is a new territory for thousands of emerging problems. "Only experience is capable of correcting and opening new ways. Only unobstructed, effervescent life falls into a thousand new forms and improvisations, has creative energy and corrects mistakes all by itself. If, therefore, the public life of countries with limited freedom is so poverty-stricken, so miserable, so mechanical, so barren it is precisely because by excluding democracy it cuts off the living sources of all spiritual riches and progress. (Proof: the year 1905 and the months from February to October 1917)." The entire populace must participate in the new life. "Otherwise, socialism will be decreed and imposed bureaucratically by a dozen intellectuals. Public scrutiny is absolutely necessary. Otherwise, the exchange of experiences will remain entirely within the closed circle of the officials of the new government. Corruption becomes inevitable. (Lenin's words, *Mitteilungsblatt* No. 29.) The practice of socialism requires a thorough spiritual transformation in masses degraded by centuries of bourgeois domination. Social instincts in place of egotistical ones; mass initiative in place of inertia; idealism which carries one beyond all the suffering, etc., etc. Nobody knows this better, describes this more impressively, and repeats this more persistently than Lenin. But he is completely mistaken in the means he employs. Decree, dictatorial force of the factory supervisor, draconian penalties, reign of terror, all these means prevent this rebirth. The only way for this rebirth is the school of public life itself, the most unrestricted, broadest democracy and public opinion. It is precisely the rule of terror that demoralises."

"But with the crushing of political life in the whole country the life in the Soviets must also become more and more crippled. Without general elections and unrestricted freedom of press and assembly, without a free struggle of opinion, life dies out in every public institution; it becomes a mere semblance of life where the bureaucracy alone remains as the active element. No one escapes this law. Public life gradually falls asleep; a few dozen party leaders of inexhaustible energy and boundless experience govern and rule. Among them, in reality, only a dozen outstanding heads lead, and an elite of the working class is invited from time to time to the meetings to applaud the speeches of the leaders and unanimously approve proposed resolutions. Basically it is a clique system – a dictatorship, however, not the dictatorship of the proletariat, but the dictatorship of a handful of politicians, i.e., dictatorship in the bourgeois sense, in the sense of the Jacobin rule." With reference to the phenomenon of corruption and of the brutalisation of public life in Germany, Rosa Luxemburg points out that it is "an overpowering objective law, which no party can evade. The only antidote: Idealism and social activity of the masses, unlimited political freedom."

"The basic error of the Lenin-Trotsky theory," it is said in the posthumously published pamphlet, "is precisely that they, just like Kautsky, put dictatorship in opposition to democracy. "Dictatorship or democracy" is how the question is posed among the Bolsheviks and by Kautsky alike. The latter, of course, opts for democracy, and indeed for bourgeois democracy, because this represents for him the alternative to socialist transformation. Lenin and Trotsky conversely decide for dictatorship as opposed to democracy, and thus for the dictatorship of a handful of people, i.e., dictatorship on the bourgeois pattern. These are two opposite poles, both equidistant from real socialist policy. The proletariat when it seizes power can now never follow the good advice of Kautsky, given under the pretext of the "lack of ripeness of the country," and thus renounce socialist transformation and devote itself solely to democracy without betraying itself, the International and the revolution. It should and must, starting immediately, embark on socialist measures in the most energetic, relentless and ruthless manner. Thus, dictatorship is to be exercised, but dictatorship of the class, not of a party or a clique. The dictatorship of the class, this means as publicly as possible, on the basis of the most active and most unrestrained participation of the masses, in an unlimited democracy."

"We have never been idol-worshippers of formal democracy, which only means that we have always distinguished the social core from the political form of bourgeois democracy, we have always revealed the bitter core of social inequality and lack of freedom hidden under the sweet shell of formal equality and freedom – not in order to reject the latter, but to spur the working class not to be content with the shell, rather by seizing political power to fill it with a new socialist content. It is the historic task of the proletariat when it comes to power to create socialist democracy instead of bourgeois democracy, and not to eliminate democracy altogether. However, socialist democracy is not something which begins only in the Promised Land after the foundations of socialist economy are laid; it does not come as some sort of Christmas present for the worthy people who, in the interim, have loyally supported a handful of socialist dictators. Socialist democracy begins simultaneously with the beginnings of the destruction of class rule and of the construction of socialism. It begins at the very moment of the seizure of power by the socialist party. It is the same thing as the dictatorship of the proletariat."

"Yes: dictatorship! But this dictatorship exists in the manner of applying democracy, not in its elimination; it consists in energetic, resolute attacks upon the well-entrenched rights and economic relationships of bourgeois society, without which a socialist transformation cannot be realized. But this dictatorship has to be the work of the class and not of a little leading minority in the name of the class, that is, it must proceed at every step with the active participation of the masses. It must stand under their direct influence, under the control of the entire public; it must emerge from the growing political education of the masses."

"Undoubtedly, the Bolsheviks would have proceeded exactly in this way, were they not suffering from the terrible compulsion of the World War, the German occupation and all related abnormal difficulties. Any socialist policy, even with the best of intentions and the noblest of principles, was bound to get distorted under such circumstances. A glaring instance of this is provided by the so very liberal use of terror by the Soviet government, especially in the period since the assassination of the German ambassador just before the collapse of German imperialism."

"Everything happening in Russia is comprehensible and represents an inevitable chain of causes and effects, whose starting and key points are the failure of the German proletariat and German imperialism's occupation of Russia. It would be expecting something superhuman of Lenin and his comrades if one were to still expect them to conjure forth the finest democracy, an exemplary dictatorship of the proletariat, and a flourishing socialist economy under such circumstances. By their determined revolutionary stand, their exemplary strength in action and their unswerving loyalty they have truly assisted international socialism as much as was possible under such devilishly hard conditions. The danger begins only when they make a virtue of necessity and establish as a complete theoretical system all the tactics forced upon them by these fatal circumstances and want to recommend it to the international proletariat as a model of socialist tactics. As they quite unnecessarily themselves stand in the way of the light in this way and forfeit their true, undeniable, historical merit under a bushel of inevitable lapses, they perform a poor service to international socialism, for whose sake they have fought and suffered. They want to place in its storehouse as new insights all the distortions inflicted by necessity and compulsion in Russia, which ultimately are only consequences of the bankruptcy of international socialism in the current World War."

"Let the German government socialists cry that the rule of the Bolsheviks in Russia is a caricature of the dictatorship of the proletariat. If it was or is such, then it is so just because it was a product of the attitude of the German proletariat, which itself was a caricature of socialist class struggle. We are all subject to the law of history and the socialist order can be realized only internationally. The Bolsheviks have shown that they are capable of everything that a genuine revolutionary party can contribute within the limits of historical possibilities. They are not supposed to perform miracles. For, a model and faultless proletarian revolution in an isolated land, exhausted by the World War, strangled by imperialism, betrayed by the international proletariat, would be a miracle. What matters most is to distinguish the essential from the inessential and the core from the incidental in Bolshevik politics. In this last hour, when we are facing the most decisive final struggles all over the world, the most important problem of socialism remains, in effect, the burning question of our time: It is not a matter of this or that specific issue of tactics, but of the proletariat's capacity for action, the masses' strength to act, the will to power of Socialism as such. In this, Lenin and Trotsky and their friends were the pioneers, who went forth as an example to the proletariat of the world; they are still the only ones to this day who can cry with Hutten: 'I have dared!'"

"This is the essential and enduring in Bolshevik politics. In this sense, theirs is the immortal historical merit of having marched at the head of the international proletariat with their conquest of political power and with the presentation of the practical problems of the realization of Socialism, and of having tremendously advanced the settlement of the altercation between capital and labour in the entire world. In Russia, the problem could only be posed; it could not be resolved in Russia. And in this sense, the future universally belongs to 'Bolshevism'."

(Translated by Tina Gopal)

III

Against a Reformist Use of Rosa Luxemburg's September Critique

The leitmotif of the September critique / Adolf Warski's analysis of Rosa Luxemburg's view of Bolshevist policy on the Nationality Question and of Levi's assertion that Rosa Luxemburg did not change her position / The fundamental difference between Rosa Luxemburg's position and that of the reformist socialists on the issue of 'democracy' / The incompatibility of the Constituent Assembly and the Soviet system / The fundamental importance of the Soviet electoral franchise / Proletarian dictatorship and terror as means of revolutionary self-defence / The creators, advocates and beneficiaries of the counter-revolutionary terror legends / The reality of Bolshevist terror and the actual conditions for its inevitability / The problem of bureaucracy in the Russian Soviet state / The relationship between the Bolshevik party and the class of the proletariat

Rosa Luxemburg's position on the Russian Revolution has been reproduced faithfully, in great detail and, important parts of it, literally. Only in its entirety can it be fully appreciated as coherent and unified genuine Marxist thought, reflecting a wealth of knowledge and ideas, and presenting a productive and well thought-out perspective of the historical process of development. This is evident in the way she has linked the past with the present and the future as one single history, and in her great, world encompassing line of the international solidarity of the proletariat of all countries.

Her critique of Bolshevist policy must be understood in its context, as an integral part of the whole. Only then can its true historical significance be understood. This context is none other than the emphasis on the deep indissoluble dependence of the Russian Revolution on the world revolution and in particular on the proletarian revolution in Germany. It was Rosa Luxemburg's basic contention that Bolshevik policy was flawed and error-ridden, but given the historical circumstances it was bound to be so since it lacked the larger historical corrective: the proletarian revolution in Germany, and in the whole world. The sharp criticism of important parts of Bolshevist tactics culminates in a scathing condemnation of the fundamental position on revolution by both strands of German Social Democracy. It was from that particular perspective that Rosa wrote to me in the summer of 1918: "The mistakes of the Russian Revolution can only be eliminated and overcome together with the German Revolution. Driving forward the German Revolution would mean not only completing the Russian Revolution but also making it perfect. Drawing from the mistakes of the Russians, we must again and yet again make the Germans aware of their own fundamental errors." How very differently the world was reflected in the brilliant mind of Rosa Luxemburg as compared to what went on in the heads of calculating, fear-ridden, overtly or covertly opportunistic social democratic politicians, whose world did not even encompass Germany and was in fact limited to the trade union, the party organisation or the parliamentary seat!

The Majority Social Democratic and Independent newspapers have remained silent on the fundamental and international conclusion of the posthumously published Luxemburgian pamphlet. It must have sounded to them like the voice of their bad consciences. So, instead they have fallen upon the critique of Bolshevist tactics with the greed of hungry mongrels. By invoking the name Luxemburg, they have, in this critique, sought to find a justification of the big sins of commission and omission by their parties with regard to the revolution. As a result of what they did to Rosa's work in the pursuit of this goal, the work is to Rosa as a scarecrow is to a beautiful human figure. But then, the Majority Social Democratic and right-wing Independent leaders needed an anti-Bolshevist scarecrow. For them, it was all about scaring off workers from pursuing what the genuine interests of the exploited demand, from what the communists call for: to form a united front against capitalism and its state.

Any assessment of Rosa Luxemburg's critique would by its very nature include taking a position on her as well. Indeed, "uncritical apologetics, instead of penetrating and thoughtful criticism" would mean the denial and belittling of the memory of the serious intellectual that she was. Comrade Adolf Warski has engaged with Rosa Luxemburg's position against Bolshevik tactics on the nationality question, as also with Paul Levi's claim that both in Bolshevik tactics and in Rosa Luxemburg's position on this issue, the old differences between her and Lenin endure – differences that were articulated clearly in Rosa's article in the *Neue Zeit* in 1904 during the dispute over organisational questions of Russian social democracy:

a mass party or small, pure sects. Adolf Warski stands much closer to Russian affairs than that of any of us. As one of the most loyal and steadfast of supporters alongside Rosa, he has literarily, politically and organisationally fought tirelessly the long and bitter battles that were waged over nationality and organisational questions within the Russian-Polish social-democratic camp that was closely linked to the revolutionary movement in Russia. What he has said should merit attention.[*]

An analysis of Rosa Luxemburg's reflections on the 'suppression of democracy' in Soviet Russia appears to me to be required. It is precisely these reflections that social democratic opponents and enemies of the Bolsheviks invoke in order to testify to their own bourgeois-uncontaminated political virtue. "We wanted and facilitated the German Constituent Assembly; we created it as our holiest of the holy. We swore by universal suffrage for all 'our countrymen.' We believe in parliamentarism and consider the system of the Soviets to be out of touch with reality. We abhor a proletarian class dictatorship that uses means other than political-ethical-aesthetic Sunday afternoon sermons. We categorically condemn all kinds of terror – with the exception of the terror that capitalism exercises day in and day out against the proletariat, and the bourgeois state with its coercive apparatus against the communists." This is how these gentlemen gloat, and they want to talk the masses into believing that they share the same views as Rosa Luxemburg, whose company they shunned during the war years and months of revolution, as a pious medieval Christian would a pact with the devil.

What the Stampfers und Hilferdings understand, praise, and quote of the observations of Rosa Luxemburg on the issue of the Constituent Assembly, suffrage, dictatorship etc. indicates mostly the 'gentlemen's own thinking'. They brush aside the essential difference separating their own position from that of Rosa Luxemburg's on the issue of 'democracy' – in order to lump together everything that could be covered by this concept. For Rosa Luxemburg, democracy is above all the instrument which, *after* the revolution, *after* the conquest of political power by the proletariat and its or-

---

[*] A. Warski: Rosa Luxemburgs Stellung zu den Taktischen Problemen der Revolution. (Rosa Luxemburg's Position on Tactical Problems of the Revolution) Published by the Communist International. [CZ]

ganisation into soviets, will serve to harness the energy and the largest possible pool of experience through the active and broadest possible participation of the masses so as to assert proletarian power. This means: Assertion of power for advancing the revolution further by destroying the bourgeois order and establishing communism, the classless society. For her, the effectiveness and primary significance of 'democracy' begins only after the culmination of class struggle, after the hammer blow of the proletarian revolution. The 'democracy' that she had in mind is the real proletarian democracy, with revolution as its goal, and not formal bourgeois democracy, which Rosa defined as a form with a bitter core of social inequality and lack of freedom. According to Rosa Luxemburg 'democracy' can only be the fruit of a revolution. It is captured and energetic, robust proletarian power, and is unfeasible so long as capitalism dominates and controls the networks of knowledge, experience and activities of the economically exploited and enslaved within the economy and the state.

The concept of 'democracy' of Kautsky, Stampfer and other like-minded persons is, in comparison, neither time-specific nor substantive 'in itself'. As soon as this concept descends from the ivory tower of desks and parliamentary speeches into the raw earthly reality of bourgeois class society, it takes the shape of formal bourgeois democracy, which has jails, truncheons and machine guns to welcome revolutionary wage slaves. Even though these can prove to be useful for the proletarian freedom struggle, yet their utility would be restricted by the bourgeois class structure. Ultimately, bourgeois democracy is an instrument to ensure the political exploitation and control of the proletariat by the bourgeoisie, since it provides the sheen of legitimacy, giving it the garb of manifesting the 'will of the people'. And the Kautskyites of both factions of the social democratic party situate this bourgeois democracy *before* the revolution, *before* the conquest of political power by the proletariat. They claim it to be the precursor to the political uprising, ushering in the proletarian revolution. Even the most unprejudiced, open-minded of them see in it a kind of 'substitute for revolution.' 'Democracy,' so they aver, will destroy the power of the capitalists through the formal value of the vote, will establish the power of the proletariat and pave the way for socialism.

The enlightened views of Rosa Luxemburg are, thus, far removed from those of the social democrats, who as idolaters of 'democracy' have been denouncing Bolshevist policy. Yet they can, with apparent justification, stake claim to Rosa's criticism of this policy. What is written in the pamphlet, published posthumously, on the 'suppression of democracy' by the Soviet Union, is, according to me, marked by the scars of Rosa Luxemburg's being imprisoned and away from the wild, passionate, stormy life of the revolution. It is also marked by the scars of the lack of access to authentic material on the situation and events in Russia. As a result, the method which has been applied so consistently in general could not be applied as successfully in the details. Rosa Luxemburg rightly accuses Kautsky of having a definition of democracy that is too rigid and schematic, not reflecting the fluid, changing social content with which historical life infuses the shell of democracy. However, she too was not always able to steer clear of a somewhat mechanical and abstract understanding of 'democracy.'

Still, the basic difference, as already pointed out, is that Kautsky's 'democracy' is retrospective and bourgeois in character, and in the prevailing circumstances non-revolutionary, in fact counter-revolutionary. Rosa Luxemburg's concept of 'democracy,' on the other hand, is imbued with the passion, blood, sweat and tears of a revolutionary. It is forward-looking and proletarian in nature. It is a revolutionary democracy. Would there be any heart that would not beat in elation in tune with Rosa's incredibly pride-inspiring hymn to the creative power of 'democracy.' And yet the 'democracy' that such a heart would be extolling is not of this world. It is not of the world of the bourgeois order, nor is it of the world of the proletarian dictatorship, of the arduous period of transition from capitalism to socialism, communism. Especially not under the inconceivably challenging, in fact barbaric conditions that are symbolic of this period of transition in Soviet Russia. On the whole, Rosa Luxemburg saw everything clearly and assessed everything correctly. The Bolsheviks had achieved the most that people in their social and historical context could have achieved. They could not transcend the historical forces of their time, could not achieve 'the miracle' of realising a perfect, ideal form of democracy. This was Rosa Luxemburg's assessment as reflected in the concluding part of her essay on Bolshevist policy. According to me, in the critical analysis of the individual measures constituting this policy, she is not able to do complete justice to the real conditions on the ground that prevented this miracle from becoming a reality. This is the other weakness from which her critique of Bolshevist policy suffers.

Rosa Luxemburg wholeheartedly endorses the dissolution of the Constituent Assembly by the Bolsheviks after the transfer of political power to the soviets. Equally strongly she condemns their not having announced fresh elections for the formation of another Constituent Assembly. She advocates: Soviets forming the strong backbone of proletarian power and a Constituent Assembly with universal suffrage. This begs the question: what should be the character of the Constituent Assembly that is being demanded, what should be its role? Should it be an institution with powers that, in addition to the soviets, would secure the interests and influence of the bourgeois classes? In that case, it is inevitable that there will be conflicts over jurisdiction, power struggles between the Constituent Assembly and the Soviets that will have to be resolved through a superior authority, and once again the question that has already been answered by the revolution will arise: dictatorship of the proletariat and the peasants, or the dictatorship of the propertied classes.

Rosa Luxemburg has evidently not taken the obstructive and dangerous nature of dual power into account. She calls for "Soviets forming the strong backbone". Should then the Constituent Assembly only have a representative, an ornamental character? Should it initially formally legitimise the Soviets as a product of the "will of the people"? But the Soviets have already legitimised themselves with the conquest of political power through the revolutionary law. As Lassalle tried to explain to the proletariat, "If you capture power, you will live in justice." Seeking to legitimise the Soviets by means of the Constitution would be as good as contesting their legal right and, in the prevailing circumstances, is tantamount to an infringement, a smashing of their power. Should the Constituent Assembly, alongside the Soviets, be just a political debating society and a social council for peer reviewing on a large scale, with a consultative voice; should it be an instrument to provoke reflection and cross-fertilisation of ideas in the Soviets and to enlighten the bourgeois classes on the political and social collaboration in the evolution of a new order?

Rosa Luxemburg did not pose these very obvious questions. I am, however, of the view that Soviet Russia has already given her a fitting reply and Bolshevik tactics have proved to be correct. Admittedly, the convening of a Constituent Assembly and the meeting of parliament flowing from universal suffrage would perhaps have weakened and overcome resistance and sabotage by a section of the bourgeois classes, at least of the 'intellectuals.' Granted also that through these mechanisms governments of capitalist countries would have been denied the excuse for not recognising Soviet power, and conspiring with their Russian arch enemies to prevent the establishment of a workers' and peasants' republic, and for arming and maintaining the White Guards against them.

Yet the influence of such a 'democracy' on the national and international counter-revolution should not be overestimated. The propertied classes of all nations are not as easily satisfied as the poor proletarian devils; they are cool, good orators and not so easily taken in by appearances, especially when political power and the power to exploit are at stake. This is true when they are fighting amongst themselves to gain political power and the power to exploit, and would be even more true when the fight is with the have-nots. At the time of the French Revolution, the National Assembly, the Constituent Assembly and the Legislative Assembly were no protection against the aristocracy or the high clergy who plotted to restore the old order, who led the Chouans of Vendee against Paris, who raised the monarchist armies of Europe against their own countries. These parliamentary bodies established by the 'will of the people' were not even able to restrain pious England – whose own system of government was the product of Civil War – from going to war against a revolutionary France with troops and counterfeit assignations. That the Russian counter-revolution was not in the least deterred by the existence of a parliament was clearly evident from the threat of a coup d'état by the tsarist military prior to the proletarian revolution of 1917. This counter-revolution and its international cohorts would have remained eyeball-to- eyeball with the Soviet Republic and they would not have laid down their weapons even before a Constituent Assembly.

On the other hand, something else would certainly have occurred. The Constituent Assembly would have become the 'legal' rallying point and haven for the counter-revolution and its offshoots in Russia and abroad. In fact, a worse outcome than the immediate strengthening of the counter-revolution was feared. Undoubtedly, the broad mass of the proletariat and peasants were irresistibly taken up by the slogan, "All power to the soviets!" and were drawn into the revolution. However, the slogan was as yet not firmly and indelibly fixed in the minds of the masses through the working and functioning of the soviets as the instrument of social transformation. The convening of the Constituent Assembly would have surely introduced contradictions, uncertainties and vacillation in the thoughts and deeds of the workers and peasants. Consequently, preserving the forms of bourgeois democracy would have resulted in the weakening and endangering of revolutionary proletarian democracy, which is the precursor to perfect democracy in a classless society. Behind the apparently harmless and, in terms of *realpolitik*, cleverly functioning Constituent Assembly lurks the dictatorship of the bourgeoisie, the counter-revolution that is ready to deal a blow. The Soviet government must experience the proletarian revolution before bourgeois democracy.

Rosa Luxemburg sharply criticizes the fact that in Soviet Russia the prevailing form of suffrage is not universal but restricted to those who live by their work. In other words, the exploiters of work are excluded from the right to vote. Her comments on this issue reveal clearly how incomplete her information on the prevailing conditions in Russia was while she was behind bars. Thus, it appears that Rosa Luxemburg is not aware that the form of suffrage introduced in Russia had been categorically declared to be 'provisional.' It is thus consistent with the precondition, under which within the framework of the proletarian revolution, even she would accept the denial of political rights as a concrete example of disciplinary action against the bourgeoisie.

In reality, the exclusion of the beneficiaries of exploitation is intended to be punitive with a view to securing proletarian power in Soviet Russia. The introduction of a system of soviets did not mean an end to capitalism. Only the path had been cleared and social forces unleashed to overcome it. The young Soviet republic felt constrained by the prevalent economic and social power of the bourgeoisie in its daily work of transformation – of dismantling and building up. In fact, it felt threatened. Should it strengthen this power further through political rights in the Soviets? Such an action would have implied the devaluing and blunting of the soviets as an instrument of power and revolution of the productive masses. That political disempowerment was not carried out as a 'punishment' due to involvement in sabotage or conspiracy etc. – as held by Rosa Luxemburg – but was instead a general disciplinary measure, is factually correct, I think. Foreseeing a problem is better than second thoughts.

Rosa Luxemburg's prediction that the electoral regulations would lead to the disenfranchisement of an increasing number of workers and petit bourgeois did not come true because Soviet Russia's ruined economy could not guarantee employment to all able-bodied persons willing to work. There is no denying that terrible economic deprivation compelled many urban proletarians to turn their backs on factory work and instead to migrate to the countryside. In such cases they did not lose their right to vote. In fact, they often functioned as political motivators who mobilized the peasantry and transformed political apathy into an interest in voting. In addition, there were other important reasons for the increase in workers and the franchised, despite the steady economic decline.

The creation of the Red Army deprived industry, agriculture and other sectors of the economy and administration of millions of capable workers. These men lost their right to vote, but substitutes now had to replace them at the anvil and the plough. The need to equip and maintain the army necessitated the harnessing of all economic forces to achieve peak performances and miracles. The fervent desire for the development and assertion of Soviet Russia was marked by the same zeal. The management and distribution of basic necessities under 'War Communism' required a large number of personnel; other Soviet organisations and offices required an equally large number of personnel. The vast and comprehensive efforts undertaken to educate the masses – the likes of which had never been seen in any other country or period till then – created a field of engagement for tens of thousands. The same held good for the public organisation of the health care system, for establishing and setting up hospitals and old peoples' homes, for establishing homes for mothers and infants, crèches and kindergartens etc. Whatever was lacking in terms of technical equipment and tools was made up for, as far as possible, by manpower. The rapid and massive integration of women in the social economy and administration of Soviet Russia was not only due to respect for the principle of gender equality, but also the result of the compulsion to meet the huge demand for manpower. That has changed now, but the involuntary unemployed still enjoy the right to vote. At the beginning of December 1920, Soviet Russia was the only modern state where unemployment was not a mass phenomenon.

Thus, unlike Rosa Luxemburg, I do not see an anachronistic precursor to a fully developed communist society in the fact that in Soviet Russia active and passive suffrage is linked to one's own output and not to exploitative work. On the contrary, in principle I believe that this link is essential, in fact indispensable. It represents a radical break with the laws of the past, a break with the bourgeois system of private property. The bourgeois revolutions have brought about political equality of bourgeois property and income with feudal property, but the continued existence of private ownership of the means of production has meant the continuation of inequality in terms of property and lack of property. This state of affairs was reflected in the old system of suffrage with its restrictions and privileges linked to the payment of taxes, the level of education etc. and its disfranchisement of the producing mass of people. The introduction of a universal, equal and direct suffrage is an indication that the exploited and dispossessed class is now pushing its way up from within the bosom of bourgeois society. A consciousness of their situation has emerged to such an extent that they assert the validity of social work output, besides possession of property, for securing political rights.

The proletarian revolution, the goal of which is to eliminate the private ownership of the means of production, to destroy the power of private ownership over employment, and the power of the owner and the exploiter over the worker must ensure that this revolution is also expressed in terms of political rights. Electoral franchise that forms the democratic basis of the legislative, executive and governing political power must be rooted in socially necessary and useful labour. It must be the franchise of productive social citizens. It must exclude the exploiters and beneficiaries of alienated labour. The electoral franchise of the Soviets is consistent with this. It is the electoral franchise of the first great victory of the proletarian revolution. Having destroyed the bourgeois state and created the system of Soviets, the proletarian revolution had to introduce an electoral franchise that conformed to its historical and social nature. If the Soviets are the pillars and instruments of political power and of the revolutionary will of the workers and peasants, then the electoral franchise of the Soviets must necessarily also be the franchise of manual and intellectual workers. The reason for this is not only due to its practical implications, but also because of the fundamental ideological significance of the same. The proclamation of the principle: "Those who do not labour, those who exploit the labour of others cannot vote, cannot be elected," is not merely intended to disenfranchise capitalists and make them powerless but also to socially stigmatize and ostracize them. Today, this is a rule of the proletarian dictatorship and in socialist education; tomorrow it will be accepted as a matter of course.

Rosa Luxemburg's posthumously published critical observations and the questions raised by her on Bolshevist policy during the proletarian dictatorship are indeed very valuable and deserve utmost serious and thoughtful attention. This does not mean that I agree with her on all counts. The importance of this publication lies elsewhere. Rosa Luxemburg is here categorically highlighting the many complex problems and huge difficulties that the proletariat encountered immediately after its first decisive victory – the conquest of political power – as well as the heavy responsibilities that fell to it. Were the workers, who were revolting against the capitalists, and we communists to simply turn a blind eye to these issues, we would be following the extremely pernicious policy of burying our heads in the sand like ostriches.

The seizure of political power does not mean an end to the proletariat's arduous struggle that has been full of dangers and sacrifices. Rather, it now stands before newer and even more difficult challenges and struggles. It cannot be catapulted into the communist paradise from the hell that was capitalism by just one single powerful yearning-driven beat of the wings. It must negotiate the purgatory of transition in a manner befitting the dictatorship of the proletariat. This is not due to the lust for revenge or power on the part of the proletariat, but rather because of the bourgeoisie fighting them tooth and nail to prevent the eradication of capitalism and the establishment of the communist system.

A clear-headed look would, however, show that the proletarian dictatorship is an act of self-defence to protect and expand the revolution and its achievements. It must deprive the bourgeoisie of the power and hope to ever again be able to restore the old order through the use of cunning or might. It must prevent any attacks on the new system and, as far as possible, defeat such attacks. The victorious proletariat requires peace to focus on cleaning up the debris of the capitalist order and on establishing a higher society. The gigantic tasks facing it demand an extremely 'humane economy.' It must not destroy people as did the blood-soaked model of capitalism. People must not be allowed to waste away. Every effort must be made to draw as many people as possible to productive labour. But: "Even the most pious person may not live in peace, if it does not please his wicked neighbour."

After the establishment of the proletarian state the still prevalent power of the propertied class, capitalist power, is and remains "a wicked neighbour"; whereas the rule and dictatorship of the proletariat is certainly a culmination, but not the end of all class struggles in a country. And dictatorship, the exercise of political power, of the one over the other implies under the circumstances the restriction, in fact, suspension of fundamental rights of the enemies of the extant regime. Under the circumstances it implies an increase in the use of violence culminating in terror. The character and the specific measures of the proletarian dictatorship reflect the power relations amongst the classes that are battling each other. They also reflect the level of maturity and power that the proletariat has achieved and the power and the spirit of resistance mustered up by the defenders of the old capitalist order. It is obvious that the dictatorship of the proletariat can be milder and more magnanimous, the stronger and more entrenched the power of the productive masses is, and the weaker and more insignificant the power of its enemies is.

The dictatorship itself is one of the most difficult problems that the proletariat has to deal with during the period of transition to communism. To what extent can fundamental rights be restricted, in fact denied and still be compatible with democracy, which is the oxygen ensuring the development and the active participation of the broad, productive masses and which is, therefore, indispensable for meeting the objectives of the revolution? Where is the boundary where the rights and duties of the majority collide violently with the rights and duties of the minority, and with those of the individual? Where is the boundary beyond which the well-being of millions, of the whole of society justifies the use of the most extreme and terrible form of violence – the extermination of human life? When does this use of violence cease to be an act of self-atonement in defence of society and become a barbaric, horrible crime, which violates against the respect for the value of every human life, and which, in contrast to capitalism, is regarded as the highest vision of communism.

During its dictatorship, the proletariat will be faced by these and other similar questions. All these questions, however, are not posed as abstract, academic award-winning questions, to be discussed calmly, only to conclude with philosophical scepticism in the manner of Pilate and exclaim with a shrug: "What is truth?" Rather, they weigh down heavily upon the proletariat and its responsible leaders in their fierce struggle against ruthless and unrelenting enemies, who endeavour to push the proletariat back into the old system of exploitation and slavery. They weigh down the proletariat day in day out, tenaciously demanding an answer in a concrete form – ranging from decisions over a counter-revolutionary pamphlet to decisions that are taken after much tortuous soul-searching.

All this is happening in the wake of the revolution that has destroyed the old social structures governing relationships and before the new superior ones have crystallised. In times of turbulent historical churning, issues that normally remain dormant in the depths of humans and society are pushed to the surface. And these are not always only golden in nature; they could also be sludge or volcanic, burnt-out slag. War is a bad 'teacher,' whether it is waged between peoples or between the citizens of the same country. It tears down the grid of civilization, of humanity, bringing to the fore the bestial in humans, in the form of addictions, obsessions, lust, passions that have been inherited by humans from their dark, animal past and which normally lie latent in the sub-conscious. The dictatorship of the proletariat puts the political and human maturity of the proletariat, of its leading party, of the revolutionary, to the test. It means moral conflict of conscience that cannot be stifled by catchwords or universal historical truths, and which has to be fought daily, on a case-by-case basis. What is at stake here is more than just the peace of mind of the decision-maker – it is, in fact, the well-being of millions, whose fate is entwined with the outcome of the proletarian revolution.

Rosa Luxemburg's critical reflections on Bolshevist policy on the dictatorship of the proletariat are coloured by her clear understanding of the complex problems posed by history and of the burden of responsibility of those engaging with them. Rosa Luxemburg's keen sense of history and her deep and pure humanity, embodied in her perception that "existence's infinite chain" binds all living beings to each other, were captured in her succinct words and often only in allusions. Rosa Luxemburg, the expert on the history of revolutions, the astute revolutionary thinker does not use the yardstick of bourgeois morality to measure the hardships during the proletarian dictatorship and the horror of terror, as reflected, according to her, in the Bolshevist policy. Nor does she take this opportunity to angrily condemn Bolshevist policy in general and terror in particular 'on principle.' She is free of any such apparently superior but childish-helpless illusion, as if this tough historical compulsion, as invoked by the counter-revolution, could be averted through solemn oaths for 'democracy,' 'just and mild' management of proletarian dictatorship and the basic rejection of terror. Terror is a tactical problem, not one of principle. It can neither be invoked nor discarded 'on principle.' Historically, it has to be understood in the context of the actual conditions in which it occurred.

Rosa Luxemburg considers Bolshevik dictatorship from the perspective of securing and advancing the proletarian revolution. According to her, this policy had exceeded the boundaries mentioned above and had, therefore, jeopardised the proletarian revolution itself, which it believed it was defending. Recall the relevant sections from the posthumously published pamphlet pertaining to the 'suppression of democracy' through the gagging of the freedom of the press, the right to form associations and to assemble; sections on the relentless struggle against the Mensheviks, the Social Revolutionaries, in brief on all the non-Bolshevik parties; sections on the terror unleashed against the bourgeoisie. These sections have been reproduced above, as also Rosa Luxemburg's views on the impending consequences of Bolshevik policy: the pauperisation and brutalisation of public life, the emergence of an autocratic and corrupt bureaucracy, the shift from class rule and class dictatorship of the proletariat to party rule, to a clique system, and to a dictatorship of individuals. The general conclusions that Rosa Luxemburg has drawn with inexorable logic stand firm as walls. But the question arises: is the concrete foundation on which they are based, on which they are premised, equally firm? This is precisely the question, the answer to which is crucial for correctly assessing Bolshevist policy.

Contrary to her normal method of working, which was to corroborate general conclusions drawn through factual evidence, on the issue of the stifling of public life in Soviet Russia by the Bolshevik Party, Rosa Luxemburg does not furnish any factual evidence. She provides merely a very general description and gives only one example: The two hundred "sacrificial victims" of the Social Revolutionary conspiracy that resulted in the assassination of the German ambassador Mirbach. This case shall be discussed in another context. Providing just one example, no matter how shocking, seems to me to be scanty evidence.

"What more do we require as further proof?" would be the cry of the self-styled guardians of 'democracy.' All of them, from Miliukov to Crispien, from Stampfer to Marlow, under the leadership of the high priest Kautsky, point to the Bolsheviks and screech to the governments of the entente imperialists: "Crucify them! Crucify them!" For them conclusive evidence of the Bolshevist terror are rumours circulated by Russian anti-Bolsheviks of all shades. Evidence for them are the allegations, imprecations, curses, lamentations and accusations made against the Bolsheviks by liberals, democrats, Mensheviks, populists, in short by all parties, whose policy was "weighed and found wanting" by the workers and peasants during the November Revolution. In addition, there is then the chorus of the big landlords, manufacturers, merchants, financers, speculators and usurers, for all of whom the country of the 'Uprising' became a place full of horror because the proletarian power dared to stretch out its irreverent and disrespectful fist for the properties of these people, who then fled with as much of their wealth as possible across the border with the help of the German Embassy, or who "shivered in their tiny cellars", where they anxiously guarded their treasure, fearing more for it than for their own lives.

Are they really impeccable, 'objective' witnesses or are they rather parties, who through their accusations of a "Bolshevist rule that is violent and bloody" seek to overwhelm and influence the 'public opinion' of the world?

Posing questions means finding an answer to them also. There is no doubt that those opposing and attacking the Bolshevik policy must also be heard – only then would it be possible to obtain a true picture of the Russian Revolution. However, it would never ever be the correct way to judge the situation solely on the basis of their statements. Who would be so thoughtless as to write the history of the great French Revolution without using any material other than the narratives of nightmares, anecdotes and grievances of the emigrant nobles and the clergy, who were stoking a desire in the German princes and their subservient subjects to destroy the 'devil's handiwork' in France.

There are many factors that must be kept in mind if we have to make a correct assessment, given the explosive accusations rending the air, emanating from the 'expropriated expropriators' thrown out from industry and from the government of Soviet Russia. Then, there is the virulent hatred of those, who in the larger framework of 'democracy' worship the golden calf, those who mourn the loss of power to greedily and hastily exploit. There is also the bitter disappointment of those civilians and social democrats genuinely harbouring the illusion of providing a panacea for social renewal, and who find that this is rejected by the "obtuse and misguided masses" in favour of the "crude political formula and brutal diktat" of the Bolsheviks. There is the extremely vitiated atmosphere caused by the longstanding battle amongst social democrats of different hues – an atmosphere that necessarily becomes even more explosive at the time of the revolution. Political in-fighting is the worst form of fighting because all sides fight with an equally impassioned belief in their cause and because hate is tinged with a bit of disappointed love.

Included in the ranks of the Russian 'anti-Bolshevists' were clever, in fact very sharp politicians, socialist and social democratic intellectuals of international repute, talented writers with connections to all the master countries. Despite the 'Cheka' and the isolation and the blockade of Soviet Russia they had at their disposal hundreds of ways and means to transmit across the world "the truth about the Jacobian-Bonapartist dictatorship of the Bolsheviks". Their moving lamentations, their 'acceptable' and 'sensible' views and objectives, or even their gold, opened the doors to innumerable publications and reception rooms of "leading personalities" abroad. In all countries, they were welcomed and supported by bourgeois parties and governments, who trembled at the thought that in their countries as well the exploited might begin to talk with their oppressors in 'Russian.' They were patronised by social democratic and trade union leaders who viewed the bold act of the Bolsheviks as the greatest historical reproach for having abandoned the proletarian class struggle, the revolution.

For Lwow, Kerensky, Alexinsky, Tschenow, Zeretelli, Martov, Abramovich and others of their ilk the "downfall of the Bolshevist terrorists" was the focus of their politics. They had nothing better to do than to work towards this goal. In the meantime, the "fanatically dogmatic perpetuators of the bloody tsarist regime in revolutionary garb" exerted all their energies, wore themselves out with worry, and toiled in battles against the offshoots of local counter-revolutionary groups and against the violence and intrigues of international imperialists in order to build up and protect Soviet Russia. Hundreds of suspicions and allegations against them and their work were topics of heated discussions, without them ever having the opportunity of repudiating even one of these.

And yet, amongst the eloquent lawyers trumpeting "civil rights suppressed" by the Bolsheviks, there was hardly anyone, who had not concurred or at least acquiesced when these oft-quoted civil rights remained on paper under the government of the liberals or at the time of 'pure democracy' under the Kerensky government – when the jails filled up with Bolsheviks, when the rebellious peasants and demonstrating workers were gunned down, and when thousands of soldiers were recruited, armed with machine guns and pushed into the imperialist offensive. Even the Kautskys of the various social democratic factions remained silent in all languages on the "desecration and murder of democracy" in Russia. Similarly, the harmoniously united Mensheviks and bourgeois democrats later denied the rule of violence and terror they had initiated in the 'model State' of Georgia with British assistance and under the British Protectorate. Of course, these impartial representatives of world history subsequently let the much discredited and abused 'democracy' come all the more abundantly into its own. That is to say, only after the workers and peasants of Georgia had liberated themselves from exploitation and slavery by this 'democracy' with the help of the Red Army. Then, before the 'whole of civilized humanity' and the two 'worthy' Internationals in particular, these expelled keepers of the grail levelled fierce charges against Bolshevist violence. In a political struggle every party and every politician claims as its 'most sacred right' what has been registered as a crime when committed by an opponent.

The above-mentioned observations may appear to some to be digressing from Rosa Luxemburg's wide-ranging reflections. Surely, not these alone, and particularly not these, should be used for Bolshevist-baiting just because of the highly respected name attached to them? And isn't just this what is jubilantly being done these days? Most definitely within Germany, but also outside Germany. All capitalist elements are involved in this. They want to gain the highest prize—i.e. the greatest opportunity to exploit—by recognising the Soviet government. And sooner or later states would be compelled to do this because of the collapse of the world economy. Falling over themselves are the Majority Social Democratic and Independent leaders, who prefer a coalition with Stinnes over one with the proletarian united front supported by the communists. They want to scuttle the forward advance of the proletariat, the call for which was given by the Executive of the Third International. Emblematic of this is the style at the Leipzig Party Congress of the Independent Social Democratic Party, where the Menshevik, Abramovich, played the role of a lead tenor to the accompaniment of Crispien's unctuous sobbing. It was 'revealed' that more than 300 Mensheviks in prison in Moscow were supposed to have been driven to undertake a hunger strike due to the most horrific torture they were being subjected to and the persistent threat of being deported to Turkestan. They were, thus, to become martyrs to their cause. A radiogram from Soviet Russia proclaimed that 34 Mensheviks were to be banished from Moscow for their counter-revolutionary activities, with the choice of settling in one of the cities under the government of Twer, Woronesch, or Jaroslawl, or be deported abroad at the cost of the Soviet government. What did this announcement achieve? The lie was celebrated in a transfigured form and will find its way around the world.

The gruesome and moving reports of the fanatic intolerance of the Bolsheviks, of their "barbaric persecution of dissenters", of the wasting of the best forces of the country are immediately revealed as lies through one fact alone: be it schools, educational or training institutions of any kind, be it shelters, homes, hospitals, be it universities, at all soviet institutions, and at the managerial level of all industrial ventures, everywhere there were several 'independents' and supporters of varied political hues. Very often they formed the majority of those employed and occupied the most influential positions. They do not make any bones about not subscribing to communism and sharply criticize the prevailing conditions. This can be verified by anyone who cares to examine the conditions impartially. What hurt Soviet Russia was the sabotage by the 'intellectuals'; it was and is not the removal of "those willing to work" on grounds of their political convictions and beliefs. How could it have been otherwise, given the huge demand for trained, skilled manpower in all sectors? The Bolshevist "burners of heretics at the stake" could not exercise any coercion in this regard. In fact, the reverse was true:

they themselves were constrained and sought to ensure that opportunity was provided to the capable to enrich and stimulate social life in Soviet Russia by contributing their talents and abilities.

The great conflict between the intellectuals and the Soviet government at the beginning of the proletarian dictatorship had nothing to do with the "violation of the freedom of expression". The roots of that tension lay in the basic assumption and valuation of intellectual and mental labour as socially necessary and useful work that was no different from manual labour and deserving of similar payment. This issue was resolved in the only way it could be during the period of transition: through the changed, necessarily pragmatic approach of the Bolsheviks to this issue. If, in this case, there is talk of "violation of the freedom of expression", then it is necessary to mention the underlying 'communist dogma' of the social parity of intellectual and physical labour. In this struggle, the 'intellectuals' were concerned about far more real and concrete things than just the "democratic freedom of expression"; their concern was over their socially privileged position and higher salary. The weapon that they unscrupulously made use of in this struggle was not in any way 'democracy' but social power based on the indispensability and importance of their work. And not a few of the intellectuals used their freedom of expression in the debate over the contentious issue to sharply counter Bolshevik politics and the dictatorship of the proletariat. What was important for them was to gain victory over the opinion of others. But now let us return to the main discussion.

These developments allayed Rosa Luxemburg's doubts that the compulsions of political dictatorship might deprive the young Soviet Republic of the productive, inspiring, valuable and indispensable contribution of men and women with the most diverse opinions. These compulsions, however, did not result in action against the diverse opinions; instead they were directed at the counter-revolutionary plots. Action against counter-revolutionary plots was necessary to ensure the survival of Soviet Russia.

From the foregoing it is obvious that the objective of Bolshevist dictatorship could not be to make its policy acceptable. It would be absurd to seek to delude oneself and others into believing that it had till then been mildly educative and politically paternal in nature. No, more often than the leading Bolsheviks would have liked, the iron fist had to be applied to secure the severely endangered rule of the proletariat. Of course, not all measures and actions of the proletarian dictatorship would in each and every case have been models of political acumen and of abstract justice 'for all times'. It is possible that individual revolutionary commissioners, lacking political understanding, could perchance have passed brutal judgements, and have had these executed without any trace of empathy. In some places, the centuries' long agony and torment the working masses had been subjected to by their 'masters' resulted in the eruption of atrocities against the 'bourgeoisie.' However, all of these are the consequences of any revolution and not the specific outcome of a particular system of Bolshevist policy. The 'terror' did create martyrs in the ranks of the anarchists, Social Revolutionaries and Mensheviks as well as amongst the bourgeois counter-revolutionaries. These martyrs died out of conviction for their cause or filled up prisons. The dead bodies of the fallen and executed were glorified by the press of all 'democrats' and of all 'lovers of law and order', including Stampfer and Hilferding. Curses against the "Bolshevik fiends" pound on the prison gates of those arrested. Unnoticed and unsung by 'public opinion' are the many dedicated Bolsheviks and communists assassinated by the anarchists and by the Social Revolutionaries, the several thousand revolutionary fighters, who were victims of counter-revolutionary conspiracies and of rebellions.

The fair and wise judges of "Bolshevik dictatorship and terrorist methods" generally overlook one fact. And yet that fact is the very basis underlying all the cases on which they pass judgement. As in all other revolutions, so too under the proletarian dictatorship in Soviet Russia, red terror is a reaction to white terror, an act of self-defence. The creation of a Soviet state did not result in internal peace, instead it ushered in the most bitter and vicious civil war. On the heels of the Soviet state came the sabotage by the intellectuals, followed by thousands of spirited, secret and open acts of resistance to the new system. The conspiracies, rebellions, troops led by tsarist generals wreaking havoc, all had the blessings and support of the Social Revolutionaries and other admirers of bourgeois democracy. This volatile situation was further aggravated by incursions of imperialist troops from the bordering states, by the blockade and the huge campaigns financed by the gold of the entente. Revolution and counter-revolution stood in close confrontation. The Soviet government had to do what Marx had described as the primary goal of any revolutionary power: "defeat the enemy". This is something that genuine, preeminent Marxist strategists of world history should be able to grasp.

Precisely at the time when the Bolshevik dictatorship aroused doubts in the mind of Rosa Luxemburg, bourgeois enemies such as the Mensheviks and the Social Revolutionary opponents could not be tackled with velvet gloves. Probably the proletarian government, the proletarian revolution in Soviet Russia had never before been confronted with graver threats than at that time. In addition to the other incidents of the civil war, they also had to contend with the revolt by the Czechoslovak Legion. The conspiracy by the Social Revolutionaries that cost Count Mirbach his life was in fact directed against the Soviet power. The assassination of the German envoy was intended to tear up the blood and sword peace of Brest-Litovsk and overthrow the government that had concluded it. Had they succeeded, the result would most definitely have been a renewed outbreak of war between the two blocs of alliances – an outcome desired by the Russian imperialists. However, of particular importance in assessing the terrible condition of the Soviet state then is that it had at its disposal only the disconnected ruins of an armed power. The Red Army, the strong rampart of Soviet Russia's freedom and existence, was yet to be organized.

The horror drama of 200 "sacrificial victims" must be viewed in the context of these facts. The heart cries out in pain at the thought of the victims. How much more it would have had to bear and bewail had the conspiracy not been relentlessly quelled in time with an iron hand. The ensuing civil war would have been even fiercer and would have consumed tens of thousands, and the concomitant renewed outbreak of an imperialist war would have resulted in the deaths of hundreds of thousands. In this case, severity prevented a greater calamity from occurring. Many thousands less have fallen victim to the much maligned Bolshevik reign of terror in comparison to the great French Revolution that is now glorified by the bourgeoisie. Equally fewer people have been destroyed by terror in the course of the Revolution in Russia than were hanged, beheaded and incarcerated every year in defence of feudal France.

Nobody, who is the beneficiary and protector of the bourgeois order—this callous and insatiable man-eater—has the right to bitterly and angrily curse the 'Bolsheviks' and their methods of struggle. The gold flow of capitalist profit is accompanied day in day out by a stream of blood, even in times of peace. In the years preceding the World War, the battlefield of labour in Germany alone was marked by an annual average of half a million wounded, and of these approximately 150,000 were seriously injured, of whom many will remain crippled for the rest of their lives; 10,000 dead are a testimony to the capitalist pursuit of profit. The reformist leaders of Labour parties and of trade unions, in particular, should out of shame not raise the matter of victims of the Bolshevik terror regime. They collaborated with the bourgeoisie and for the benefit of the latter led the workers into the bloody World War. This is the case especially in Germany, where the hands of Ebert, Noske and their consorts are stained with the blood of the fallen and assassinated revolutionaries, including Rosa Luxemburg, in whose shadow they squat, and childishly hurl invectives against Soviet Russia.

The revulsion of the Majority Social Democrats and Independent leaders against the "terror" and "brutally violent methods" of the Russian communists conceals their aversion towards revolution itself. Those desiring revolution cannot shy away from its excesses, intemperateness and horror. The revolution has to be viewed as a whole. Even the smartest and the strongest do not have the power to take merely the 'best' and to contemptuously push away with a foot the bad, in order to ensure a 'clean and beautiful' revolution. Rosa Luxemburg, who read the past and present with a scientific spirit and a revolutionary heart in order to provide insights for the future, was conscious of this fact. Even when the shadow of the Chimborazo of anti-Bolshevik allegations and calumny reached her Breslau jail cell, she did not on grounds of morality contemptuously turn up her nose or indulge in smart talk to distance herself in principle from Bolshevik tactics. Instead she restricted herself to critically appraising its limitations and appropriateness. She would not have been the conscientious researcher and fighter that she was, if she had not focused keenly and sharply on the maze of intersecting and contradictory tendencies of old and new historical thought in an effort to distinguish between what she believed would secure the proletarian revolution and what would jeopardise it.

In this context what Rosa Luxemburg said about the dangers of an excessive bureaucracy and on the proletarian class rule getting restricted to a party and clique rule is remarkable. However, I believe that in her appraisal of anticipated developments she overstates the accountability of Bolshevik policy and its "suppression of democracy" for this. Her position on this is probably coloured by the vestiges of her past opposition to the Bolsheviks that was mired in the fear that the 'Lenin Party' would ossify into a formula and dogma-ridden party, lacking the necessary revolutionary flexibility to adapt to existing historical conditions. Nonetheless, as regards the issue itself, Rosa Luxemburg correctly identified it. The bureaucracy is an evil that the Soviet Republic has to resist with all its might. The bureaucracy is primarily the by-product of the rapidly increasing and expanding responsibilities of the proletarian state. The state, however, does not have at its disposal a concomitantly large and appropriately well-trained, experienced workforce to deal with these.

The bureaucracy, its role in the proletarian state, its relationship with the masses and with 'democracy' is a thorny problem. It also includes the vexed issue of the social status of intellectual and manual work, which in the future will create difficulties for every socialist and communist country. There were specific circumstances in Soviet Russia which resulted in such a rampant spread of bureaucracy that the negative features associated with it mushroomed exponentially: the backwardness and the collapse of the economy, the as yet insufficiently developed competence and proficiency to rationally organize activities, the enormous number of illiterates, the severe shortage of trained manpower for both intellectual and manual work, the as yet poor work discipline of the proletariat, the functions of 'War Communism', the defensive wars the Soviet Republic was forced to enter into, the urge of the established bourgeoisie to secure for itself a life that is as far as possible non-proletarian in nature. It is not without reason that in Soviet Russia there is much and not very positive talk about an emerging 'Soviet bourgeoisie'. Incidentally, currently there are similar occurrences *mutatis mutandis* in all countries and not least since the revolution in Germany. In this case the conquest of political power by the proletariat is casting an ugly shadow in the form of party and trade union bureaucrats rapidly morphing into bureaucratic bourgeois, who as ministers will also function as lackeys of the bourgeoisie.

Again, Rosa was right in warning that the communist party must not transform itself from being a party of the proletariat into a party that dictates to the proletariat. During the destructive struggle and subsequent work of construction, the party must educate and create awareness among the working masses regarding their historical role and task. The party should not become an isolated authority-wielding, oppressive entity, issuing commands to the masses. It is an indisputable fact that in Soviet Russia there are indications that the opposite is true. If this trend continues without any hindrance, the communist party in Soviet Russia will be transformed into an authority outside and above the proletariat. There are definite internal and external connections between such tendencies and the threat of the mushrooming and degeneration of the bureaucracy. The bureaucracy is partly drawn from the communist party. It is the potential for such a career that has attracted some new communists who lack the necessary political conviction and it has also undermined the political conviction of some old communists. It is for this purpose that they display unprecedented energy, work non-stop totally consumed by their work, take pride in responsibility, and demonstrate unconditional devotion to the party as a whole and to the best leaders. But even in this relationship quantity can turn into quality. The ability and habit of providing leadership can change into the brute power of commanding, the confidence of the committed masses can change into vacuous subservience. The bourgeois and social democratic 'anti-Bolsheviks' perceive this to be the relationship between the party— or to be frank—between the party leaders and the masses in Soviet Russia.

No other party than that of the Bolsheviks so keenly spots its deficiencies and mistakes, admits to these with scrupulous honesty, and energetically seeks to overcome them. And, of all parties, is it supposed to not be open to the disastrous consequences of the mushrooming and degeneration of bureaucracy, and to the reduction and ossification of the party as the mouthpiece of the leading clique? The graver the impending crisis appears to be, the more conscious and vigorous is the effort to ward it off. Evidence of this is provided by every congress of the party with its heated and tough debates on contentious issues as well as by every meeting of the Soviets carrying out their multifarious tasks.

The Communist Party of Russia fully recognizes what needs to be done so that with the consecrating penance of the proletarian revolution a new and higher life can blossom from the ruins. The party and the masses have to mutually support each other; through the give and take between them they will be more closely bound to each other and form an inseparable whole. In the long term, the party can only sustain an inspired and productive life among the masses, if the drive and desire to act creatively comes from the masses themselves. This does not, however, preclude it from being ideologically and organisationally a coherent whole as though cast in one mould with the masses. On the contrary, this is a prerequisite for its influence on the masses and by the masses. The party interacts with and educates the masses not by treating them as an amorphous, malleable, adaptable entity, but rather by developing their intellectual and political individuality in a clear-cut way so that a distinctive face emerges that is clearly recognisable in fair weather or foul, that can never be mistaken for anybody else and not ever be misunderstood. The bond of the communist party with the masses is not a mechanical one of the 'social revolutionary' type; rather it is a live one of action and the most knowledgeable, decisive and wholehearted representation of the interests and demands of the masses. This is the constant, abiding fundamental principle that distinguishes it from all other parties. The life of the party must be intimately connected with that of the masses. Thousands of nurturing veins and capillaries must criss-cross between the two. However, the life of the party must reach beyond the life of the masses. If this were not the case, it would cease to be the leader of the masses. Such a life does not in any way imply the narrowing of the mass party to a sect. There is room in it for growth, for expansion, but as an organic whole and not in the mechanical aggregation of alien elements. The consequence of this is that the party is able to carry and lead the masses not just at specific historical moments, but that it continuously assimilates the most advanced forces among the masses and a firm spiritual bond exists between them.

Incidentally, Rosa Luxemburg had recognized that for the victory and defence of the revolution it would be necessary to single out and organize minorities from among the masses as cohesive entities—within defined parameters—who would lead an 'independent existence'. In the "Spartacus Programme" under the section on "Immediate Measures to Secure the Revolution", she demands "the arming of the entire adult male population as a workers' militia, the formation of a Red Guard of proletarians as an active part of the militia for the permanent protection of the revolution against counter-revolutionary attacks and intrigues". What is the Red Guard, separated out from the general workers' militia, other than the communist party transiting from the political to the military? For the party should also be a consolidated, well-equipped, trained, permanent strike force, the active part of the masses. Besides, the demand for arming the proletariat is merely a component part of denying electoral franchise to capitalists in Soviet Russia; it supplements the "suppression of democracy" by the "restriction and suspension of the right to freedom of expression of the press, of the right of freedom to form associations and of the right to freedom of assembly". If I deny my arch enemy possession of a military weapon, with which he murders the supporters and protectors of the revolution, then what is the point in leaving him in possession of intellectual instruments with which he can influence the proletariat, converting them from revolutionaries, who overthrow the bourgeois order, into those who become supporters and protectors of the selfsame order? A carbine in the hands of a bourgeois, the power over a machine gun is harmless as compared to the formidable counter-revolutionary power of a Stinnes, as a newspaper proprietor and publisher, or of a publishing house such as Mosse, etc.

Had the Bolsheviks, the communists of Soviet Russia, actually ceased to be the party of the revolutionary proletarian masses, then these masses themselves would long ago have swept them into the garbage heap of history. The revolution cannot carry any sects, much less be led by one such. It sounds very mundane, but articulates the reality very clearly: the masses remained with the Bolsheviks because the Bolsheviks remained with the masses as the ruling party. This is 'the secret' of the effervescent and vital source of their power and not 'unprecedented terror' as imagined by the petty bourgeoisie – from Gottlieb Wilhelm Schulze to Karl Kautsky. Conscious of this fact, the "ossified zealots of the Bolshevik sect" utilised every opportunity and each minute to consistently and assiduously consolidate their bonds and solidarity with the mass of the workers, to draw them into the mental and political orbit of the party and retain them there.

Through innumerable channels, both direct and indirect, they set about introducing into the lives of the masses the revolutionary fervour of the party and filling their lives with a clear focus and indefatigable energy. The history of the West European workers' movement and particularly that of old German social democracy had taught them that well organized and disciplined comrades could march in splendid suffrage parades, but no revolution could take place without intellectually and politically aware and inspired masses. The influence of 'Bolshevism' was felt in Soviet Russia well beyond the confines of the party. It awakened interest, unleashed energies and multiplied activity. The programme to educate the masses in multifarious ways was a huge achievement in terms of its outreach – no words suffice to do justice to that enormous effort. The education and politicisation of the Red Army which, while defending the Revolution, simultaneously emerged as one of the strongest intellectually sound educational institutions was something a country could be proud of. A country could be proud of the social welfare facilities and the trade unions and co-operatives that were established and the functions and responsibilities of which were increasing with each passing day. That was and is the awakening of the masses, of the masses becoming active. In them beat the heart of the party, and in them lived the soul of the party. The Soviets and their institutions are the universities for the humane and social maturing of the masses. Even without the sanction and co-operation of a Constituent Assembly, without electoral franchise for the exploiters and despite the Bolshevik dictatorship, democracy, proletarian democracy, had begun to function here. Agreed it was not perfect and still somewhat disfigured by the birth marks of the period of transition; yet it remained strong and focused enough to secure the future.

In Soviet Russia under the proletarian dictatorship, a wonderful abundance of active forces have suddenly sprung up like mushrooms after a warm thunder shower. Undreamt of potential has been tapped. Many thousands, who were culturally impoverished prior to the Revolution, are taking the lead in establishing a higher culture. Thousands of unnamed and unknown people are their insightful, skilled and loyal co-workers in this venture. Admittedly, all these forces were not sufficient, with enemies and enormous difficulties all around, of catching up within these few years with all that capitalism had transformed and created over the centuries in other countries. Despite all this, they proved to be so strong and creative and titanic in their achievements that Soviet Russia, although abandoned by the proletariat of the whole world, dares to permit capitalism to be an assistant in the painful and difficult beginning. With manly confidence in its own strength it hopes to subdue this dreadful and dangerous assistant so that it remains a reluctant servant doing the economic spadework for communism and does not become an overbearing arbiter of Russian economy and politics. For as yet all power belongs to the Soviets.

Rosa Luxemburg was concerned and ruminated on approaching dangers for the proletarian revolution. Her clear eyes closed before she could witness the seriousness and energy with which Soviet Russia under the leadership of the Bolsheviks sought to beat back these dangers. However, Rosa Luxemburg lived long enough to clearly work out her fundamental position on the main issues: dictatorship of the proletariat, the Soviet system, the Constituent Assembly, bourgeois or proletarian dictatorship. If the voice of the Russian Revolution did not penetrate the walls of the Breslau prison loudly or convincingly enough, then soon the German Revolution unambiguously raised these issues. Unrestricted study and free discussions with well-informed friends certainly played an important role in the quick development of her understanding. More than this it was the outbreak of the German Revolution that enabled her to connect fully with the Russian Revolution and to formulate her own fundamental position on the important characteristics of a proletarian revolution in general. The times demanded revolutionary action from her and with Rosa Luxemburg thought always preceded action.

(Translated by Chitra Harshavardhan)

IV

Rosa Luxemburg's Attitude towards the Russian Revolution after the November Revolution in Germany

Rosa Luxemburg's 'revised' opinion of the problems of the Russian Revolution, a product of historical analysis / The Rote Fahne, the classic testimony for this / The Rote Fahne as the leading organ of the German Revolution, Rosa Luxemburg's work and her political testament / The Rote Fahne against the National Assembly, the German Constituent Assembly, and in favour of the Power of Councils / Criticism of the Congress of Councils and its position regarding proletarian dictatorship and bourgeois democracy / The Councils' Constitution as a means of overcoming 'separatism' / Civil liberties and terror / Position on the January Uprising in Berlin and criticism of the 'Independent' leaders during the struggle / Non-discussion of the theories and methods of the Bolsheviks, their practice under the banner of the Russian Revolution / The Paul Levi of 1918/19 against the Paul Levi of 1922 / The collaboration of Rosa Luxemburg and Karl Liebknecht during the months of the revolution, a proof of Rosa's change in attitude to the Russian Revolution / Rosa Luxemburg's alleged 'fundamental' rejection of terror

Rosa Luxemburg would not have been herself if, following her release from prison, she had not immediately thrown herself into the thunderous rapids of revolutionary events. However, she did not let herself be swept away or overwhelmed by these events, unlike the leaders of the Majority Social Democrats* and the Independents†,

* Also known simply as the Social Democratic Party of Germany (S.P.D.), it played an openly social-chauvinist role in World War I, calling for the support of German imperialism.

† The Independent Social Democratic Party of Germany (U.S.P.D.), formed in 1917 after an earlier split from the S.P.D. It tried to follow a centrist path between the S.P.D and the Spartacus League, later the Communist Party of Germany (K.P.D.), which played an independent role within the U.S.P.D. In December 1920 the U.S.P.D. split, with a majority of 400,000 members joining the K.P.D. and the remaining 340,000 staying with the U.S.P.D. In 1922 the U.S.P.D. merged with the S.P.D.

who on the eve of November 9 had either tried to prevent the Revolution or did not believe it was happening. On the contrary, she concentrated her greatest energy in understanding and thus guiding the revolutionary events and in how to bring their meaning to the consciousness of the masses and thereby to raise the uncertain and vacillating rebels into becoming focused and determined actors in the Revolution. The Majority Social Democrats and Independent 'anti-Bolsheviks' slander Rosa Luxemburg, when they try to portray her commitment to the proletarian dictatorship and the council system, her passionate struggle against the National Assembly and her exposure of bourgeois democracy as if it were some sort of temporary misunderstanding, a mistaken, careless accident, an emotion-driven lapse that swept her away, as if her clear mind was carried away by her warm heart. For this sharp and bold thinker, the thought that arose from her historical conviction was never the burnt out, gray ashes left over from the action, but rather the luminous flame that set the deed afire.

Thus her changed attitude toward the most difficult problems of the proletarian revolution was the result of careful consideration and the intellectual mastery of the historical situation and the basic conditions that set the stage for the working people's struggle for liberation. Rosa Luxemburg arrived at a fundamental outlook that guided her activity during the revolutionary period she was able to experience. This activity was the most determined and devoted struggle to push the revolution forward by the proletarian masses, to rid them of all the bourgeois and petty bourgeois illusions, which the competing Majority Social Democrats and the Independents had made their concern to build up. She did this before the broadest public, and it can be found in a classic document: The *Rote Fahne*[*]. This document proves that a little more than a week of reflection was enough for Rosa Luxemburg's superior mind to give a clear and firm answer to the questions that had been put on the historical agenda by the November Revolution in Germany as well: Council state power or National Assembly? Bourgeois democracy or revolution? That is, civil war or dictatorship of the proletariat?

The *Rote Fahne* waved for the first time before the proletarian masses on November 9 as the second evening edition of the *Berlin-*

[*] The *Rote Fahne* was the organ of the Spartacus League, later the Communist Party of Germany.

er Lokalanzeiger[*], which had been occupied in the late evening hours by members of the "Spartacus[†]" group. Due to technical difficulties the 'revolutionary' content of the improvised first issue had to be limited to incomplete reports on the political uprising in Berlin. The second issue, on the contrary, shows the desire to elevate the political uprising to the level of proletarian revolution. At the top of the sheet was the announcement of the conclusions that had been unanimously decided on by the just elected workers' and soldiers' councils. They were: "All men and women workers shall assemble in the factories on Sunday, November 10, at 10 a.m. and elect workers' councils. Women are eligible for election. (Employees are to be regarded as workers.) All soldiers should assemble in the barracks and military hospitals and elect soldiers' councils.... At 5 p.m. the chosen workers' and soldiers' councils should assemble in the Busch Circus and choose the provisional government."

A call: "To the Workers and Soldiers in Berlin," commented on the events and set forth a programme of 10 demands, which the proletariat "with full determination and indomitable fighting spirit" must carry out. Under item 1 it called for "disarming all police, all officers, and the soldiers who did not stand with the new order; arming the people; all soldiers and proletarians, who are armed, should keep their weapons." It is characterised by the following demands: "Elimination of the Reichstag[‡] and all parliaments and the existing imperial government; the takeover of the government by the Berlin workers' and soldiers' council until the establishment of a national workers' and soldiers' council; Item 7. Election of workers' and soldiers' councils throughout Germany, which will hold exclusive legislative and administrative authority. The entire adult population of working people in the cities and the countryside are to participate in the vote, without distinction by gender...."

"Item 10. The immediate recall of the Russian Embassy to Ber-

---

[*] A reactionary, pro-Kaiser Berlin daily newspaper.

[†] The Spartacus League was the group of German revolutionaries formed during World War I that included Rosa Luxemburg, Karl Liebknecht, Wilhelm Pieck, Leo Jogiches, Paul Levi and others. Initially working as an independent group within the U.S.P.D., in December of 1918 it became the Communist Party of Germany.

[‡] German Parliament, or Parliament of the German Empire.

lin." The call is not signed; it was directed either by the editors or by the Berlin Spartacus group to the workers and soldiers. There follows a "Greeting to the Russian Soviet Republic" from the *Rote Fahne* (Spartacus tendency). In other articles in this issue "the Spartacus group calls for meetings of factory employees, soldiers' councils, workers' committees, trade unions and political organisations." Among other things it asks: "In addition to the other most loyal and courageous comrades, Comrade Luxemburg should be sent to participate in the executive committee of the Central Workers' and Soldiers' Council of Germany or of any other similar political organ of this level that is formed."

The *Rote Fahne* that resulted from the transformation of the infamous court scandal sheet consisted only of these two issues. The power of the 'Spartacists' over it ended quickly. This was an indication that initially in Germany 'order' and bourgeois property was to triumph over the proletarian revolution, just as the first proclamation of the Provisional Government of the People's Representatives solemnly swore it would. During its one-day existence the newspaper had firmly and clearly struck its guiding principles, which were consistently continued in the later *Rote Fahne* issues. It unequivocally aroused the reaction that the 'bad example' of the Bolshevik methods and goals were beginning to ruin the 'good morals' of the German proletariat.

On Monday, November 18, the *Rote Fahne* appears again (No. 3), and this time as the central organ of the Spartacus League, Editorial board: Karl Liebknecht and Rosa Luxemburg. And now for the first time from a revolutionary newspaper it becomes the leading organ of the revolution, the only organ of the revolution. The *Rote Fahne*, for the proletarian revolution of 1918/1919, had the same overriding historical significance as that of the *Neue Rheinische Zeitung* under Marx's editorship for the bourgeois revolution of 1848. That it had this importance was due to Rosa Luxemburg's work and merit. Engels had declared: "The editorial staff of the *Neue Rheinische Zeitung* – that was the dictatorship of Karl Marx." With the same right we can claim that the management of the *Rote Fahne* was the dictatorship of Rosa Luxemburg. Those who find the word dictatorship harsh as it enters their delicate ears can replace this expression with 'authority' or 'acknowledged superiority' of the leadership. The *Rote Fahne* was Rosa Luxemburg herself with her clear, well-grounded insight into the course, the laws, the goal, of historical development in the conditions of the proletarian revolution; with her iron will she would pull the German revolution forward as far as possible, corresponding to its enormous international significance; with her warm heart, ready for self-sacrifice, that beat with the stormy rhythm of the times.

As valuable as the collaboration of other leading Spartacus League members was— especially that of Karl Liebknecht— without Rosa Luxemburg the *Rote Fahne* would not have been the *Rote Fahne.* She was the living soul of the newspaper, making it the clearest, most decisive and fiery voice of the revolution, the unerring beacon for the proletariat propelled forward. Without regard for her poor health – she had suffered greatly during her years in prison and from the emotional shock of the war years – with contempt for and even abuse of her needs, with every longing obliterated by the one great wish and desire, she gave herself entirely to this task. With scrupulous conscientiousness, she took care that in each issue the character of the *Rote Fahne,* its opinion on the issues and demands of the day raised by the revolution, would be expressed as clearly and sharply as possible. No news item was to appear without its content and form first having been approved and sanctioned by Rosa Luxemburg.

Thanks to her work and leadership the *Rote Fahne* was of one piece. From the first issue that appeared under Rosa's editorial leadership, until the last one she signed off on the day before her murder on January 14, the newspaper appeared as a unified whole regarding its fundamental and tactical approach to revolution, without cracks and fissures from contradictions, without spots, confusion and haziness. However unclear and confused the situation was, no matter how violently the storm of the counter-revolution rumbled, the *Rote Fahne* held straight to its course, Rosa Luxemburg at the wheel. Ebert's[*] and Scheidemann's[†] open betrayal of the revolution re-

---

[*] Friedrich Ebert was a leader of the S.P.D. who directed the S.P.D. Reichstag members to vote for war credits in 1914. He was instrumental in crushing the German revolutionary uprisings at the end of World War I and later became President of Germany from 1919 until he died in 1925.

[†] Philipp Scheidemann was also a leader of the S.P.D. He joined the German government in October of 1918. Although he fought for amnesty for political prisoners he was strongly opposed to a Workers'

vealed itself more and more shamelessly. Under Haase's* and Kautsky's† leadership the Independents reeled back and forth between paying lip service to the dictatorship of the proletariat and offering a humble worship of bourgeois democracy, and they turned themselves from shield-bearers for Scheidemann's group into their accomplices. The workers' and soldiers' councils did not know how to use the power that the revolution had turned over to them and threw it to the Government of People's Representatives and then to the National Assembly, like primitive people who do not know what to do with a gun. The broad proletarian masses let it go, let it happen, thus heralding their own immaturity and the immaturity of the revolution itself. Immutable and undiscouraged, the *Rote Fahne* adhered to its fixed line based on political principles given by Rosa Luxemburg.

All power to the Councils! No National Assembly! Not bourgeois, but proletarian democracy! Dictatorship of the proletariat! Social revolution! These are the slogans which the *Rote Fahne* carried to the masses of the working people. They showed once more Rosa Luxemburg's conviction. They form the essence of the articles that she writes – really only writes? – No, that she experiences deeply and inwardly, so strong and on fire does Rosa Luxemburg's soul speak to us. She filled each page of the newspaper with content, meaning and character. One might pick out some portion of an article from the *Rote Fahne* under Rosa Luxemburg's leadership;

Republic and became chancellor of the Weimar Coalition Government in 1919.

* Hugo Haase was a supposed anti-war member of parliament from the S.P.D., but when that party voted to support the war, he declared: "We won't abandon the Fatherland in the hour of danger." He became chair of the U.S.P.D. in 1917 and joined the Provisional Government in November 1918, but resigned together with the two other U.S.P.D. representatives on December 29, 1918 after the crushing of the revolt of the People's Navy Division a few days earlier. He was shot to death in 1919.

† Karl Kautsky was a once revolutionary leader of the German Social-Democrats. During and after World War I he became a leading opportunist, against whom Lenin wrote many polemics (see in particular his book, *The Proletarian Revolution and the Renegade Kautsky*, written in 1918).

wherever and whatever you choose, the fragment shows the essence of the whole. The Conference Report from Berlin, the situation reports from all over Germany bring the attitude of the workers and soldiers to the idea of the councils into print. The political overview, social news items, but especially the critical and polemical debates with the two social democratic parties, with the executive council* of the Berlin workers' and soldiers' councils, with the National Congress of Councils have the following as their goal: To erase every false evaluation of formal bourgeois 'democracy' to the very last remnants from the consciousness of the working class and to mobilize the workers against the convening of a National Assembly and against the government, which handed the power of the young, immature councils bit by bit to the counter-revolution; to mobilize the working class in the struggle for the proletarian dictatorship.

Not always, and not always as loudly as it would be necessary, does "the mass march of revolutionary workers' battalions," wanting to make the councils take power in truth and deed, echo in the streets of German cities and industrial centres. But from the *Rote Fahne* comes constantly the same clarity, resolution, passion and determination of the will to reach the goal; it calls the proletarians to such an act. The *Rote Fahne* is thus Rosa Luxemburg's last and decisive political declaration and testament. Between it and the main experiences and main slogans of the Russian Revolution there exist no contradictions. Not that Rosa Luxemburg would have mechanically transferred "the Bolshevik slogans and methods" to the German situation, as she was criticized for doing by the two social democratic parties that clung tenaciously to the illusion of a peaceful revolution. Rosa Luxemburg rather seized on the living historical meaning of these solutions and methods and applied them creatively and effectively, taking German conditions into account. Taking into account the national and momentary conditions, the differences and the changes in Russia and Germany, she astutely recognized the common international features of the great proletarian revolution here and there. Quite independently, her free, proud spirit had sought the path of revolution. But lo and behold! It led her in Lenin's footsteps. This is what the *Rote Fahne* proved first from the

* The Executive Council was dominated by the two opportunist Social-Democratic Parties that opposed a workers' revolution in Germany.

general content of the paper, then by Rosa Luxemburg's words themselves.

In one article entitled, "They even Threaten," the *Rote Fahne* stands against the National Assembly, the German Constituent Assembly*, with these remarks: "That cute little plan of Haase and Kautsky has already been quashed, sabotaged by the ruling class on this very day. As its essential point it was thought that the National Assembly should not be expeditiously convened without further ado, but should be prepared for by a series of strong actions of the Provisional Government. Basically these are their tactics: first a brief dictatorship of the proletariat, then the National Assembly and the majority vote, then the introduction of socialism by an act of parliament. This confused and ambiguous plan thus also includes the application of the [proletarian] dictatorship.

"Yes, obviously even the Independents feel that the National Assembly without a prior dictatorship in a socialist sense amounts to nothing more than smoothly handing over the revolution to the ruling classes. That is why they so desperately resist the intention of the Scheidemann group to convene the National Assembly immediately and without further ado.

"Thus Haase and his comrades also want the dictatorship of the proletariat, thus they also admit that the dictatorship is inevitable, if they are not to make an outright betrayal of socialism. Only, being wise guys, they want to put the cart before the horse. They want at first a dictatorship and a little socialism, and then want the proletariat to lay down its power and hand over the main work of introducing socialism to the parliamentary system.

"It now appears, however, as might be expected, that even at the first announcement of the most rudimentary measures in the direction of the socialist dictatorship, the threatened bourgeoisie leaps to its feet and carries out the sharpest resistance. The bourgeoisie comes out in the open: National Assembly! The slogan of the National Assembly is such that hardly had it escaped the lips of Haase and Kautsky that it was used as a weapon against their socialist intentions and against themselves.

"The astute guardians of the ruling classes have shown always

---

* The bourgeois parliament in Germany from February 1919 to June 1920. It drew up the Constitution of Germany that was in effect until 1933 and even technically under Nazi rule until 1945.

and in all situations what the oppressed classes, unfortunately, so often lack: an unerring instinct for their own class interests. If the bourgeoisie so emphatically and stormily demand the National Assembly as their protective wall against socialism, is this not a striking confirmation that the National Assembly as an institution of planned "parliamentary socialisation" is a sword made of cardboard?

"The Independent supporters of this solution want to outsmart the bourgeoisie. They want to catch them in the trap of an Act of Parliament and believe that this will be the least painful way to overcome their opposition to socialism. But being too wily in great events has already cost many a head. It is not the bourgeoisie that the National Assembly would catch in its trap, but the proletariat. "

In No. 8, the newspaper wages a polemic against the Independents, who with devout fervour were demanding that the National Assembly produce a Constitution. The news item bears the distinctive headline: "The Road to Nowhere."* The polemic against this party and the struggle against the threat of the National Assembly continue in No. 14 of November 29. The *Rote Fahne* calls for the speedy convocation of the Congress of the Independent Social Democratic Party and justifies this call, in particular as follows:

"Its true mission as shareholder in the Scheidemann-Ebert company is to mystify its clear and unambiguous character as a force protecting bourgeois class rule in a system of ambiguities and cowardice.

"This role of Haase and his comrades finds its classic expression in their attitude to the main slogan of the day: the National Assembly.

"There are only two positions possible in this matter, as in all others. Either one wants the National Assembly as a means to cheat the proletariat of its power by paralyzing its class energy and dissolving its ultimate socialist goals in a blue haze. Or one wants to put all the power in the hands of the proletariat, to develop the revolution that had already begun into a powerful class struggle for a socialist society and for that purpose to establish the political rule of the great mass of the working people, the dictatorship of the workers' and soldiers' councils. For or against socialism, against or for

* This article is by Rosa Luxemburg herself as I am told by someone who is well informed [C.Z.]

the National Assembly, there is no third choice.

"The Independent Party is also desperately working here to bring together mountain and valley, mix fire and water in the name of 'unity.' It wants the National Assembly to be the supreme directing and deciding authority, but it wants to postpone this National Assembly as long as possible and before it is convened to implement policy in its broad guidelines through dictatorial measures of the present government.

"As usual, the entangled centrist position leads to ambiguity, to political dishonesty. Either one truly intends to make the National Assembly the qualified decision-making body that represents the people – in which case it would be inappropriate to confront this highest authority with accomplished facts, as it would then find itself behind the major social upheavals. Or one truly believes in the socialist dictatorship of the proletariat in which case one should not promote it as a stopgap measure in a corner of revolutionary history nor hand over its barely begun efforts to the conclusive judgment of a bourgeois-democratic assembly.

"A party that in a historical moment demanding great, clear, bold decisions of world historic importance only promotes ambiguities, fluctuations and half-truths, a party which wants to pursue foreign policy with the imperialist annexationist David, to direct culture and primary school education with the German national-chauvinist Haenisch[*], and build socialism with Ebert—the executioner of the revolution—a party which through Barth's[†] voice urges the striking masses to desist from struggle and remain in slavish obedience to the whip of the bosses, such a party is judged by every one of its words and every one of its deeds. This party is a product of decades of stagnation of the German workers' movement. What the German proletariat needs at its head today is a socialist party that is equal to occupy the role required at this decisive hour. There is no place in the revolution for a party of indecision and ambiguity." The article ends with the demand for "the speediest convocation of the Party Congress to bring clarity and decisiveness."

At a meeting of the Spartacus League on 1 December Rosa

---

[*] Eduard David and Konrad Haenisch were both S.P.D. politicians during and after World War I.

[†] A Swiss-born theologian educated in Germany.

Luxemburg delivered a speech that won the audience's approval for her point of view, as expressed in the following resolution:

"The People's Assembly called on 1 December in the Teachers' Union Building on Alexander Street declares its agreement with the remarks of Comrade Luxemburg. It considers the convening of the National Assembly a step that strengthens the counter-revolution and betrays the proletarian revolution and its socialist goals. It calls for handing over all power to the workers' and soldiers' councils, whose first duty is to drive the traitors to the working class and socialism out of the government: Throw out Scheidemann, Ebert and their comrades; arm the working people to protect the revolution and with all energy take decisive actions to bring about the socialisation of society."

In the "Political Overview" of 3 December the news item "Dictatorship or Democracy?" denounces ironically the snivelling about the "dictatorship of the left" and the insecurity of the leaders of the Independents, who count the buttons of their vest to see if and when a national assembly should be elected. On the following day, the news item: "A Foretaste of the National Assembly" says you can deduce the following conclusion from the bourgeois demonstration in the Busch Circus: "These people know very well why they are pushing for the National Assembly and what is hidden behind the much-vaunted 'democracy.' The audacity and self-confidence in the behavior of all these elements allow one to measure with mathematical accuracy the weakness of the current government."

With programmatic focus and determination the political standpoint of the *Rote Fahne*— Rosa Luxemburg's political position—is expressed in the issues published from December 10 to December 22. These issues deal with the meeting of the Workers' and Soldiers' Councils in Germany, the Congress of Councils: Preparation and agenda; attitude and behaviour of the Executive Committee of the Berlin Workers' and Soldiers' Councils; the Ebert-Haase parties, the relationship of the Congress to the masses of the Berlin proletariat and of these masses to the Congress; its deliberations, decisions, and the end result; in short, its total contents, its meaning and its historical essence. In the caustic criticism as also in the urgent positive demands and blazing anger, with which this is done, in the mixture of profound realism and passionate impetuosity the awareness comes through that the Congress is deciding the central problem of the proletarian revolution in Germany. The Congress will decide for or against it, certainly not as a final and irrevocable decision but only for the time being and until the proletarian masses themselves—ripe for revolution through their will to seize state power—shall correct its decision.

Council rule or a bourgeois parliamentary state symbolized and embodied in the National Assembly? Proletarian dictatorship or bourgeois democracy? 'Socialisation' of the economy or capitalist production for profit? Revolution to overthrow capitalism or reform to preserve and strengthen capitalism? These were the long-range issues before the Congress. The *Rote Fahne* answered unequivocally, without any evasive 'on the one hand' and 'on the other hand,' without clauses beginning with 'if' and 'but.' It answered them in the spirit of the Russian November Revolution*, the first decision on these questions of world historic significance. Some of the relevant contributions show without any ambiguity Rosa Luxemburg's clear, firm, characteristic handwriting. It is a piece of German revolutionary history, captured in the *Rote Fahne,* every day, a piece of the agony of the German Revolution, but also an overview showing its road to the future. Whoever wants to 'make' history cannot afford to ignore these pages, nor can those who want to write about history. Have the best and most important lessons about the principles and tactical issues of the proletarian revolution on the occasion of the Congress of Councils, really 'already' been written three years ago in the *Rote Fahne*? It might be written today, not only because of the freshness of tone and colour, but also because of the relevance of the lessons as a guide to action. What appeared to be within reach in December 1918 has still not been realized. Germany's proletariat still lets the mill of bourgeois parliamentarism grind on; it still stomps forward on the road of bourgeois democracy, torn apart by its condemnations of terror and its bullets ripping into every revolt against the power of capital. Even its most bitter experience crystallized slowly, despairingly slowly, to insight and action.

Rosa Luxemburg had called for the convocation of the Constituent Assembly in September 1918 in Russia, after the victory of the proletariat. However, under her leadership, the *Rote Fahne* fought in December of that same year with tenacious passion to convince

---

* The October Revolution was called that because of the Julian Calendar in use in Russia at that time. It actually took place on November 7, 1917.

the [German] Congress of Councils to most sharply reject the demand for a Constituent Assembly that would write the Constitution. Right from the beginning it must instead establish the sovereignty—born from the will of the proletariat and supported by the will of the proletariat—of the power of the Councils in all areas. There must be no deals, no toying around with the counter-revolutionary slogan "to convene a National Assembly"; no wavering in its resolve to push aside the Provisional Government of the House of People's Representatives and to concentrate all power in the Councils. Deceptive hopes about the nature and the value of bourgeois democracy, outdated political views and new fears of big decisions and responsibilities all jumble together with parliamentary routine and with blatant privileges to form a trap, in which workers' power gets more entangled every day. If the Congress of Councils of December 16 were to write the Magna Carta of the Rule of the Councils, of the proletarian seizure of power, it would be necessary to undermine the influence of the leadership of the two social democratic parties and overcome uncertainty and indecision within its own ranks. It would be necessary also to overcome the betrayal of the councils and their organs, especially within the Executive of the Berlin Workers' and Soldiers' Councils, which should have led, but instead could only stagger, topple over and capitulate.

On December 10, the *Rote Fahne* presented the main ideas of the agenda of the Congress that the Executive Council had set up: Point 2 read: "National Assembly or Councils' Constitution?" Speaker: Cohen-Reuss, Discussion: Daumig-Berlin[*]. "The significance of this agenda is twofold. First, the formulation of the central problem of the revolution as an alternative: National Assembly or Council Constitution? Here at least it was openly admitted that the National Assembly is synonymous with the destruction of the workers' and soldiers' councils and their political role." And day-by-day the articles follow, with the cold, unrelenting spotlight focusing on and illuminating the situation. It is tempting to reproduce the articles almost completely in order to convey the full sense of what the *Rote Fahne* was at that time, and how it guided the blade of its

[*] Ernst Daumig was co-chair of the U.S.P.D. and chief editor of its newspaper, *Die Freiheit*. He briefly became a member of the K.P.D. when the majority of the U.S.P.D. joined that party in 1920, but resigned together with Paul Levi in 1922.

sword. Each article strikes an unerring blow. Thus in no. 26 of December 11, "On the Executive Council,"[*] in No. 27 of December 12, it scourges the Executive Council with the headline: "The Executive Council Knuckles Under," and it characterizes the Russian Soviets (councils) as a positive example.

Thus, on December 15, the *Rote Fahne* formulated the task of the Congress as follows:

"By fulfilling four urgent measures, the Central Council can make up for lost opportunities and assure for itself the place it deserves:

"1. It must eliminate the nest of counter-revolution; it must eliminate the place where all the threads of the counter-revolutionary conspiracy converge, it must eliminate the Ebert-Scheidemann-Haase Cabinet;

"2. It must demand the disarming of all front-line troops who do not unconditionally recognize the supreme power of the workers' and soldiers' councils and who will otherwise become the personal bodyguard of the Ebert-Haase Cabinet.

"3. It must demand the disarming of all officers and of the White Guard trained by the Ebert-Haase government and create the Red Guard.

"4. It must reject the National Assembly and identify it as an attack on the revolution and the workers' and soldiers' councils.

"By immediately taking these four steps, the workers' and soldiers' councils can still put themselves at the head of the revolution. The proletariat is willing to follow the councils' leadership if they show strong leadership against capitalism. The proletariat is willing to give everything to them and to raise them to the highest level with the cry: All power to the workers' and soldiers' councils!"

The article, in which this appears, has the characteristic headline: "To the Barricades."[†] The 'call' on 16 December for a demonstration to greet the Congress of Councils makes this exhortation ring with even more force. The protesters should, among others, raise the following demands: All power to the workers' and soldiers' councils. The Executive Council, elected by the Central Council of the workers' and soldiers' councils, is the highest organ

---

[*] Rosa Luxemburg was the author. [C.Z.]

[†] It is written by Rosa Luxemburg [C.Z.]

of legislative and governmental power. The Eberts-Council of People's Representatives is to be eliminated. The call reads:

"It is the first time that representatives from all over Germany, workers and soldiers, organized as a class for their own interests, have come out on the political scene; for the first time the proletarians of all of Germany have embodied themselves in this Central Council; they see themselves united, struggling and fighting.

"And will they see themselves as the victors?

"That is the question that moves us today. The enemy, which the proletariat has to defeat today, is a dangerous enemy. It is not an enemy that declares itself openly; no, it is one that rises from within its own ranks and sows doubt within the ranks of the proletariat. This enemy has carried out an appalling campaign. For weeks it has been busy. It has whispered into the ears of the proletarians in town and country, in their work shirts and soldiers' uniforms, that they are not the ones who are or can be capable of accomplishing the mighty work of human liberation. It has whispered this in a thousand voices, it has painted on the wall the devil of anarchy, it brought in lies from abroad and invented new ones to prove to the proletariat that its organisation could not lead to peace; the Ebert-Haase government has done everything it can to take from the proletariat its belief in the power of the Councils and the victory of the revolution....

"But what would all delegates or all councils be without the great mass of the proletariat behind them? A resounding gong or a clanging cymbal? The masses themselves must appear on the scene. Their fate will indeed be forged now. They must unite with the councils, they must show that they want to live and that, going beyond all the wavering and feeble elements, they have realized that the struggle is over their destiny.

"Individual human weakness and procrastination cannot destroy the work of the Revolution. It can only be destroyed if the proletariat itself abandons it. If they, the proletarians, have reached the point when they are animated by the desire to win and have decided to take action, then the Revolution has to be victorious. And that is why: proletarians out into the streets!"

The proletarians of Berlin had understood the call. The *Rote Fahne* of December 17 reported with satisfaction that 250,000 impressively determined protesters filled the streets to guide the meeting of the Central Council of Workers' and Soldiers' Councils in

Germany. The above demands were backed up by the marching masses. As its convinced spokesperson—for neither the first nor the last time—Paul Levi stepped before the Berlin workers; he spoke to them while standing in a window of the Prussian parliament building. Doesn't it seem today like a fairy tale, which begins: "Once upon a time"?

The demonstrating masses jubilantly agreed with the revolutionary demands. But the counter-revolution was also at work. This was emphasized in a December 18 article "The Second Menetekel.*" We read there:

"... In its process of self-clarification, the national conference is under pressure from two antithetical forces. From the top in the Ebert-Scheidemann's headquarters the concentrated bourgeois counter-revolution is exerting the strongest pressure on the national conference, to demoralize it, to rob it of its self-confidence, to move it to abdicate its role as an organ of the Workers' and Soldiers' Councils by convening instead the National Assembly. That is what the December 6 putsch was for, and the demonstration at the arrival of the Guard troops, the disarming of the proletariat and the formation of the 'volunteer militia.'

"At the same time, from below the resolute mass of the proletariat, its goal clear, was putting pressure on the national conference to strengthen its revolutionary will, to keep it focused on maintaining a socialist class standpoint and turn it from the chaotic condensation of the November Revolution into a sharpened weapon for the further development of the socialist revolution.... "

From its earliest meetings the Council Congress documented that its majority, and especially the leaders of the two social democratic parties, had neither the ability nor the will to forge the councils into a tool of proletarian power. Its ear was sensitive to the needs of the bourgeoisie, to the boasts of the counter-revolution, to the whining and stuttering of the vacillators and cowards, to the betrayal of the social climbers and the successful low-level operators within the workers' movement. It lacked the organ of thought and the spirit of the language of the masses in the streets that is tuned to the revolutionary situation and aware of the duty the masses have imposed on it. Instead of connecting with the masses on an

---

* "Writing on the Wall," a biblical reference from the Book of Daniel.

intimate level and drawing its revolutionary life force from them, it shut itself off from them. Without dignity and greatness, in the barren parliamentary shop talk, in feeble, foolish and treacherous decisions it wasted the treasure that the proletarian power had entrusted to it and delivered it instead to the National Assembly, to the bourgeoisie. The reports in the *Rote Fahne* about the Congress, the articles, "Behind Walls," and "Ebert's Mamelukes*" sharply define what is going on. Instead of revolutionary self-awareness, counter-revolutionary self-exposure; instead of strengthening the power of the councils, it encourages the suicide of the councils; instead of struggling against the bourgeoisie, it makes a defenceless capitulation to the bourgeoisie. Despite everything, the newspaper's voice is clear and unwavering and it speaks with the conviction that the proletarian masses will lead the revolution on to victory. The triumph of the counter-revolution in the Council Congress was: "A Pyrrhic Victory," as the *Rote Fahne* expressed it in the December 21 issue: "The first meeting of the Council Congress has ended. Looking over its accomplishments as they are presented in the public debates and decisions, they amount to a victory of the Ebert regime, a victory of the counter-revolution all down the line. The revolutionary 'street' was locked out, and the political power of the Workers' and Soldiers' Councils nullified, the convening of the National Assembly, which represents the dictatorial power of the December 6th clique – in the present climate what more and better could the bourgeoisie wish for?

"'The dictators didn't want to know anything about their intended dictatorship," triumphantly exclaims the newspaper *Freiheit*†, the sad organ of political ambiguity.

"For sure, the self-elected body of the Workers' and Soldiers' Councils, instead of seizing political power for itself to promote revolution, which was its mission, cut off its own limbs and handed the power entrusted to itself over to the enemy.

"What is involved here is not just the general inadequacy of the

---

* This article is by Rosa Luxemburg. [C.Z.]. The mamelukes were a military caste in Egypt from about 1250 until 1811, shortly after Napoleon's conquest of that country. They were originally made up of slaves from Turkey.

† Newspaper of the U.S.P.D.

first immature stage of the revolution, but also the special difficulty of this proletarian revolution, expressed in the unique character of its historical situation. In all previous revolutions the fighters openly came to the barricades: class against class, manifesto against manifesto, shield against shield. In the current revolution, the shock troops of the old order do not enter the fray with the placards and emblems of the ruling classes; they do so instead under the banner of a 'social democratic party.' If the cardinal question of the revolution was to be raised openly and honestly: capitalism or socialism, any doubts or wavering among the great mass of the proletariat would be now impossible.

"With every passing day the situation is sharpened, the world-historical predicament heightened, unrelentingly and with greater intensity. The retreating mass of soldiers gradually changes into a mass of workers, as they take off the uniforms of imperialism and put on the clothes of the proletariat. The soldiers are back on their home soil, in which their class consciousness is rooted, and the threads that bound them temporarily to the ruling classes are torn asunder. At the same time, they confront the huge and growing problems of unemployment, the economic struggles between capital and labour, and financial bankruptcy of the state. The internal dissolution of the capitalist economy shows its Medusa's head. Here in the economic contradictions is the hot forge, out of which the new fires of the class struggle will be kindled daily.

"And it is thus a given that the revolutionary tension, that the revolutionary consciousness of the masses grows more acute and sharper every day. The Council Congress, through the rugged, unmediated contradiction in which it was confronted with the situation and mood of the masses, has itself done the best job possible to bring education and clarification. In the few days of its discussions, it has demonstrated to the proletariat and to the masses of soldiers the need to fight to the death against the counter-revolutionary regime as the inevitable question of survival. Only confusion, indecision, only veil and fog are dangerous to the cause of the revolution. Any clarity, any revelation is oil on the fire of the revolution.

"The Congress of Councils has done in the few days such a thorough, complete work, has torn away all the veils from the core of the counter-revolution, that like an exploding mine it must arouse the conscience of the proletarian masses. From this hour onward, now that the council delegates have finished speaking, the workers' and soldiers' councils in Germany and the working masses have the word. They will speak, and they will act. The victory of the Ebert regime—like all the victories of the counter-revolution—will remain a pyrrhic victory."

This is one of many examples of the consistency with which the *Rote Fahne,* headed by Rosa Luxemburg, described all emerging controversial issues from the angle of the rule of the Councils. On November 27, she spoke of a 'national conference' of representatives of various German "closer fatherlands":

"... What is separatism? Certainly there was separatism even before the Revolution. People railed against the 'Prussians' and wished the Berliners to go to hell, but the railing has now changed its historical meaning. The railing against the 'Prussians' during the war was the manifestation of resistance of the South German proletariat against the most extreme representatives of aggressive war, the Prussians. The railing against the 'Prussians' now is the manifestation of the fear of the South German bourgeoisie concerning the proletarian revolutionary struggle in North Germany. Separatism in this sense was revolutionary before the [November] revolution, now its social content has become reactionary.

"And this realization leads to different tactics. Only on the basis of the Councils' Constitution is unity of the country possible. Only the Councils' Constitution, the developed proletarian struggle, which has progressed furthest in north Germany, will resolve for the south German proletarians and small farmers their entanglement in separatism, in which the bourgeoisie has placed them."

The 'Russian methods' that the *Vorwärts* * and *Freiheit* newspapers cursed and proscribed in unison obviously had a contagious affect on the editorial board of the *Rote Fahne,* judging from its assessment of the Councils and its rejection of the National Assembly. The paper reported on December 19 without any moral indignation about "terrorist actions out of Munich." Red soldiers there had sinned against the sanctity of 'democracy' by dispersing a meeting of real live democrats. And still more. Soldiers wearing red emblems entered a bourgeois printing house and confiscated 100,000 leaflets "against Bolshevism." It was stamping out 'freedom of expression,' not to mention assaulting bourgeois 'property.' But the condemned *Rote Fahne* added to that dreadful event this afterword:

---

* Newspaper of the S.P.D.

"...So, the privilege of the ruling class to dissolve meetings of the proletariat by armed gendarmes, the privilege of Ebert and Wels to order protesters shot down, was interfered with by armed soldiers; the soldiers believed that freedom of the press did not include freedom to print slanders and they stopped the lies of the bourgeois press that had continued for four years. That is what the pack is howling about! Which is greater: their stupidity or their hypocrisy?"

With the worsening of the situation in Berlin it would become even 'madder.' Emboldened by the [weakness of the] Congress of Councils, armed and blessed by the Ebert regime, the counter-revolution turns on the soldiers of the Peoples Navy, these brave revolutionary fighters, on the bloody Christmas holiday. The revolutionary instinct of the masses rears its head against the agents of the bourgeoisie. Masses of workers occupy the editorial offices of the *Vorwärts* on 25 December. "The revolutionary shop stewards and representatives* of the large enterprises of Greater Berlin" take a position on the 'terrorist' operation and declare themselves against a minority:

"The Assembly of revolutionary shop stewards and representatives of Greater Berlin on 26 December, 1918 fully understands the anger of the masses of workers that led to the occupation of the *Vorwärts* enterprise on December 25. The egregious breach of the law, carried out two years ago against the workers of Berlin, will today be perceived as all the more provocative by the revolutionary working class, as the *Vorwärts* most recently in the most shameless way insulted all honest and resolute revolutionary circles, as well as the People's Navy Division. The revolutionary shop stewards therefore consider the lesson meted to the *Vorwärts* people to be well deserved. But they do not consider the action against the *Vorwärts* an opportunity to take up the comprehensive final battle against the open and covert counter-revolution.

"The Assembly of revolutionary shop stewards, therefore, recommends the ending of the occupation of the *Vorwärts* building. It commits itself to use all its powers to push forward the revolutionary development and the struggle for socialism to the end. Included in this fight, of course, is the struggle against the Ebert regime and

---

* The revolutionary shop stewards and representatives were delegates elected by the workers in the enterprises who were not part of the official trade union structure.

their lackeys in *Vorwärts*. The Assembly of revolutionary delegates recognizes the right of the Berlin workers to the *Vorwärts*. It believes that the matter of the *Vorwärts* in this revolutionary era must be immediately resolved by the Executive Council of the Greater Berlin working class."

The *Rote Fahne* published this resolution in its No. 41 on December 27 and also published the other decisions of the revolutionary shop stewards. Namely, to insist that the editors of the *Vorwärts* print the declaration at the top of their front page, without comment; otherwise the workers would continue the occupation. Thus coercion, terrorism from the Left. The *Rote Fahne* writes about this: "This was a completely spontaneous mass action and therein lies its great political importance. The masses have once again proved that they have that unerring revolutionary instinct, which is the living source of the revolution's momentum that renews itself again and again. The re-conquest of the *Vorwärts*, which had been stolen from the Berlin socialist proletariat under the protection of Kessel's [military] sabre dictatorship by a despicable act of violence, represented an outstanding debt owed to the Revolution, which should have already been taken back on November 9. To leave the rightful property of the Berlin workers any longer in the hands of the Ebert-clique, which will use it as the meanest reptile in order to inject poison into the revolutionary proletariat, is untenable. It is only a matter of time before this mockery of the basic rights and interests of the revolution must come to an end. If today some doubts among the revolutionary shop stewards and representatives still keep them from rallying in close support of the masses, who on their own initiative want to redeem those irrefutable debts to the revolution, and if these doubts cause the *Vorwärts* to be returned to the counter-revolution, nevertheless this question, which has now been put on the agenda in such a determined manner, will not disappear. For our part, we will continue to support the mass of the Berlin workers in their intended aim with all the strength at our disposition, and we do not doubt that the courage, determination and initiative that they demonstrated on that day will soon lead them to their goal."

The inevitability that the proletarian struggle will turn against the blessings of 'democracy' is demonstrated in this article: "How they perceive freedom of the press." "The Ebert crony, August Müller, sustainer and director of the Economics Office, explains that he can supply no additional paper to the *Rote Fahne* other than what it has at the moment. We want to show the gentlemen and the Berlin proletariat what freedom of the press means in Germany. Last Sunday there appeared: the *Vorwärts* with 16 pages, the *Deutsche Zeitung* of 16 pages, the *Berliner Tagesblatt* in 20 pages, the *Vossische Zeitung* with 24 pages. On Wednesday of this week the same newspapers appeared in the same number of pages again, that is, a total of 76 pages. If we add to this all the rest of the Berlin press, such as *Tägliche Rundschau*, *Kreuzzeitung*, *Morgenpost*, *Volkszeitung*, *Germania*, *Freisinnige Zeitung*, *Lokalanzeiger*, *Tag*, and whatever the rest are called, that means that the bourgeois press appeared with at least 300 pages. In contrast, the *Rote Fahne* appears with 4 (four) pages! It could not get more paper!

"Is not it time for the Berlin proletariat to teach Dr. Müller a lesson to remind him that out in the world besides the profit interests of the Mosses, Scherls, Ullsteins and the fraudulent interests of the *Vorwärts* there are also proletarian interests?"

Almost without realising that there was a short breathing spell, in the beginning of January 1919 the revolution and counter-revolution again clash violently with each other and wrestle hand to hand. With the zeal of well-trained, dutiful servants of a good bourgeois establishment, the reigning Scheidemann cronies continue their work of disarming the proletariat and arming the bourgeoisie. They deliver into bourgeois hands another major power position. The Independent Eichhorn is deposed as chief of police. At the same time, the government orders a strong counter-revolutionary troop contingent deployed around Berlin and prepares an invasion by General Lequis and the imposition of martial law. The workers cannot take this brazen slap in the face without reacting. The pavement resounds with the steps of hundreds of thousands who demonstrate, including many tens of thousands who want to fight. The burning breath of revolution wafts through the streets. "Eichhorn stays" – this authoritative slogan rings in the ears of the regime. Workers and soldiers have seized the police headquarters, and occupied *Vorwärts* again, without any respect for the 'freedom of opinion' of its editors and the swindled legal title of its owners:

"The working masses have again occupied *Vorwärts*. The brutal provocations in recent days of that reptile Ebert have put the patience and kindness of the Greater Berlin workers to severe tests. To leave such a dangerous weapon in the hands of the enemies of the Revolution any longer would indeed amount to a betrayal of the most vital interests of the revolution. Taking back the *Vorwärts*, the stolen lawful property of the Berlin workers, is an obvious act of revolutionary self-defence. Hopefully the workers won't let it slip away again this time!

"The workers and soldiers have also occupied other bourgeois newspapers. They may continue to appear, but under the control of the Workers' and Soldiers' Council, which is thus only exercising its duty as an organ of the threatened revolution."

Occupation of the police headquarters and occupation of the *Vorwärts* building was the beginning of the revolutionary January fighting that devoured Karl Liebknecht and Rosa Luxemburg. "Karl and Rosa have fulfilled their ultimate revolutionary duty," Leo Jogiches wrote to Lenin, when the bloody murders of the two great leaders were no longer in any doubt. In his terse message he gave the most moving and most glorious tribute to them.

Paul Levi's[*] publication [in 1922] has given Arthur Crispien[†] grounds for the contention that Rosa Luxemburg rejected the January uprising. This is untrue. What Rosa rejected was not the revolutionary struggle of the Berlin proletariat, but the wrong target, the incorrectly chosen object of the struggle: the overthrow of the Ebert-Scheidemann regime. It is clearly documented that it was the left wing of the Independent Social Democracy, the revolutionary shop stewards of Berlin's large enterprises, who set this goal for the struggle under Georg Ledebour's[‡] leadership. The fact stands in an interesting and instructive parallel to the March Action of 1921 concerning the political attitude of a significant portion of the motive forces, such as the choice of a goal for the struggle that could

---

[*] A member of the Spartacus League and then the Communist party of Germany (K.P.D.), Levi became chair of the K.P.D. after the assassinations of Luxemburg and Liebknecht, and later in 1919 of Leo Jogiches. In 1921 he was expelled from the K.P.D. and in 1922 he published Luxemburg's pamphlet "The Russian Revolution" with his own introduction. Also in 1922 he joined the U.S.P.D. and returned with them to the S.P.D. He died in 1930.

[†] Arthur Crispien was a leader of the U.S.P.D. He was a U.S.P.D. delegate to the 2nd World Congress of the Comintern but refused to accept its conditions of admission.

[‡] Georg Lebedour was a leader of the U.S.D.P. who took part in the January 1919 uprising.

not be the starting point for a mass action.

Rosa Luxemburg saw the events—as significant and hopeful as they were—not from the perspective of the Berlin City Hall tower. She grasped them in their relation to the given situation and in particular the level of political development of the broadest sections of the population in all of Germany. Accordingly, the overthrow of the Ebert government could at first be only a propagandistic slogan of the revolutionary proletarians, not the tangible object of revolutionary struggles. Under the given circumstances, in the main limited to Berlin, in the best case this would lead to a Berlin 'Commune,' and on top of that probably on a small historical scale. The struggle's objective could only be a powerful defence against a counter-revolutionary blow. Thus: Reinstatement of Eichhorn to his post, the removal of the troops – whose job it would be to carry out a bloody suppression of Berlin's revolutionary proletariat – the arming of the workers and the transfer of the military chain of command to the revolutionary political representatives of the proletariat. To pursue these demands, deeds were needed; they couldn't be won by striking any deals.

Under these conditions the young Communist Party led by Rosa Luxemburg faced a difficult, conflict-ridden task. It could not make the goal of the mass action—overthrow of the government—its own; it had to reject it. But at the same time it could not separate itself from the masses who had taken up the struggle. Despite these contradictions it had to stay with the masses, and remain among the masses in order to strengthen them in their struggle with the counter-revolution and promote the process of their revolutionary maturing during the action, while bringing to their consciousness the prerequisites for their advance. To this end, the Communist Party had to show its own face, to work out a sharply defined evaluation of the situation, without violating the revolutionary proletarian solidarity that it owed to the combatants. Its participation in the struggle had to be both negative-critical and positive-advancing at the same time. Leo Jogiches justified this view of the January fighting in Berlin thoroughly and convincingly in a lengthy letter to me. It forms the basis of the description of the Berlin January uprising that Caius set down in his booklet that is well worth reading. Supported by facts, the pamphlet throws a bright light on the situation, and in particular on the complicated, great internal and external difficulties, among which Rosa Luxemburg's conception had to prevail. Thus, this booklet is an important contribution to the history of the revolutionary struggles of the Berlin proletariat in January as well as to the history of our Party.

The *Rote Fahne* itself is in those memorable days a singular document showing Rosa Luxemburg's attitude to the January uprising, her superiority as a leader, her expertise in turning theory into practice and historical insight into revolutionary struggle. The combatants do not experience the *Rote Fahne* as a nagging schoolmaster on their backs, draining their energy and their joy in struggle. Rather, it directs their attention, their will again and again to fight for the limited concrete goal: disarm the counter-revolution, arm the workers. It does not use any propagandistic slogan; it leaves no phenomenon unnoticed, from which strength would be gained in action. In the same issue in which the *Rote Fahne* reports the occupation of the *Vorwärts*, it urges the masses to take up the urgent need to act to avert the impending horrors of unemployment. The article thus rings out: "Jobs! Socialisation! All power to the workers' and soldiers' councils! This three-sided formula of the revolution is now the cry of the starving masses, the practical solution of the hour." Again and again, it demands the speedy new election of the workers' and soldiers' councils.

All individual claims and individual considerations are drowned out by the need of the hour: "Deeds, deeds, not deals." As an indication of the significance of the events, as a warning against the unsafe back and forth movement between fight and surrender by the Independent leaders, faced with the naked betrayal of Scheidemann and his supporters, with the failure of the workers' and soldiers' councils, and acting as a wake-up call of the highest impulse to struggle; as an expression of the conviction that the revolution must be the work of the masses themselves, as a reaffirmation of the confidence in the revolutionary self-awareness of the workers. "Deeds, deeds, not deals," that is the tireless battle cry of the *Rote Fahne* against the counter-revolution dripping with the workers' blood, it is the "Carthage must be destroyed" of the Roman senator.

On January 7 the lead article of the *Rote Fahne* raises the question: "What are the leaders doing?"* After a look back at the overwhelming mass demonstration in the Sieges alley on the previous day it says: "Yes, it is a revolution, with all its externally chaotic

* By Rosa Luxemburg [C.Z.]

movements, with its alternating ebb and flow, with momentary rushes toward seizing power and equally momentary retreats of the revolutionary waves. And through all these apparent zigzag movements, the revolution moves step by step toward victory, pushing inexorably forward. Through their struggle the masses must themselves learn to fight, learn to act. And you can feel today that the working class of Berlin has learned to act to the highest degree; it thirsts for resolute action, for clear situations, for sweeping measures. It is not the same as it was on November 9; it knows what it wants and what it should do.

"But are its leaders, the executive organs of its will, up to the task? Have the revolutionary shop stewards and representatives of the large enterprises, have the radical elements of the Independent Social Democratic Party in the meantime increased their energy and determination? Has their capacity for action kept pace with the growing energy of the masses? We are afraid that we cannot answer this question with a straight yes. We fear that the leaders are still the same as they were on November 9; they have learned little since then.... It may well be that the representatives of the working class deliberate thoroughly and extensively. Now, however, is the time for action... Deeds! Deeds! To be courageous, determined, consistent – that is the darned duty of the revolutionary shop stewards and the sincere socialist party leaders. Disarm the counter-revolution, arm the masses, occupy all positions of power. Act fast! The revolution demands it. Its hours count for months in world history, and its days for years. Let the organs of revolution be conscious of their high responsibilities! The call for a new demonstration is confronted with the fact that "Haase and his associates mediate" and do not know how to lead the advancing masses. Some 700,000 proletarians eager for action and bursting with revolutionary energy are wandering the streets of Berlin without direction, and the revolutionary headquarters – deliberate on a 'settlement' with Ebert and Scheidemann."

The article "Failure of Duty"* in a special edition of the *Rote Fahne* of January 8 raises the same accusation and ends with the same reminder. It was not enough to call out the masses; what was needed was to keep their revolutionary energy alive and ready to act. It was not enough to wrest power positions from the counter-

* By Rosa Luxemburg [C.Z.]

revolution; they had to be put fully at the service of the revolution. That did not happen, neither with the Wolff Telegraph Bureau* nor with the *Vorwärts*. The leading corporations had "to provide editorial leadership in the spirit of the revolutionary workers of Berlin. Where have the editors gone? What did Daumig and Ledebour—reputable career journalists and editors—who now as the left wing of the Independent Social Democratic Party have no political organ, do. Why did they leave the masses in the lurch? Was it perhaps a more pressing business to 'deliberate' instead of acting? ... The masses must not simply be called upon; they must also be politically activated. They must above all be called upon to decide on what is to be done and left undone... The experience of the last three days calls to the leading bodies in a loud voice: Don't talk! Stop these endless deliberations! No deals! Deeds!"

"The Lessons of the Crisis" are drawn on January 9 in the following sentences: "The mass of Berlin workers has no hard-hitting organisational centre ready for action that understands how to utilise and direct the aroused energy of the masses. The revolutionary shop stewards, the Central Committee of the Independent Social Democratic Party of Greater Berlin, have not proven to be such a centre.... Where then is the workers' council, the working masses' appointed revolutionary organ? The workers' council does not exist, does not meet, it leads a shadowy existence. Or maybe it comes on stage in the form of the Executive Council... to betray the cause of the revolution right in the midst of the revolutionary crisis.... It is essential today to newly elect the workers' and soldiers' councils, to vote new members into the Executive Council under the slogan: Out with Ebert and his followers! It is essential today to express the experiences of the past eight weeks in the workers' and soldiers' councils, to elect those workers' and soldiers' councils whose goals are consistent with the views, objectives and aspirations of the masses. In a word, it is essential above all to eliminate the Ebert-Scheidemann group from the fundamental basis of the revolution, the workers and soldiers' councils. Then and only then will the Berlin masses and the masses in the whole country have in the workers' and soldiers' councils the revolutionary organs that will provide real leaders, real centres of action, struggles and victories in all decisive moments."

---

* One of the leading press agencies in Europe.

The same warning would be emphasized after the declaration of a general strike on 10 January in the article: "The Death Agony of Ebert-Scheidemann."

"The workers' councils since the November 9 days have not become organs of power. They have led the wretched life of plants that do not come to the light. Within the factories they had to give way to the omnipotence of the trade union bureaucracy and in political life they had to give way to the State Council democracy: They would soon find a less than honourable burial under the dunghill of the National Assembly. Now they must become the first arena of victory of the true proletarian revolution. The cry: Down with Ebert and Scheidemann, which has become the battle cry of the militant proletariat, must find its first implementation in the workers' councils. Get all the Ebert people out of the workers' councils. No conscious or unconscious servant of capital dare sit in the workers' councils! The workers' councils for labour and not capital: that is the watchword."

On the following day, "The Failure of the Leaders"* during the struggle would be once again denounced. The behaviour of the leading Independents receives particularly sharp criticism, which is summarized in these phrases: "The Independent Social Democratic Party once more proved to be the redeeming angel of the counter-revolution. Haase and Dittmann have resigned from the government, but they follow the same policy in the streets of being the fig leaf of the Scheidemann group. And the Left of the Independent Social Democratic Party supports and joins in this policy! The conditions for the recently approved negotiations with the government, which were adopted by the revolutionary shop stewards, were formulated by Ledebour. As the price for the surrender of the workers, they demand, among other things, the resignation of Ebert, Scheidemann, Noske† and Landsberg from the government. As if what was involved were individual personalities, not specific policies! As if it were not tantamount to creating complete confusion

---

* By Rosa Luxemburg [C.Z.]

† Gustav Noske was a leading S.P.D. politician. He was commander of the Freikorps, the German reactionary military units during the period after World War I, at the time of its suppression of the January 1919 uprising and the murder of Luxemburg and Liebknecht.

and misleading the masses by removing the typical and well-established representatives of the infamous Scheidemann policy from the front stage and replacing them with some colourless functionaries, who will remain as front men for the same policy, while the Ebert-Scheidemann group will pull the strings from behind the scenes, thus trying to escape the judgment of the masses!

"One way or the other all of the politics of negotiations that the Independent Social Democratic Party initiated and the revolutionary shop stewards collaborated with amounts to a headlong rush toward capitulation of the revolutionary working class, toward covering up the inner conflicts and contradictions. They want to scale back the situation that has matured during the last eight weeks and the political harmony of the masses to the policy of November 9.... Clarity, the sharpest, ruthless struggle against all attempts at covering-up, brokering and stagnation, concentration of the revolutionary energy of the masses and creation of the appropriate institutions for their leadership in the struggle: these are the most urgent tasks of the next period; these are the most important lessons from the last five days of the masses' stormiest offensives and the leaders' pitiful failure." In the same issue the article "Swamp Gas" ends the same way. "So it is indeed. They have remained the same from the first day of their existence, the Haase followers. They learned nothing during the war; they learned nothing from the Revolution! Their horror at the revolution determined their reactions from beginning to end. Now, startled by the insistence of the masses, they led with unfailing certainty back into the swamp of compromise, of false peace, of confusion. The liberation of the masses from the leadership of the Independent Social Democratic Party, the disposal of this corpse: from now on, this task is the indispensable prerequisite for the ability of the proletariat to take revolutionary action; it is the next stage of the struggle."

The counter-revolution, which had in Ebert and Scheidemann its Thiers, in Noske its Gallifet*, has used every day of the 'negotiations' to massively arm itself. They and their accomplices grow progressively more impudent and unscrupulous. They take terrible, inhuman revenge for having trembled before the revolutionary

* Adolphe Thiers and Marquis de Gallifet were respectively the political and military leaders responsible for the suppression of the Paris Commune in 1871.

masses. However, through the heavy bitterness and the spilled blood of the day, the *Rote Fahne* sees the transitory character of the counter-revolutionary victory and the provisional character of any solution to the crisis. There is nothing but a "House of Cards"* that the counter-revolutionaries and their Independent shield-bearers built on the ruins of the revolutionary battlefield. "The entire political sense and historical content of the crisis this past week lies precisely in the fact that its inner strength and logical development drives the revolution forward toward a serious push at the conquest of power by the proletariat and the realization of socialism, while it is now hemmed in at every turn in the road. It may be that these enemy forces gain the upper hand for the moment by brute force; but to hold back the further course of development, the drive to sustain the victory of the revolution, they are completely powerless..... Even if the naked power of the machine-gun or the ambiguity of the Independent Social Democratic Party's concealment plans gain the upper hand, after a short while the elemental forces of the revolution—the economic struggles—will cross out all these calculations. The revolution will again and again put the basic problem on the agenda: the general showdown between labour and capital. And this showdown is a world-historical conflict between two mortal enemies, which can be fought out only by a long power struggle, face to face, hand to hand. Hardly will the debris and the corpses of this latest episode be carried away than the revolution will step in to do its tireless daily work."

On the following day, January 14, the *Rote Fahne* brought out Rosa Luxemburg's monumental article: "Order Reigns in Berlin." Her last work. This special occasion was not required for it to secure its place of importance. Its worth speaks for itself. This article illuminates the breadth of Rosa Luxemburg's knowledge and being, it sparkles with her talent. It is as much the expression of her clear, deep historical mind as of her rock-solid, passionate commitment to the revolution. It stays far away from any attempt to whitewash, reduce or cover up the defeat and yet is a "song of victory, song of triumph, a song of the future's great day." The article was meant to introduce Rosa's critical analysis of the January Uprising, a critique that she intended to be the starting point for new preparations, for further struggles for the revolution.

---

* This article is also by Rosa Luxemburg [C.Z.}

Perhaps the above excerpts of the *Rote Fahne* would not satisfy some people as evidence of Rosa Luxemburg's attitude to the January Uprising in Berlin, and beyond to the proletarian revolution itself. Those people may search then through the organ of the Spartacus League from A to Z in the weeks when it was led by Rosa Luxemburg. Their overall impression will be unable to escape the sharply defined, unified, revolutionary physiognomy of the newspaper, which I have tried to present here in detail. This physiognomy disproves line by line the old wives' tale that Arthur Crispien told in *Freiheit*. He did this obviously out of a desire to prove that, as a former party pupil, and in spite of his eternal fear and trepidation that left him in suspended agony between revolutionary programmatic points and unadulterated opportunistic phraseology, he had not strayed too far from his great teacher. Even more comforting: that the latter, to paraphrase Paul Levi, had been on the way to developing herself to the height of "genuine Marxist conviction" of the Hilferding variety.

The attitude of the *Rote Fahne* during the Berlin January struggles ruthlessly shreds much worse arguments: Paul Levi's myth of Rosa Luxemburg's fundamental opposition to the Bolshevik conception and tactics of proletarian revolution. Certainly! The *Rote Fahne* of those days contains no treatises comparing bourgeois and proletarian democracy, about proletarian dictatorship and terror, about rule by councils and parliaments. It barely mentions the National Assembly, and just fleetingly on the eve of its election. It does not discuss "the lessons and experiences of the Russian Revolution." Theory was, for the moment, overtaken by practice, debate overtaken by the struggle. It was not only the 'lessons' of the proletarian revolution in Russia that confronted Rosa Luxemburg, but even more so the proletarian revolution in Germany itself. It raised as an imperative its right to life; it ordered: Deeds, deeds!

The fight against the deceptive theory of all-liberating 'democracy' had been transformed from an abstraction – from an academic matter for the leaders – into the struggle of the proletarian vanguard with the very real political and military power of 'democracy,' that is, of the bourgeoisie, masked and hidden by the Ebert-Scheidemann camp, which in turn received cover and protection from the Kautsky-Haase camp. The issue of the dictatorship of the proletariat would be answered by the forced battle against the dictatorship of the propertied classes. The reasoned rejection of the National Assembly was continued by the struggle in the streets with massive demonstrations, strikes, bullets, under the slogans: Down with Ebert and Scheidemann, down with the government! Was it about the truly insignificant individuals in government office? Not at all; it was about their genuine bourgeois counter-revolutionary politics. Only because they act as the Thiers and Gallifet of the German bourgeoisie, as its servants, have these members of the government gained a historical significance that extends beyond the scope of social democratic evenings to make contributions, party conferences, battles for seats in parliament, and party archives.

Indeed! In the struggle of the revolutionary vanguard of the German proletariat against the Ebert government the fundamental and tactical problems that the Russian Revolution had raised came alive. How could it be otherwise, once history had placed the proletarian revolution itself on its agenda! The policy of the Ebert government, of the Majority Social Democrats, was the consistently embodied response to these disputes in practice. It was the same regarding the policy of the leading Independents, but with variations and without consequence, partly conscious, partly unconscious. The 'uncouth' policies of the Bolsheviks answered the pressing problems to be resolved from the proletarian, from the revolutionary point of view. The 'soulful' policy of Germany's 'true Marxists' did the same but from the bourgeois, from the counter-revolutionary side. They led, therefore, not only with each opportunity to solemn abjuration of Bolshevik tactics and methods, but inevitably to the denial and abandonment of the proletarian revolution itself.

When in the struggle against this policy the basic problem of the proletarian revolution rose up ever more powerfully, then despite 'the German soul,' 'Bolshevik ideas and methods' appeared. Not in adoring uncritical imitation of the 'Russian role model,' but in order to put into effect the basic conditions of the proletarian revolution. It also is not done, as the enemies of the revolution curse and its lukewarm friends moan, by making a "mechanical transfer" to "such a very different situation in Germany"; no, it is done while adjusting to the historically given conditions of the revolution in Germany. From this self-evident fact, another one follows.

The debate over the controversial fundamental and tactical issues was and is in Germany only in its beginnings. It corresponds to the degree of development of the German Revolution. It is not, therefore, the gigantic, thoroughgoing and sharply intensified one of

'Bolshevism.' It will only reach that level in its further stage of development, namely, at the boiling point of the historical situation, immediately prior to the conquest of political power by the proletariat, and after the conquest, when the victory of the proletariat begins to express itself through its dictatorship. In this sense, 'Bolshevik tactics and methods' do not belong, as they do according to the well-known superior insight of social democratic and trade union leaders, to the "easily and quickly surmounted past" of the proletarian revolution in Germany, but to its approaching future. Nevertheless, the contentious issues in the first revolutionary struggles of the German proletariat came into play in such a tangible and pervasive way that Rosa Luxemburg's attitude toward them in the *Rote Fahne,* in her overall political activity could in no way be uncertain, wavering or doubtful. The passionate, revolutionary fighter, who always remained the thinker thirsty for clarity, had to master them mentally. She was driven to this by the practice of the German revolution and not, like Karl Kautsky, by the need to check out, in his role as schoolmaster in world history, whether the theory and practice of 'Tatar socialism' coincides with the finished, well-seasoned revolutionary recipes on his writing desk. The incarnations of 'German socialism' in the *Vorwärts* and the *Freiheit* correctly concluded from the blows that Rosa Luxemburg directed at them what her fundamental and tactical conception of the problems of the revolution was. Even as the assassins had destroyed the body of the great communist leader, they imagined they should stone her spirit in front of the masses, as they declared the "strong Bolshevik contamination" of the dead leader.

Paul Levi was part of the editorial staff of the *Rote Fahne*. He was one of their most valued colleagues. In the political physiognomy of the *Rote Fahne,* with its indelible 'Bolshevik' family resemblance, it is also undeniable that his own personal view of fundamental and tactical issues of the proletarian revolution would be expressed. Here is some evidence. The headline of the *Rote Fahne* of November 23: "Here Scheidemann - there the Proletariat" points, in massive polemics, to the contradiction between the working masses and the Majority Social Democratic leaders. It includes these sentences:

"For all of them the twilight of the gods approaches. They felt it, and hand in hand with their comrades-in-arms of four years,

Erzberger[*] and company, they look to change destiny through the National Assembly. 'The members of the government'—says the *Vorwärts*— 'cannot let go of this plan, because it corresponds to the social democratic programme.' We do not know where in the social democratic programme there is something about a National Assembly, but when the Scheidemanns and their journalistic satellites swear on the social democratic programme, it is the same as a streetwalker swearing to her innocence. It is also stated in the social democratic programme that one should grant no military credits and that one should not enter into any government together with bourgeois forces. The social democratic programme is in tatters, even more gruesomely shredded than the famous 'scrap of paper,' the Belgian neutrality treaty."

The article is signed: Paul Levi.

On 6 December, we read in the article "The New March" from Paul Levi's pen:

"... How did this change come about? The convening of the National Assembly has reassured all the gentlemen of the bourgeoisie about their future and that the great stock market of parliamentary seats can begin again.

"But if we compare the position of the parties now with their positions immediately before the revolution, then something reveals itself. The social democracy of Mr. Scheidemann and Mr. Ebert is in itself no more in that bloc. The large 'German Democratic Party,' which includes everything with which Mr. Scheidemann and Mr. Ebert persevered for four years through thick and thin, in which Hausman and Payer, Stresemann and Friedberg[†] sit, has constituted itself, temporarily without the government socialist accessories.

"This of course does not mean that these accessories have ceased to be part of the political constitution of the bourgeoisie. The Ebert-Scheidemann group during the war became the ever more powerful and important leading champions of the capitalist war policy. Without their active participation, German capitalism and impe-

---

[*] Matthias Erzberger was a parliamentary representative of the Catholic *Centre* Party who supported Germany's role in World War I until 1917, when he saw that Germany was going to lose. He signed the armistice with the Allies for the German government.

[†] German bourgeois politicians who took part in the Weimar government in Germany after World War I.

rialism long ago would have faced bankruptcy – even though one not as big as the present one. They were the influential promoters and protectors of pro-war sentiment, they were the ones whose rich phraseology magically disguised policies promoting capitalist interests as 'defense of national assets' and tried to make the proletariat believe it was in its interests to be involved in imperialist exploitation and cash boxes.

"And now today. Like those 300 Lacedaemonians, who stood at the narrow pass of Thermopylae and blocked the way of the invading Persian hordes, while at their backs the hordes of Greeks armed themselves, lined up and prepared for the fight, so today the Scheidemann-Ebert gang is standing. They sit in the 'socialist' people's government and battle against the proletarian onslaught. The embryonic council organisation that is forming is reduced to objective powerlessness by being restricted to pure control activities; the socialist organisation of industry, begun by the election of workers' councils, is strangled through the award of government omnipotence to the unions and the 'socialization commission.' The living will of the working class to struggle for its economic power is answered by the requirement that human beings should work six days. The deceptive lure of the National Assembly is placed in front of the proletariat's desire for political power."

Paul Levi is neither a political sleepwalker nor one whose left hand does not know what his right hand is doing. He wrote and acted in full awareness of his 'Bolshevik' attitude to the problems of the proletarian revolution. He was aware of the fundamental and tactical position of the *Rote Fahne* under Rosa Luxemburg's leadership, precisely due to her leadership. He could not doubt that this attitude had required a revision of Rosa Luxemburg's earlier conception of the problem that had been sharply chiseled out by the Bolshevik policy in Russia. Or would you seriously believe that the Rosa who fought with passion against the emergence of the National Assembly in Germany would get enthusiastic about a Constituent Assembly in Russia? That here she would use all her power to hasten the hour of the proletarian dictatorship, but in Soviet Russia she expected the salvation of 'democracy'? That she sought council rule for Germany but there she sought the parliamentary system? That she mustered the full weight of her knowledge and talent to bring down the politics of Ebert, Scheidemann and Haase, but considered a repentant return to Kerensky's policies in Russia as a "goal devoutly to be desired."? Only fools could associate such a dichotomy of thought, with Rosa Luxemburg of all people, who, when confronted with the multi-faceted and much intermingled historical conditions of the proletarian struggle for emancipation in each country, always sought the broad, unified, international unifying guidelines. Moreover, Karl Liebknecht's name—a historic symbol—would not have stood next to Rosa Luxemburg's at the head of the *Rote Fahne* for even 24 hours had there not been agreement between the two outstanding fighters in the presentation of the basic international questions of the proletarian revolution. This framework of agreement was—notwithstanding differing nuances in detail—the foundation of the solid, loyal personal friendship and revolutionary comradeship in arms that bound together Rosa Luxemburg and Karl Liebknecht until their tragic deaths. And Karl Liebknecht's position of support for the Russian Revolution is well known.

But what about 'terror,' the Bolshevik 'terror' of the proletarian revolution in Soviet Russia! With grand gestures it is assured that Rosa Luxemburg rejected terror 'in principle' to the very end. There are two authentic expressions of her opinion about terror. One was in the *Rote Fahne* of 24 November, 1918 in the article "A Dangerous Game." The article is obviously not an exhaustive treatise on the historical role of terror in revolutions. It is a brilliant sword's thrust written from the situation and for the situation. But it was guided by the spirit of Rosa Luxemburg's in-depth historical understanding and sought out from the situation of the day some general, basic lessons. The article reveals that the counter-revolution behind their cries and rumors of impending coups by the revolutionaries was preparing to wield terror against the forward-driving proletariat. It points out that the proletariat does not need to use terror the way the bourgeoisie and the petty bourgeoisie did in order to liberate themselves from historical illusions or in a desire to rescue historically untenable positions. It culminates in the view that the terror of the counter-revolution will be answered by the terror of the masses. The readers can themselves judge according to the central points made in the article: "From the *Kreuzzeitung*[*] to the *Vorwärts* the German press echoes invective against 'terror,' 'putschism,' 'anar-

---

[*] German conservative newspaper, whose symbol was an Iron Cross.

chy,' 'dictatorship.' *Quis tulerit Gracchos de sedition querentes?* Who wouldn't be aroused when the capital's guardians of bourgeois anarchy, those who within four years have turned Europe into a pile of rubble, scream about 'anarchy' of the proletarian dictatorship?

"The propertied classes, who in thousands of years of history never shrank from any act of violence and meanness to protect the 'palladium of order'—private property and class rule—when confronted with the slightest rebellion of their slaves, always wail and moan about violence and terror – of the slaves. The Thiers and Cavaignac*, who in the June butchery of 1848 slaughtered tens of thousands of the Parisian proletarians—men, women and children—filled the world with howls about the alleged 'atrocities' of the Paris Commune.

"The Reventlows, Friedbergs, Erzbergers, who without batting an eyelid drove one-and-a half million German men and youths to be slaughtered—at Longwy and Briey—for the sake of new colonies; Scheidemann-Ebert, who for four years authorized all means to carry out the greatest bloodletting that humanity experienced, they now cry in a raucous chorus about the 'terror,' of the alleged 'reign of terror' that is threatened by the dictatorship of the proletariat! The gentlemen should flip through the pages of their own history...

"Terror and reign of terror in the bourgeois revolutions were a means to destroy historical illusions or to defend hopeless interests against the tide of history.

"Thanks to the theory of scientific socialism, the socialist proletariat steps into its revolution without any illusions, with a full insight into the final consequences of its historic mission, in irreconcilable contradiction and deadly enmity to the entire bourgeois society. It joins the revolution, not to chase utopian fantasies against the tide of history, but supported by the cast-iron engine of development to accomplish what is the need of the moment in history: making socialism a reality. As a mass, as a huge majority of the workers, the socialist proletariat is bound to fulfil its historical mission.

"It is, therefore, not necessary for them to first destroy their own illusions through bloody acts of violence, to first dig an abyss between themselves and bourgeois society. What are needed are the

* Representative of the French National Assembly, which granted him full powers to suppress the 1848 insurrection in Paris.

entire political power of the state and the use of that power to carry out the ruthless abolition of capitalist private property, of wage slavery, of bourgeois class rule, to build a new socialist society.

"But there are others today who urgently need terror, a reign of violence and anarchy: these are the gentlemen of the bourgeoisie, all the parasites of the capitalist economy, who are quaking in their boots for their possessions, their privileges, their profits and prerogative to rule. They are the ones who are trying to place the responsibility for anarchy and for coups on the socialist proletariat in order to be able to carry out actual coups, to unleash real anarchy at an opportune moment with the help of their agents, in order to strangle the proletarian revolution, to sink the socialist dictatorship into chaos and to erect on its ruins a class dictatorship of capital forever.

"The brain and heart of today's smear campaign against the revolutionary vanguard of the proletariat is formed by capital and its struggle for survival. Its handmaiden is subservient social democracy. The relationship of servitude has survived the [November] revolution; the government as well as its servants have only pinned red badges on their clothes...

"We are watching the spectacle from the historical perspective, with a cold-blooded smile. We understand the play, the actors, the director and the roles.

"But what should one think, what should the masses of revolutionary proletarians do, if the slanders achieved their purpose, if even one hair on the head should be hurt of those they have taken from the prison and recognized as their appointed leaders? Who then would have the power to preach to these masses a cool-headed attitude? ...

"You bourgeois gentlemen and you servants of moribund capital of *Vorwärts*, you speculate as bankrupt gamblers do on the last card: on the ignorance, on the political inexperience of the masses. You long for the moment, you long for the laurels of Thiers, Cavaignac and Gallifet. It is a dangerous game. The moment belongs to the dictatorship of the proletariat, to socialism. Whoever stands against the bulldozer of the socialist revolution will lie on the ground with shattered limbs."

Rosa Luxemburg's second statement regarding terror, which the 'anti-terrorists' of the workers' movement rely on, is included in the "Spartacus Programme." The section in question is initiated by these remarks:

"During the bourgeois revolutions bloodshed, terror and political assassination were indispensable weapons in the hands of the rising classes.

"The proletarian revolution requires no terror for its goals; it hates and abhors killing. It does not need these weapons because it is combating not individuals but institutions, because it does not enter the arena with naive illusions, which when disappointed must be avenged in blood. It is not a desperate attempt by a minority to mould the world forcibly according to its ideal, but the action of the great mass of millions of people, destined to fulfil a historic mission and to transform historical necessity into reality. "

It has been rumoured that the first two sentences were "coined specifically against the Bolsheviks," and were the beginning of a fundamental dispute by Rosa Luxemburg with Bolshevik theory and practice, of their fundamental condemnation by her. The old opposition to the 'party of Lenin'—which had found its expression in the article of the *Neue Zeit*[*] of 1904—had allegedly continued unabated or even sharply exacerbated. Just as old fortunetellers read the future from tea leaves, so these oracle-like rumours arise from the backstairs, muttering about occasional angry expressions of opinion on the part of Rosa Luxemburg, which are bound to happen from time to time whenever temperamental people are involved. Only a complete lack of theoretical sense would allow anyone to fabricate a fundamental historical theory from such expressions of opinion. Besides, nothing was further from Rosa Luxemburg's character than to struggle with pin pricks in an offhand or surreptitious manner. Refusing such a style of struggle cloaked in impotent 'femininity', she always sought an open struggle with the opponent.

But if one really wanted to distill from these two sentences a hidden relationship with the 'Bolshevik policy,' they could mean something else entirely: the rumble of a retreating storm and not the first thunder of an approaching one. The leading party of the Russian Revolution of 1917 and of the Russian proletariat in 1918 was not the rigid social democratic émigré organisation of 1904. A world of revolutionary development, of maturing, lay between 1904 and 1918; these were months that played the role of years, and years

[*] The German S.P.D. journal that had published Luxemburg's article: "Organisational Questions of Russian Social Democracy", published in Russian in *Iskra* (see Introduction).

that played the role of decades. Let us recall Lenin's words about the shift in the party, as what was needed after the March 1917 revolution was to impel revolutionary politics on Russian soil. Rosa Luxemburg's position on the 'Bolsheviks' given this state of things could not remain unaffected. Of course, this is not to say that she would have said 'Yes' and 'Amen' to each single move, to every action of their policies. But the question at issue is not about the individual 'errors' and 'stupidities' of Bolshevik policy, as they were often sharply and openly criticized by Lenin and his friends themselves. An international problem of the struggling proletariat is at stake. On this Rosa Luxemburg continues in her "Spartacus Programme":

"But the proletarian revolution is at the same time the death knell for every kind of servitude and oppression. That is why all capitalists, Junkers, petty bourgeois, officers, all opportunists and parasites of exploitation and class rule rise up against the proletarian revolution as they would for their own life and death.

"It is sheer insanity to believe that the capitalists would willingly obey the socialist verdict of a parliament or of a National Assembly, that they would calmly renounce property, profit, the right to exploit. All ruling classes have fought to the end, with tenacious energy, to preserve their privileges.

"The imperialist capitalist class, as the last offspring of the exploiting classes, outdoes all its predecessors in brutality, in open cynicism and treachery. It defends its holiest of holies, its profit and its privilege of exploitation, with tooth and nail, with every method of cold evil which it has demonstrated throughout its history of colonial politics and in the recent World War. It will mobilize heaven and hell against the proletariat in motion. It will mobilize the peasants against the cities, the backward strata of the working class against the socialist vanguard; it will use officers to instigate atrocities; it will seek to paralyze every socialist measure with a thousand methods of passive resistance; it will force a score of Vendées[*] on the revolution; it will invite the foreign enemy, the murderous weapons of Clemenceau, Lloyd George, and Wilson[†] into the coun-

[*] Symbol of the destruction of the Paris Commune.

[†] Representatives of French, British and U.S. imperialism respectively in World War I.

try to rescue it; it will turn the country into a smoking heap of rubble rather than voluntarily give up wage slavery.

"All this resistance must be broken step by step, with an iron fist and ruthless energy. The violence of the bourgeois counter-revolution must be confronted with the revolutionary violence of the proletariat. Against the attacks, insinuations and slanders of the bourgeoisie must stand the inflexible clarity of purpose, vigilance, and ever-ready activity of the proletarian masses. Against the threatening dangers of the counter-revolution, the arming of the people and the disarming of the ruling classes.

"The fight for socialism is the mightiest civil war ever seen in world history, and the proletarian revolution must procure the necessary tools for this civil war; it must learn to use them – to struggle and to win.

"Such arming of the solid mass of labouring people with all political power for the tasks of the revolution – that is the dictatorship of the proletariat and therefore true democracy. Not where the wage slave sits next to the capitalist, the rural proletarian next to the Junker in fraudulent equality, to engage in parliamentary debate over questions of life or death, but where the million-headed proletarian mass seizes the entire power of the state in its calloused fist—like the god Thor his hammer—to smash the head of the ruling classes: that alone is democracy, that alone is not a betrayal of the people."

The meaning of these statements is clear. Here it is as with Luther: "They shall allow the word to stand." Does anyone believe that Thor's hammer of proletarian state power could be forged out of the paper of the *Mitteilungsblatt* or of *Unser Weg* and *Freiheit*? "From cardboard I cannot forge a sword," sings young Siegfried to the dwarf called Mime.

(Translated by John Catalinotto; Revision by George Gruenthal; German consultant: Michael Schiffmann)

V

Further Evidence of Rosa Luxemburg's Revised Viewpoint

Excerpts from characteristic articles of Rosa Luxemburg in the Rote Fahne / Excerpts from the "Speech on the Programme" at the Founding Congress of the Communist Party / Leo Jogiches on Rosa Luxemburg's and his own change of attitude to Bolshevik policy / Rosa Luxemburg's entire political activity since the November Uprising, an expression of her changed attitude to the Russian Revolution

Excerpts from some particularly characteristic articles of Rosa Luxemburg* in the *Rote Fahne* may indicate from her position on German affairs the close and strong inner contact she had arrived at with the Russian Revolution since September 1918. Her first lead article of 18 November is an affirmation of the Council system and the proletarian dictatorship, in short a programme of revolutionary action in which the spirit, the experience of the Russian revolution breathes. Under the telling title "The Beginning" Rosa Luxemburg writes:

"The revolution has begun. What is appropriate now is not jubilation over what has been accomplished, nor triumph over the defeated enemy, but the most rigorous self-criticism and iron concentration of energy in order to continue the work begun. Because what has been accomplished is small and the enemy is not defeated.

"What has been achieved? The monarchy has been swept away, supreme government power has passed into the hands of workers' and soldiers' representatives. But the monarchy was never the real enemy; it was just a facade, it was the sign-board of imperialism.

"The abolition of the rule of capital, the realization of the socialist social order: this and nothing less is the historical theme of the present revolution. A mighty work that is not accomplished in an instant by a few decrees from above, that can only be brought to

---

* Of these articles only the first two and the last are signed with Rosa Luxemburg's name. A well-informed and reliable friend of Rosa's confirmed that the lead articles, "The Acheron in Motion" and "A Dangerous Game", similarly "National Assembly or Council System," also come from Rosa's pen. Strong reasons of content and form speak for the authorship of the other specified examples. [C.Z.]

life by the conscious action of the masses of working people themselves in town and country, that can only be brought through all storms safely into the harbour by the highest intellectual maturity and inexhaustible idealism of the masses.

"The path of the revolution follows clearly from its goal; its method follows from its task. All power in the hands of the masses, in the hands of the workers' and soldiers' councils, the securing of the work of the revolution from their lurking enemies: this is the correct line for all measures of the revolutionary government.

"Every step, every act of the government must point like a compass in this direction:

"Expansion and re-election of the local workers' and soldiers' councils so that the first chaotic and impulsive gesture of their formation is replaced by a conscious process of understanding the objectives, tasks and methods of the revolutionary government.

"Permanent Congress of these representatives of the masses and the transfer of actual political power from the small committee of the Executive Council to the broader base of the workers' and soldiers' councils.

"Speediest convocation of the national parliament of the workers and soldiers in order for the proletariat of all Germany to constitute itself as a class, as a compact political power and to place itself behind the work of the revolution as its military thrust and momentum.

"Immediate organisation, not of the 'peasants' but of the rural proletariat and small peasants, who as a stratum still remain outside the revolution.

"Formation of a proletarian Red Guard as a permanent defence of the revolution and the training of a workers' militia, in order for the whole proletariat to be on guard at any time.

"Removal of the organs of the absolutist military police state that have been taken over from the administration, judiciary and army.

"Immediate confiscation of dynastic wealth and possessions as well as of landed property as the first provisional measures, in order to ensure food supply for the people, because hunger is the most dangerous ally of the counter-revolution.

"Immediate convocation of the World Workers' Congress in Germany in order to emphasize sharply and clearly the socialist and international character of the revolution, since the future of the

German Revolution can only be secured through the international, the world revolution of the proletariat.

"We have enumerated only the most necessary first steps. What is the current revolutionary government doing?

"It still calmly leaves the state as an administrative body from top to bottom in the hands of yesterday's pillars of Hohenzollern absolutism and tomorrow's tools of the counter-revolution.

"It is convening the Constituent Assembly, thus creating a bourgeois counterweight to the workers' and soldiers' representatives, and thereby shifting the revolution onto the track of a bourgeois revolution, conjuring away the socialist goals of the revolution.

"It is doing nothing to smash the remaining power of the capitalist class rule.

"It is doing everything to reassure the bourgeoisie, in order to proclaim the sanctity of property, to secure the untouchability of capitalist relations.

"It quietly permits the step by step active counter-revolution, without appealing to the masses, without warning the people loudly.

"The picture of the German Revolution corresponds to the inner maturity of the German situation. Scheidemann and Ebert are the appointed government of the German Revolution in its present stage. And the Independents, who believe that they can make socialism together with Scheidemann and Ebert, those who attested solemnly in the *Freiheit* that together with them one can form a "purely socialist government", qualify themselves as the appointed shareholders of the company in this first provisional stage.

"But revolutions do not stand still. Their law of existence is a rapid forward march, outgrowing themselves. Through its internal contradictions the first stage already impels a forward advance. The situation is understandable as a beginning, but it is untenable in the long run. If the counter-revolution is not to win out all along the line, the masses will have to be on their guard.

"The beginning has been made. The rest is not in the hands of midgets who hold back the course of the revolution, who want to put a spoke into the wheel of history. Today, the agenda of world history is: the realization of the ultimate goal of socialism. The German Revolution has come onto the path of this shining star. It will continue to proceed step by step, through storm and stress, through struggle, pain and suffering to victoriously attain its goal.

“It must!"

Two days after the unmistakable "Beginning" Rosa Luxemburg's position on the "National Assembly"—the German Constituent Assembly—confirms how quickly and far behind she has left her September view.

"From the *Deutsche Tageszeitung*, the *Vossische* and the *Vorwärts* to the independent *Freiheit*, from Reventlow, Erzberger, Scheidemann to Haase and Kautsky, one hears a unanimous call for the National Assembly and an equally unanimous cry of anguish at the idea of the power in the hands of the working class.

“The whole ‘people’, the whole ‘nation’ should be called upon to decide on the further fate of the revolution by a majority vote.

“For open and covert agents of the ruling classes, the slogan is self-evident. We do not talk with the guardians of the vaults of the capitalist class either in the National Assembly or about the National Assembly.

“But on this crucial issue the Independent leaders also stand in the ranks of the guardians of capital.

“In this way, as Hilferding points out in the *Freiheit,* they want to spare the revolution the use of violence, civil war with all its horrors. Petty bourgeois illusions!

“Indeed, the relatives of Lamartine, Garnier Pages, Ledru-Rollin, the petty bourgeois deluded ones of 1848 and their relatives are not extinct, they resurface—without the brilliance and talent and charm of novelty—in Kautsky, Hilferding, and Haase, in a boring, pedantic and erudite German version.

“These profound Marxists have forgotten the ABC of socialism!

“They have forgotten that the bourgeoisie is not a parliamentary party, but a ruling class, which is in possession of all the economic and social means of power.

“As soon as the famous National Assembly really decides to bring about socialism fully and completely, to eradicate the capitalist rule root and branch, then the battle begins. Once the bourgeoisie is struck in the heart—and its heart beats in the money vault—it will be a life and death struggle for its control, it will carry out thousands of open and hidden measures of resistance against the socialist measures.

“All this is inevitable. All this must be fought, repelled, overpowered – with or without the National Assembly. The ‘civil war’, which they want to banish from the revolution with anxious concern, cannot be banished. Because civil war is just another name for class struggle, and the thought of being able to introduce socialism without class struggle, by decision of a parliamentary majority, is a ridiculous petty bourgeois illusion.

"So what is gained by this cowardly detour of the National Assembly? It strengthens the position of the bourgeoisie and weakens and confuses the proletariat with empty illusions, it dissipates and loses time and energy in 'discussions' between the wolf and the lamb; in a word it plays into the hand of all those elements whose purpose and intent it is to swindle the proletarian revolution of its socialist goals, to emasculate it into a bourgeois democratic revolution.

"But the question of the National Assembly is not one of expediency, not one of what is more 'convenient.' It is a question of principle, a matter of the socialist self-realization of the revolution.

"The workers' parliament, the representative of the urban and rural proletariat, arises as a symbol of the new socialist system, whose bearer the current proletarian revolution is. The class character of its actual task is also the class character of the political organ that should carry out the task.

"The National Assembly is an outlived inheritance of bourgeois revolutions, a shell without content, a relic of the days of petty bourgeois illusions of 'one people,' of 'liberty, equality and fraternity' of the bourgeois state.

"Whoever takes recourse to the National Assembly today, consciously or unconsciously drags the revolution back to the historical stage of the bourgeois revolutions; he is a disguised agent of the bourgeoisie or an unconscious ideologue of the petty bourgeoisie.

"The fight for the National Assembly is carried out under the battle cry: Democracy or dictatorship! This slogan of counter-revolutionary demagogy is also taken over by obedient socialist leaders, who do not realize that the alternative is a demagogic falsehood.

"Today it is not a question of democracy or dictatorship. The question placed on the agenda by history is: bourgeois democracy or socialist democracy. For the dictatorship of the proletariat is democracy in the socialist sense. The dictatorship of the proletariat does not mean bombs, coups, riots or 'anarchy', as the agents of capitalist profit purposefully falsify it, but it is the use of all political means of power for the realization of socialism, for the expropriation of the capitalist class – in the mind and through the will of the revolutionary majority of the proletariat, that is, in the spirit of socialist democracy.

"Without the conscious will and conscious action of the majority of the proletariat there is no socialism. To sharpen this consciousness, to steel this will, to organize this activity, a class organ is needed, the national parliament of the proletarians in town and country.

"The convocation of such workers' representation in place of the traditional National Assembly of the bourgeois revolutions is in itself an act of class warfare, a break with the historical past of bourgeois society, a powerful means of arousing the proletarian masses, a first open abrupt declaration of war on capitalism.

"No excuses, no equivocation; the die must be cast. Yesterday parliamentary cretinism was a weakness, today it is an equivocation, and tomorrow it will be a betrayal of socialism."

In the article "The Acheron in Motion" the petty bourgeois hopes for the National Assembly are contrasted with the forward-driving force of the strike movement:

"...The masses are fed with the hope of the coming golden fruit, which is supposed to fall into their lap through the National Assembly. Through long debates, talks and decisions of a parliamentary majority, we are supposed to gently and 'quietly' slip into the promised land of socialism.

"The healthy class instinct of the proletariat rises up against the schemes of parliamentary cretinism. 'The emancipation of the working class must be the work of the working class itself,' says the *Communist Manifesto*. And the 'working class' does not mean a few hundred elected representatives who control the fate of society through speeches and arguments; even less is it the two or three dozen leaders who occupy government posts. The working class are the broadest masses themselves. Only through their active involvement in the overthrow of capitalist relations, can the socialisation of the economy be prepared....

"This incipient strike movement is at the same time the most succinct criticism by the masses of the chimera of their so-called 'leaders' about the 'National Assembly'. They already have the majority, the striking proletariat in the factories and mines! The fools! Why don't they invite their bosses to a little 'debate' and then vote them down by an ‘overwhelming majority’ and enforce all their demands in a smooth and ‘orderly manner’? It is above all and formally about real trifles, about the purely superficial features of the wage relation!"

The criticism of the *Vorwärts* of a session of the Berlin soldiers' councils in the parliament building on December 3, received this answer in the lead article entitled: “The Immature Masses”:

"But the *Vorwärts* has not had enough. The one meeting of the soldiers' councils in Berlin, which does not appeal to its ‘political’ and ‘parliamentary trained’ taste, provides it the occasion to generalise the case and to conclude further: ‘If one had experiences such as those of yesterday, one could honestly understand what a malicious deception is the Russian Soviet government that is praised by fools. Our soldiers and workers are—it can be said without nationalist arrogance—greatly superior to the Russians in general education and political training. If the system of a ‘council constitution’ has failed with us, this is the best proof that even with the most educated and intelligent people this system is unworkable, simply because it is an intrinsic impossibility.’ Whereby, ‘without nationalist arrogance,’ two observations can also be made:

“First, that the German workers and soldiers are vastly superior to the Russians in general education and political training.

“Next, that the whole system is not feasible, it suffers from an internal impossibility, because the education and intelligence even of the most educated and intelligent people are not sufficient, and then all this leads to a third observation: ‘Only the Constituent National Assembly can rescue us from chaos.’

“This is absolutely correct. On an average the German people attend school longer, have learned to write better and do mental arithmetic better than the Russians. They have also—one of the foundations for the ‘political and parliamentary training’—had religious instruction and patriotic education longer than the Russians, and have then gone on for further education to the high school of ‘political and parliamentary training’ run by German Social Democracy. This teacher bid them to consider the most shameless predatory war of the world as a defence against a ‘shameful attack’, to consider the threatened money vaults of the capitalists as their ‘house and home,’ the rape of Belgium and northern France as ‘our just cause,’ and the murder of proletarian brothers in Finland,

Ukraine, in Livonia, Estonia, and the Crimea as a fight for 'order and peace'.

"The whole point of this revolution is the fierce rising up of the masses against these results of the 'parliamentary and political training,' of the school as well as the schoolmaster, and the *Vorwärts* is already at hand to take them back to school with the 'Constituent Assembly'.

"Certainly, they would all come back, all the 'politically and parliamentarily trained' gentlemen such as Westarp and Erzberger, Stresemann and Grober, Payer and Haussmann, all heirs to an art acquired by the bourgeoisie through centuries of deceiving people. And with them came Scheidemann and Ebert, David and Lensch, who have learned how to clear one's throat and how to spit. They would all come together again and would continue their trade in deceiving the people, which they recently carried on in the four war years with the most horrible virtuosity, which came to an end on the bloody battlefields of France and with the first mass action of the German workers and soldiers.

"With the trick that the *Vorwärts* has played here, it places itself worthily on the side of its master, Friedrich Ebert. If he tried to kill the revolution physically through starvation hand-in-hand with Mr. Wilson, then the *Vorwärts* is trying to mentally assassinate it, as it again erects before the masses that bronze plaque held out to the oppressed for thousands of years by the bourgeoisie and every ruling class. And on it is written, 'You are not mature, you never will be'; it is an 'inherent impossibility'; you need leaders, we are the leaders."

The agenda of the Council Congress led Rosa Luxemburg to the following exposition: "National Assembly or Council Government?"

"This is the second item on the agenda of the national assembly of the German workers' and soldiers' councils and this in fact is the cardinal question of the revolution at this moment. Either a National Assembly, or all power to the workers' and soldiers' councils; either a renunciation of socialism, or the sharpest class struggle in full armour by the proletariat against the bourgeoisie. This is the dilemma.

"This is an idyllic plan: to achieve socialism by parliamentary means, by a simple majority decision! Unfortunately this sky-blue fantasy from the clouds of cuckoo land does not take into account even the historical experience of the bourgeois revolution, much less the nature of the proletarian revolution."...

The article points out that, despite the significant historical achievement of parliamentarism in England and France through the glorious struggles of Marstonmora and Naseby, the fate of the revolution there was decided by the battles of the French sans-culottes. It then continues:

"So little was the parliamentary majority of use to fight the bourgeois revolutions. And yet, what is the conflict between the bourgeoisie and feudalism, as compared to the yawning chasm that has opened up today between labour and capital! What was the class consciousness on both sides of the fighters, who in 1649 and 1789 stepped on to the barricades as compared with the deadly ineradicable hatred that blazes today between the proletariat and the capitalist class! Not for nothing did Marx turn his scientific lantern on the hidden mainsprings of the economic and political mechanisms of bourgeois society. Not for nothing did he analyse its activity and behaviour down to the finest change in its feelings and thoughts as the result of the great fundamental fact, that it feeds its life, like a vampire, from the blood of the proletariat.

"It is the great final conflict, on which depends the existence or non-existence of exploitation, the turning point of human history, a conflict in which there can be no excuse, no compromise, and no mercy.

"And this final conflict—in which the enormity of the task exceeds all that has been—must achieve what no class struggle, no revolution has ever accomplished: to dissolve the life and death struggle between two worlds into a gentle rustling of parliamentary debates and majority decisions!

"The parliamentary system was also an arena of the class struggle for the proletariat, as long as the quiet day-to-day life of bourgeois society remained; it was the tribune which brought the masses together around the flag of socialism, to be trained for the fight. Today we are in the midst of the proletarian revolution, and it is now up to us to lay the axe to the tree of capitalist exploitation. Bourgeois parliamentarism, as bourgeois class rule, whose finest political goal it is, has forfeited its right to exist. Now the class struggle steps with its bare, naked figure on to the barricades. Capital and labour have nothing to say to each other anymore, they have only to seize each other in an iron embrace and decide the final conflict: who gets thrown to the ground.

"Lassalle's word applies today more than ever: the revolutionary act is always to express the reality. And the reality is: labour is on one side and capital on the other! No hypocrisy of amicable negotiation when it is a matter of life and death; no victories of togetherness, where there is only opposition. Clear, open and honest and deriving strength from clarity and honesty, the proletariat has to constitute itself as a class, to take the entire political power in its hands.

"'Political equality, democracy!' the big and little prophets of bourgeois class rule have sung to us for decades.

"And 'political equality, democracy,' like an echo, the henchmen of the bourgeoisie, the Scheidemanns, sing today.

"Yes, it should first become reality. For the word 'political equality' will become real as soon as economic exploitation is eradicated root and branch. And 'democracy', people's rule begins only when the working people seize political power.

"It is time that the words misused by the bourgeois classes for one-and-a-half centuries should be critiqued by means of the practice of historical actions. It allows 'Liberte, Egalite, Fraternite', which was proclaimed in France by the bourgeoisie in 1789, to be made into a reality for the first time by the abolition of the class rule of the bourgeoisie. And as the first act of this liberating action, it loudly proclaims before the whole world and before the centuries of history: What hitherto was considered to be equal rights and democracy: Parliament, the National Assembly, the equal ballot was a lie and deceit! All power in the hands of the working masses, as a revolutionary weapon to shatter capitalism – that alone is true equal rights; that alone is true democracy"!

The article of 23 December: "Elections to the National Assembly" was evidently meant to prepare the standpoint of the upcoming Founding Congress of the Communist Party. The following passages are reproduced from it:

"...As we took advantage of the infamous Prussian three-class right to vote, to fight within the three-class parliament against the three-class parliament, so we will use the elections to the National Assembly to fight against the National Assembly.

"Here, of course, the analogy is at an end. For the real advocates of the revolution and socialism today, participation in the National Assembly can have nothing in common with the conventional pattern, with its time-honoured 'utilisation of Parliament' for so-called 'positive achievements'. We shall not take part in the old rut of parliamentarism, nor present bills to bring about small, cosmetic improvements, nor shall we parade an army of followers in order to 'match forces', in line with the well-known phrases from the era of bourgeois parliamentary treadmills and the vocabulary of Haase and comrades.

"Now we are in the midst of the revolution and the National Assembly is a counter-revolutionary fortress, which is raised up against the revolutionary proletariat. Therefore, it is important to attack this fortress and raze it to the ground. The elections and the tribune of the National Assembly must be used in order to mobilize the masses against the National Assembly and call them out to the sharpest fight.

"The participation in the elections must not be used to make laws together with the bourgeoisie and its supporters; it must be used to drag the bourgeoisie and its supporters from the temple, to storm the fortress of the counter-revolution and victoriously hoist the flag of the proletarian revolution upon it.

"...They, the masses, have to decide on the fate and history of the National Assembly. Their own revolutionary activity will determine what takes place inside and outside of the National Assembly. The emphasis is on the action outside, which must furiously pound on the doors of the counter-revolutionary parliament. But even the elections themselves, and the action of the revolutionary representatives of the masses inside must serve the cause of the revolution. The task of participation in the National Assembly is to ruthlessly and loudly denounce all the tricks of the esteemed Assembly, to unmask its counter-revolutionary work step by step in front of the masses, calling the masses to decide, to intervene.

"The gentlemen bourgeois, with the Ebert government at the top, want to ward off, to paralyze the class struggle through the National Assembly, to evade the revolutionary decision. In defiance of this plan the class struggle itself should storm into the National Assembly, it should utilise the elections as well as the negotiations of the National Assembly precisely in order to speed up the revolutionary decision,"...

To conclude our review of Rosa Luxemburg's writings in the *Rote Fahne*, we take excerpts from the article "Order Prevails in Berlin," which she wrote with murder stalking her from all sides.

"...'Order prevails in Warsaw!' 'Order prevails in Paris!' 'Order prevails in Berlin!' So every half-century run the announcements of the guardian of order from one centre of world-historic struggle to another. And the exultant 'victors' do not realize that an 'order' that must be maintained periodically by bloody massacres is inexorably approaching its historical destiny, its doom. What was this last 'Spartacus week' in Berlin, what were its results and what are its lessons? Even in the midst of battle, in the midst of the victory cry of the counter-revolution, the revolutionary proletariat must account for what has happened; it must measure the events and their results with a large historical yardstick. The Revolution has no time to lose; it rushes on – over still open graves, over 'victories' and 'defeats'– towards its great goals. For the fighters for international socialism to consciously follow its guiding principles and course is the first task.

"Was an ultimate victory of the revolutionary proletariat, were the overthrow of Ebert and Scheidemann and the establishment of the socialist dictatorship to be expected in this clash? Certainly not, if one maturely takes into consideration all the deciding factors. The sore point of the revolutionary cause at this moment: the political immaturity of the masses of soldiers, who still let themselves be misused by their officers for anti-people counter-revolutionary purposes, is itself proof that a lasting victory of the revolution in this clash was not possible. On the other hand, this immaturity of the military is itself only a symptom of the overall immaturity of the German Revolution.

"The rural districts, from which a large percentage of the masses of soldiers come, are still barely touched by the revolution. Berlin is up to now as good as isolated from the country. Certainly there are revolutionary centres in the provinces – in the Rhineland, on the North Sea coast, in Braunschweig, Saxony and Württemberg – that stand body and soul on the side of the Berlin proletariat. But missing for the time being are the immediate uniform step of the forward march, the direct unity in action, that would make the advance and the battle readiness of the Berlin workers incomparably more effective. The economic struggles—the actual volcanic source—which feed the revolutionary class struggle continuously—

are only in their beginning stages, and this is the deeper context of the political immaturity of the revolution.

"From all this it follows that a final lasting victory could not yet be counted on at this moment. Therefore, was the struggle of the past week a 'mistake'? Yes, if it is treated in general as a deliberate 'advance', as a so-called 'coup'! But what was the starting point of the last week of fighting? As in all previous cases, as on 6 December, as on 24 December, it was a brutal government provocation! As before, the bloodbath against unarmed demonstrators in Chaussee Street, the slaughter of the sailors, this time the attack on the Berlin police headquarters was the cause for all further events! The revolution does not always operate by choice, in an open field, according to a clever, correctly defined plan of 'strategists'. Its opponents also have the initiative; yes, they exercise it as a rule much more than the revolution itself.

"Faced with the fact of a brazen provocation by Ebert and Scheidemann, the revolutionary workers were forced to take up arms. Yes, it was a matter of honour of the revolution, to immediately meet the attack with vigour, in order not to encourage the further advance of the counter-revolution, in order not to shake the revolutionary ranks of the proletariat, the moral reputation of the German Revolution internationally.

"The immediate resistance arose spontaneously with such an obvious energy from the Berlin masses that already at the first attempt the moral victory remained on the side of the 'street'.

"Now it is an internal law of the revolution to never remain passively inactive at the stage achieved. The best defence is a good offence. This elementary rule of every fight certainly dominates every stage of the revolution. It goes without saying, and provides evidence of the healthy instinct, of the inner fresh strength of the Berlin proletariat that it was not satisfied with the restoration of Eichhorn to his office, that it spontaneously proceeded to occupy the other commanding heights of the counter-revolution: the bourgeois press, the semi-official news bureaus, the *Vorwärts*. All these measures were carried out by the masses from an instinctive understanding that on its part the counter-revolution would not calmly suffer defeat, but would proceed to a general trial of strength.

"Here we are also faced with one of the great historical laws of the revolution, against which all the sophistries and claims of knowing it better by the little 'revolutionaries' of the type belonging to the Independent Social Democratic Party are smashed to pieces, who in each fight are only striving to find excuses for retreat. Once the basic problem of the revolution has been clearly established—and in this revolution it is to overthrow the government of Ebert and Scheidemann, as the first obstacle to the victory of socialism—then this basic problem appears again and again in all its topicality. With the inexorability of a natural law every single episode of the fight unfurls to its full extent, however unprepared the revolution still is to resolve it, however immature the situation may still be...

"From this contradiction between the intensification of the task and the lack of prerequisites for its solution in an initial phase of revolutionary development, it follows that the individual battles of the revolution formally end in defeat. But the revolution is the only form of the 'war'—and this is their special law—that the final victory can only be prepared by a 'series of defeats.'

"What does the history of modern revolutions and socialism show? The whole path towards socialism—as far as revolutionary struggles are taken into consideration—is strewn with nothing but defeats. And yet, this same history leads step by step inexorably towards final victory! Where would we be today without those 'defeats,' from which we have drawn historical experience, knowledge, power and idealism! Today, when we are standing just before the final battle of the proletarian class struggle, we are based directly on those defeats, none of which we could do without, each of which is part of our strength and clarity of purpose...

"The revolutions have brought us nothing but defeats so far, but as these inevitable defeats pile up they guarantee the future final victory. But on one condition! The question is under what circumstances each defeat was suffered, whether it was due to the fact that the forward-storming combat power of the masses crashed at the barrier of the lack of maturity of the historical conditions, or whether the revolutionary action itself was paralyzed by half-measures, indecision, internal weakness...

"How does the defeat of this so-called 'Spartacus week' appear in the light of the above historical question? Was it a defeat because of stormy revolutionary energy on the one side and the insufficient maturity of the situation on the other, or because of the weakness and indecisiveness of action?

"Both! The ambiguous character of this crisis, the conflict between the powerful, determined, offensive rising of the Berlin masses and the indecisiveness, timidity, half-measures of the Berlin leadership is the special hallmark of this latest episode.

"The leadership failed. But the leadership can and must be recreated by the masses and come out from the masses. The masses are the decisive ones; they are the field on which the final victory of the revolution is accomplished. The masses were up to the mark, they have made this 'defeat' into one link in the chain of those historical defeats, which are the pride and strength of international socialism. And that is why the future victory will bloom from this defeat.

"'Order prevails in Berlin!' You unintelligent henchmen! Your 'order' is built on sand. The revolution will again, already tomorrow 'furiously rise up' and announce with fanfare to your terror: 'I was, I am, I will be!'"

Besides, another classic document from the *Rote Fahne* provides the answer to the international proletariat as to whether or not its leader maintained her September attitude to the fundamental issues of the Russian Revolution and thus to the proletarian revolution in general or not. And it is only these fundamental issues that are at stake, not some mistakes in the outcome. This document is Rosa Luxemburg's "Speech on the Programme", held at the Founding Congress of the Communist Party of Germany (Spartacus League) from 29 to 31 December, 1918 in Berlin.

After a sweeping overview of the working class movement, since Marx and Engels wrote the *Communist Manifesto,* the original charter of scientific socialism, Rosa Luxemburg explains:

"What has this war left of bourgeois society other than a huge pile of rubble? Formally all the means of production, and also most, almost all significant instruments of power still remain in the hands of the ruling classes: let us not deceive ourselves about this. But what can they do with them, except make frantic attempts to reestablish exploitation through bloodbaths, which will be nothing but anarchy. They have gone so far that nowadays the dilemma facing humanity is: either sink into anarchy, or attain salvation through socialism. It is impossible for the bourgeois classes to find a way out of the results of the World War on the basis of their class rule and capitalism. And so it has come about that we are experiencing the truth that Marx and Engels expressed for the first time as the scientific basis of socialism in the great document, the *Communist Manifesto*: Socialism will become a historical necessity, in the most exact meaning of the word today. Socialism has become a necessity, not merely because the proletariat is no longer willing to live under the conditions of life that the capitalist class make for it, but because, if the proletariat does not fulfil its class duties and bring about socialism, the downfall of all of us together will be imminent" (p. 10).

Rosa Luxemburg considers it particularly important and urgent "that we come to an understanding about how the specific circumstances are to be assessed, how the tactical lessons and practical solutions are to be formulated, which follow from the political situation, from the course of the revolution and from the foreseeable further direction of its development" (p. 11).

The result of the first phase of the German Revolution from November to December 1918 looks to Rosa Luxemburg like this:

"Thus there is mutual disillusionment on all sides! The proletariat has lost any illusion about the union of Ebert, Scheidemann and Haase as a so-called socialist government. Ebert and Scheidemann have lost the illusion that in the long run, with the help of the proletarians in soldiers' uniforms, they could keep down the proletarians in workers' shirts, and the bourgeoisie has lost the illusion that by means of Ebert, Scheidemann and Haase they could swindle the whole socialist revolution in Germany of its goals. It is nothing but a negative balance, nothing but tatters of destroyed illusions. But especially since only such torn-up tatters remain from the first phase of the revolution, the proletariat is the greatest winner, for there is nothing that is so harmful for the revolution as illusions, there is nothing as useful to it as the clear, open truth.

"...What then is the further perspective of the development, once we have its first phase behind us? Of course, it cannot be a matter of prophecy, but only of deducing the logical consequences from previous experiences and making inferences as to the likely paths of the forthcoming development in order to subsequently amend our tactics, our own way of fighting. Party comrades, where does the way forward lead? (p. 15)...

"That we are coming directly through the previous development, through the logic of the events themselves, and through the violence that weighs down on Ebert and Scheidemann; in the second phase of the revolution we will experience much sharper conflicts, much more violent class struggles (very true!), than was the case earlier, a much sharper conflict not merely because the political factors that I have enumerated previously will lead to this, without illusions, face to face, head on, to take up the fight between the revolution and the counter-revolution; but because a new fire, a new flame is spreading from the depths of the whole, and those are the economic struggles.

"Party comrades, it is characteristic of the first period of the revolution, one might say until 24 December, which I have described—we must with full consciousness become clear about this—that it was still an exclusively political revolution, and therein lies the beginning stage, the inadequacy, the unfinished character and lack of consciousness of this revolution (p. 17)…

"Only in recent weeks have the completely spontaneously strikes become noticeable. We want to say again: it is precisely the very essence of this revolution that strikes will increase more and more, that they will have to become more and more the central point, the main component of the revolution. (Quite right!) Then it is an economic revolution and with that it will become a socialist revolution (p. 17)...

"Socialism will not be made and cannot be made by decree, not even by a socialist government, no matter how outstanding it is. Socialism must be made by the masses, by every proletarian. Where they are forged to the chain of capital, there the chain must be broken. Only this is socialism, only in this way can socialism be made (pp. 17 and 18)...

"As a result: in the coming phase of the revolution, the strikes will not only expand more and more, but they will be the central point, the decisive point of the revolution, pushing back the purely political questions (p. 18)...

"It is also difficult to foresee what will develop out of the National Assembly in the second phase of the revolution. It is possible that, if it comes into existence, it will be a new school of education for the working class; or it may also be that nothing will ever come of the National Assembly; nothing can be predicted. I will only add parenthetically, so that you can understand from what standpoint we defended our position yesterday: we were only against basing our tactics on one alternative. I will not start a new discussion, but only say this, lest any of you, listening only superficially, thinks: aha, now we are hearing something different. We stand decisively united on the same position as yesterday. We do not want to base our tactics toward the National Assembly on what could possibly but not definitely happen, namely, that the National Assembly does not come into existence. We want to prepare for all eventualities, including the revolutionary utilisation of the National Assembly, if it comes into existence. Whether it comes into existence or not is immaterial, the revolution can only win in any case (pp. 20 and 21)...

"I have tried to show you that the revolution of 9 November was above all a political revolution, while in the main it must still become an economic one. But it was also just a revolution in the cities, while so far the broad countryside remains almost unaffected. It would be insane to think that one can realize socialism without agriculture. From the standpoint of a socialist economy one cannot even transform industry without its immediate amalgamation with a socialist transformation of agriculture. The main idea of the socialist economic system is the abolition of the distinction and separation between town and countryside. This separation, this contradiction, this conflict is a purely capitalist phenomenon that must be eliminated immediately if we place ourselves on the socialist standpoint. If we are serious about a socialist transformation, you must pay attention to the countryside, as well as on the industrial centres, and here we are, unfortunately, not even at the beginning of the beginning (p. 23)...

"I would like to summarize our next tasks: We must henceforth above all build up in all directions the system of workers' and soldiers' councils, particularly the system of workers' councils. What we undertook on 9 November are only the weak beginnings and not even that. In the first phase of the revolution we have again lost great instruments of power. You know that a continued abolition of the workers' and soldiers' councils system is planned by the counter-revolution. In Hesse, the workers' and soldiers' councils were completely abolished by the counter-revolutionary government; in other places the instruments of power are being ripped from their hands. We must therefore not only build up the workers' and soldiers' councils system, but also bring the rural workers and small farmers into this system of councils. We need to seize power; we have to formulate the seizure of power as the question: what does, can and should each workers' and soldiers' council in Germany do? (Cheers!) Therein lies the power; we must undermine the bourgeois state from the bottom up by no longer separating public power, legislation and administration, but unite them and put them into the hands of the workers' and soldiers' councils.

"Party comrades, this is a huge field to plough. We have to prepare from below up to give the workers' and soldiers' councils such power that, when the government of Ebert and Scheidemann or any similar one is overthrown, then this is just the final act. Thus, the seizure of power should not be a single act but a progression, in which we penetrate into the bourgeois state until we have occupied all positions, and then defend them tooth and nail. In my view and the view of my closest party friends, the economic struggle should also be led by the workers' councils. Also the leadership of the economic conflict and its channelization into ever more spheres should lie in the hands of the workers' councils. The workers' councils should have all power in the state. We have to work towards this in the near future, and from this it is also evident that when we set ourselves this task, we will have to reckon with a huge intensification of the struggle in the near future. Because here it is necessary to fight step by step, face to face, in every State, in every city, in every village, in every community, to transfer all powers of the state, which must be ripped away from the bourgeoisie step by step, to the worker' and soldiers' councils. To do this, however, our party comrades and the proletarians must be trained. Even where workers' and soldiers' councils exist, consciousness is still lacking as to what the workers' and soldiers' councils are called upon to do. (Very true!) We must first train the masses in the fact that the workers' and soldiers' council should be the lever of the state machinery in all spheres, that it must take over all powers and must lead them all in the same current of the socialist revolution. There are still those masses of workers who are already organized into the workers' and soldiers' councils, but who are far removed from this, except of course a small minority of proletarians who are clearly aware of their responsibilities. But this is not a defect, it is normal. By exerting power, the masses must learn to exercise power. There is no other way to teach them. The proletarians will be trained by taking recourse to action. Here we can say: In the beginning was the deed, and the deed must be that the workers' and soldiers' councils feel called upon and learn to be the only public power in the whole country. Only in this way can we undermine the ground to such an extent that it will be ready for the overthrow, which will then crown our work. (pp. 24 and 25)...

"History does not make it as easy for us as it was in the bourgeois revolutions; that it was enough to overthrow the official power in the centre and replace it with a few or a few dozen new men. We have to work from the bottom up, and that specifically corresponds to the mass character of our revolution according to its goals which reach into the base and foundation of the social structure. This corresponds to the character of the present proletarian revolution, that we must make the seizure of political power not from above, but from below. The bigger the task, the more we will unite all forces; and let us not forget, the revolution expects its work to be accomplished with tremendous speed. I do not attempt to predict how long this process will take. Who among us will make an estimate; who cares, if only we live long enough to bring this about." (P. 26)

It seems to me that Rosa Luxemburg's relationship to the Russian Revolution and to the 'Bolshevik' slogans also burns with a bright flame in her Speech on the Programme. Her review of the first weeks of the revolution and her outlook on the next tasks of the revolutionary proletariat in Germany Rosa begins with these remarks:

"What we experienced on 9 November was much more the collapse of existing imperialism than the victory of a new principle. (Agreement.) It was simply that the moment had come when imperialism, inwardly rotten, had to collapse like a colossus with feet of clay. What followed was a more or less chaotic, unplanned movement with very little awareness. The unifying bond and the abiding and redeeming principle were summed up only in the slogan regarding the formation of workers' and soldiers' councils. This is the slogan of this revolution, which immediately gave it the special character of a proletarian socialist revolution – with all the shortcomings and weaknesses of a first step. We should never forget that, if they come to us slandering the Russian Bolsheviks, we must reply: Where have you learned the ABC of your present revolution? You have adopted the workers' and soldiers' councils from the Russians. (Agreement.) Those little people who now see it as their duty, at the head of the German so-called socialist government, to assassinate the Russian Bolsheviks, hand in hand with the English imperialists, they are likewise formally based on workers' and soldiers' councils, and they must admit: it was the Russian Revolution that issued the first slogans for the world revolution. We can certainly say— resulting from the entire situation itself—in whichever country after Germany the proletarian revolution breaks out, its first act will be the formation of workers' and soldiers' councils. (Very true!) Precisely here we have the unifying international bond of our actions, that is the slogan that distinguishes our revolution completely from all previous bourgeois revolutions, and it is very characteristic of the dialectical contradictions, in which this revolution, like all other revolutions, moves, that already on 9 November, as it uttered its first cry, its birth cry, it found the word that guides us to socialism: workers' and soldiers' councils."

Paul Levi published Rosa Luxemburg's September 1918 critique of Bolshevik tactics disregarding Leo Jogiches' expressed will. If he thought he was entitled to do this, it would have been his most elementary duty to place this criticism in its historical context. It must be stated that it was the beginning, and not the conclusion of Rosa Luxemburg serious grappling with the problems of the Russian Revolution. One could not help but realize that the astute theoretician of the proletarian revolution had changed her September view. It was of course Paul Levi's good right to reproach this development as a serious, unforgivable case in chorus with the Kautskys and Hilferdings of the whole world. But he should not have overlooked it without a word. Instead of doing the obvious, what he has done is really incomprehensible. In the *Mitteilungsblatt* of the C.W.G. [Communist Workers' Group] on 6 January of this year, he explained: "No, Rosa Luxemburg did not change her viewpoint on the tactics of the Bolsheviks during her lifetime, as Leo Jogiches also did not. Yes, I think the Polish friends of Rosa Luxemburg only changed their views, conforming to those of Rosa, long after her death."

"The Friends of Rosa Luxemburg" will know how to answer this—let us politely say— bold statement themselves. As far as the murdered Leo Jogiches is concerned, I deny its accuracy in the strongest terms. Not merely on the basis of occasional remarks in his letters, but most of all due to very detailed discussions with him in the week before his assassination. Already many years before the outbreak of the World War, I turned to Leo on Rosa's advice, when my studies alone did not provide satisfactory information about the revolutionary movement in Russia. Now that the Russian Revolution itself stands tall among us, it was natural that during our get-togethers I asked him for his opinion. The great, long-range problems of the Russian Revolution, the position of the Social Revolutionaries, of the Mensheviks and the Bolsheviks, the leading personalities, etc. were repeatedly the subject of our conversations. And I am to this day firmly convinced that this rare man, a friend of Rosa's, expressed his opinion openly and frankly to me, as he always used to do.

Leo Jogiches had at first observed, examined critically, and yes, was to a certain degree 'distrustful' of Bolshevik policy in the Russian Revolution. At that time he feared that the 'party of Lenin' after the first brilliant start—the seizure of political power by the proletariat and the securing of power in the Soviets—could "lose the stamina for a revolutionary *realpolitik* in grand style". However, the longer the course of the Russian Revolution continued the more his doubts were refuted. "The revolution has educated Lenin", Leo told me; "the man has learned, he has learned tremendously. How he has developed! Who among us would have imagined it! The revolution has created in the Bolsheviks the leading party, which it had to have. We may believe that the party has really 'blossomed.' The Mensheviks and the Social Revolutionaries are the ones with stereotyped beliefs. They have lost their connection with the life of the revolution. What has become of such a witty and theoretically educated person as Martov! A sterile critic and whiner! Now, after the Kerensky period with its unequivocal experience, after the seizure of power by the proletariat, now in the most terrible struggle with the counter-revolution to quarrel over the 'true meaning' of Marx' and Engels' quotes and about democracy in the abstract, instead of inexorably carrying out the proletarian dictatorship! Now to talk about history, instead of making history! It is incredible! The Bolsheviks have learnt what is required. They act, daily, hourly, with a clear consciousness of the need to make the masses actively take part. They now stand on the broad, solid basis of being connected with the masses, without which a revolutionary party would remain a shadow."

This is essentially the reason that Leo Jogiches gave for abandoning his earlier hesitant attitude toward the Bolsheviks and standing side by side with them, approving their policies as a whole. Leo Jogiches of course did not assess every single measure of their policies as the pinnacle of wisdom. His concerns about the revolutionary correctness, the consequences of the agrarian policies, for example, had not yet completely disappeared. He was imbued with the conviction that the proletarian revolution in Russia, "was not yet over the hill, but only stands close to it." However, in his opinion the policies of the Bolsheviks will help it over the hill—if they are consistently carried out and developed. It is understood that Leo Jogiches also took into account the significance of the proletarian revolution in Western Europe and especially in Germany. He particularly appreciated that Lenin, from the outset, considered the Russian Revolution not as a 'national affair,' but as an international one. Regarding the controversial issues—Constituent Assembly, proletarian dictatorship, 'democracy', he viewed the policy of the Bolsheviks including their toughness—as a historical necessity, rooted in the given concrete circumstances. Undoubtedly, Leo Jogiches' evaluation of Bolshevik tactics was an especially significant influence that led to Rosa Luxemburg also changing her earlier opinion of them.

Rosa's entire political activity from early November 1918 until the day of her death demonstrates most effectively her later changed opinion of the controversial fundamental and tactical questions of Bolshevik politics. This activity was not a private matter in a narrow political 'family circle'. It was openly carried out as a revolutionary struggle, as a cause of the German and international proletariat. And this activity is a monumental whole, lasting longer than iron. Its meaning, its character cannot be distorted or misinterpreted. However, for Paul Levi, Rosa Luxemburg's work in the active weeks of the revolution seems to be lost and forgotten. As Joshua in the Old Testament makes the sun and moon stand still until his people win the battle, so Paul Levi decrees that for him until he has won his battle against the heathens of the executive in Moscow, Rosa Luxemburg's process of arriving at an understanding about the mightiest event of our time was completed with her September treatise. With one sentence he strikes out the further development of the views of this tireless thinker, although the result embodied in flesh and blood in Rosa's activity, in the action of the proletarian vanguard that she led, has become a part of history. How else is one to understand the statement in the *Mitteilungsblatt*? No one will dare to suspect that Rosa Luxemburg had a public and a secret view of the basic problems of Bolshevik revolutionary politics; that in articles and speeches she had passed the fiery wine of the 'Russian example' to the masses, while alone in her little private room she brewed a soft democratic reform lemonade for the posthumous domestic use of Paul Levi. The utter ridiculousness of such a conjecture deals a death blow to her infamy.

Energetic salesmanship has decreed that Paul Levi is Rosa Luxemburg's ‘political heir’, and his ‘petty little followers’ echo this dictum to the four winds. But the gentlemen forget that political inheritance cannot be established by the possession of literary remains; rather it must be earned through work and struggle. However, Paul Levi’s political activity since the “Third World Congress” of the Communist International really proves over and over how essentially alien this ‘struggle companion’ of the first revolutionary period has become to the bold and consistent leading pioneer of the proletarian International. Such action is the expression of an inner development, which inevitably distances itself further from the historical content of Rosa Luxemburg's thought and intended goal. Publication of the ‘posthumous pamphlet’ seals the process. But this is not merely because it is outwardly in opposition to Rosa’s future intentions and Leo Jogiches explicit will, but because internally in its tendency and purpose it is a negation of the essence, the activities of these two great dead persons. Assuming the differences in talent, etc., etc., Paul Levi proves as much to be the ‘political heir’ of Rosa Luxemburg, as Bernard Becker, Mende and so many other secretaries were Lassalle's ‘political heirs’. By seeking to lock the legacy she has left to the international proletariat in the cage of his personal opinion and harnessing it in the service of his personal politics he is abusing it.

As little as the now overcome, extravagantly romantic "revolutionary March philosophy" was nurtured in the bright, deep spring of Rosa Luxemburg's thoughts, so little has the super-clever pretending to be wise theory of a ‘great Social Revolutionary Workers’ Party’, whose prophet Paul Levi would like to be, drunk of Rosa Luxemburg's passionate heart’s blood. The cleverest play with the concepts of ‘sects’ and ‘masses’ does not create the historical preconditions of a mass party, nor does the criticism of the ‘rotting’ Communist Party of Germany and of the aberrant Executive in Moscow. This criticism may be a pleasant literary pastime, self-satisfying in the consciousness of one’s political godliness, but by itself it is not a creative, political act. It is not so because it does not open up new historical perspectives on the road that leads the proletariat out of the Egypt of capitalist slavery to the Canaan of socialism and communism. Conversely, it points unmistakably to the old, well-worn reform roads leading to a kingdom of a capitalism that has regained its strength and become young again, and in which the proletariat should make itself at home.

Therein lies the break with and abandonment of Rosa Luxemburg's world of thought. The imperishable historic achievement of our leading theorist, when war broke out, was to focus the will of the international proletariat in clear recognition that, after the imperialist mass killings there should not be a 'renaissance' of capitalism, that the world proletarian revolution must be the world's judgment of it. Whether a 'mass party' or a 'Social Revolutionary Workers' Party', in Rosa Luxemburg's mind and heart it truly does not depend on the extent and the garnering of cheap momentary results. It is decided solely by the will and purpose of the party, its historical life content. On the relationship between party and masses Rosa Luxemburg had always held the view that Blanqui's theory of 'revolutionary cadres' modified historically and further developed was correct. Namely in the sense that an ideologically and organisationally united, unified party must be the solid backbone and the thinking, leading brain of the revolutionary mass movements and mass struggles, their driving force, but also their enduring capacity. In Germany, an unyielding party such as 'Spartacus' should carry the banner of revolution ahead of the slaves of our days.

Rosa Luxemburg's 'political heirs' will not be individual personalities, who give lip service to her theory with more or less talent and skill. They will be in the form of the proletarian masses, who act and fight in the spirit of the immortal leader. They must take up her legacy. Therefore: that to the international proletariat which belongs to it. They must adopt as their own the very rich political legacy left to them by Rosa Luxemburg. Leo Jogiches' last will was clear and is mandatory as the authority of the international proletariat itself. The friends, who accordingly together with him were expected to publish Rosa's entire writings, were initially hindered by the daily tasks of the situation from fulfilling their duty. Last summer they undertook the preparatory steps to do so. The Executive of the Communist International provided the means for the publication of Rosa Luxemburg's Collected Works. Paul Levi's influence has so far prevented the necessary inventory and cataloguing of Rosa Luxemburg's literary remains from being made. Why? Because it contradicts his personal opinion about the Executive of the Third International, which is carrying the initial costs of publication. His behaviour in this matter together with the nature, the presentation, the purpose of the posthumous pamphlet, is part of his political-theatrical hara-kiri as a communist, which he is carrying out in public, and which emits the most unpleasant odour of decay. The misleading picture of Rosa Luxemburg's attitude to the Russian and to the proletarian revolution that Paul Levi would like to present disappears like an apparition in front of her clear, powerful voice, murdered but still so alive. Her last work must be published first. Her articles in the *Rote Fahne* are Rosa Luxemburg's political testament. They belong together as a booklet in the hands of the masses. The latter will decide. Not between the Rosa Luxemburg of September 1918 and the Rosa Luxemburg of the week of the revolution, because she is one and the same. Much more one must choose between all those, who want to justify their development backwards by reference to the great dead one, and a Rosa Luxemburg storming forward toward the proletarian revolution.

(Translated by George Gruenthal)

VI

Paul Levi's 'Introduction' – a Misuse of Rosa Luxemburg's September Critique

Why bring out the 'posthumous pamphlet'? / The non-Marxist method of the 'Introduction' / The frank characterization of the 'new policy' as an imposed policy of concessions to capitalism and an incisive formulation of the communist ideal by the Bolshevists / The need for the Bolshevist policy to consider the mentality of the Russian small peasant / The tragic historical contradiction of the Russian Revolution as the background for the Bolshevik policy of concessions

The rationale for the posthumous publication of this pamphlet at precisely this point is given in the 'Introduction' which follows the 'Foreword'. According to this, Paul Levi clearly felt the need to cover up his own sharp clash with the Bolshevists using the authority of a communist theoretician. Indeed the 'Introduction' does not serve as an insight into Rosa Luxemburg's struggle with the most important issues of the Russian Revolution. Rather, it gives us Paul Levi's assessment and condemnation of the policies of the Bolsheviks. That too while invoking Rosa's critique and in a manner as if Paul Levi's position was its logical continuation. At first glance this could appear to be justified. Are not the subsequent developments in Soviet Russia, particularly the policy of concessions and the relationship of the communist party to the proletarian masses repercussions of the 'mistakes' pointed out earlier in Rosa Luxemburg's study of September 1918, undertaken out of her concern for the revolution? This is what the editor of the 'posthumous pamphlet' believes and he flatly states that on the basis of her critical analysis Rosa "came to conclusions which even allow us to surmise her opinion about the present policy of the Bolsheviks."

All that is missing from this 'conjecture', as the decisive factor of historical evaluation, is table rapping and pronouncements by a medium as statements in the Luxemburgish spirit. If Rosa were still alive, she would have brusquely dismissed such political spiritualism.

Her innermost essence was absolute determination and precision – consequently her incomplete September treatise also aims at being understood and not being 'conjectured'. Given the present

Bolshevik policy, what matters is not the 'postulation' of a final judgment – even if it is pronounced by such an illustrious personality as Rosa Luxemburg – but a sober, conscientious examination of the historical conditions under which this policy exists and exerts its impact. This is what is missing in Paul Levi's 'Introduction'.

To be sure, he declares in an attitude of exalted objectivity that one should not reproach, but analyse and understand that the policy of concessions and the evolution of the Bolshevik party must be understood in their historical context. However, this remains a mere genuflection before the Marxist method; Paul Levi did not use it. His evaluation of Bolshevik policy is based on quotations. On citations from Lenin, Zinoviev, Trotsky, Radek, and from Rosa Luxemburg; on industriously collected, cleverly chosen quotes about the altered position of the Bolsheviks on the question of building the economic structure, about the assessment of the Soviets, the unions etc. etc. Paul Levi himself realizes that with such a juxtaposition of quotes "nothing is proven". Nevertheless, he is satisfied to pile opinion on opinion, instead of tracking the historical circumstances from which these opinions emerged and from which they get their meaning. Thus, these pillars of his assessment are without substance, they are lifeless.

In Paul Levi's 'Introduction' it is neither a revolutionary politician nor a Marxist historian who is examining the Bolshevist policies. Here it is a lawyer who has the say, and stepping forth as prosecutor and in the manner of a public prosecutor, wants a conviction at any cost. Over and over again his arguments resound: "Accused, you are guilty! *Russische Korrespondenz* in volume such and such, on page number such and such it is written. In such and such pamphlet you have stated." … Quotations play the role of circumstantial evidence for the culpability of Bolshevik revolutionary politics. At the present time only a very sectarian lawyer would pronounce guilt merely on the basis of such circumstantial evidence disregarding the social ramifications of the allegations in his investigation.

The 'Marxist' Paul Levi did not consider it necessary to examine his charge against the Russian communists in connection with the historical reality of the Russian Revolution. And this, despite the fact that Rosa Luxemburg, whose authority he after all adheres to, had strongly emphasized, that the tactics and the politics of revolutionary parties were not accidental, superficial or specious, but were rather a specific product of concrete historical conditions which the parties become conscious of or which assert themselves unknowingly. Worse still, occupied with judgments and verdicts, Paul Levi has even lost the inner contact with the vitality of the Russian Revolution. Consequently his 'Introduction', in relation to Rosa Luxemburg's critique, seems like a withered graft on an alien plant on which it is incapable of growing. The shimmering green around the aridity does not signal the presence of sap bursting with the promise of fruit; it is smeared on literary veneer and ingenuity.

Were Paul Levi's perception of the development of things in Soviet Russia correct, Bolshevik revolutionary politics could most aptly be characterized with Schiller's distich: "Into the ocean sails with a thousand masts the youth; peacefully, on a rescued boat the old man drifts into the harbour'.

The 'Introduction' makes the so-called 'new policy,' inaugurated in early 1921, appear as the 'rescued boat', on which the resigned old Bolshevik seeks refuge in the harbour of capitalism, after the stormy sea journey, without a reliable compass towards the shores of communism, broke and split the masts of the hopeful and jubilant youth. For Paul Levi the policy of concessions is a 'complete reversal' of Bolshevist politics, an expression of its bankruptcy. Not because it made compromises with capitalism. For the realization of communism, compromises can be necessary, an unavoidable result of the power relations between classes which fight for and against it. However, for communists compromises are allowed only under two circumstances: no concealment, a frank characterization of the compromise as a compromise; a resolute unshakable adherence before the people to the goal that transcends the compromises. In short, what determines the admissibility of compromises is that it does not cause the dulling of the revolutionary consciousness and the weakening of the revolutionary will of the masses.

According to Paul Levi, Bolshevik politics has not been mindful of these circumstances. It had abandoned not just economically, but also 'conceptually its old goals' and capitulated before capitalism. In its objective effects it is not revolutionary, but counterrevolutionary. By no means does its fall into sin originate in the deficit of its measures in the course towards communism, but rather in the steps taken in the direction of capitalism. As proof for his evaluation of Bolshevik policies Paul Levi juxtaposes two statements of Lenin's from the years 1918 and 1921. In 1918, Lenin declared the task of the Communist Party to be: "the creation of such conditions which will not allow the bourgeoisie to exist or re-emerge". In 1921, he writes 'Tax in Kind': "Inasmuch as we are yet unable to pass directly from small-scale production to socialism, some capitalism is inevitable as the elemental product of small-scale production and exchange; so that we must utilize capitalism (particularly by directing it into the channels of state capitalism) as the intermediary link between small production and socialism, as a means, a path, and a method of increasing the productive forces." Elsewhere Lenin stated: "Not only through enthusiasm, but rather with the help of personal interest, personal interestedness, with the help of economic calculations one, for the time being, builds a firm bridge, which in the country of small peasants will lead from state capitalism to socialism." Can Paul Levi's assertions claim evidentiary strength? Judge for yourself!

It is puzzling that Paul Levi, for whom world history is made up of quotes, remained ignorant of those statements by leading Bolsheviks, which incisively and in all certainty characterized the concession policy as a forced compromise. The number of such statements is legion. Paul Levi obviously missed the wood for the trees. The Communist Party of Russia certainly does not let the masses grope in the dark about the fact that the concessions to capitalism were a hard necessity, but not the goal or ideal. "We must now take two steps back in order to be sure of the ground, to hold our position in order to once again push forward." This is the leitmotiv of all Bolshevik statements about the concession policy. On the basis of all actually prevailing national and international situations, it has been demonstrated that in the battle for communism, compromises are unavoidable, bitterly felt and risky transitional measures.

Had the Bolsheviks wanted to conceal the compromise character of the new policy, necessity would have forced them to tear down all the deceiving wrappings. The proletarian masses must understand the concession policy in order to tolerate it. Day after day, the consequences of this policy encroach pitilessly into the life of the worker. After these long years of communist aspirations and painful realities the heart and will could have been overpowered by demoralization, disappointment and bitterness. Only an understanding of the why and whereof of the new policy will be able to counter this, will be able to strengthen the ability to persevere. The incisive characterization of the compromise contains simultaneously the sharpest formulation of the lofty goal which the compromise has to serve. Every dismantling of a communist institution, every capitalist measure spurs the proletarian masses to compare communism with capitalism. Whereof the stones speak, thereof the Bolsheviks cannot be silent. To speak out openly about how things are and to unswervingly hold on to the ultimate goal and path is, in the given situation, fundamental to Bolshevik tactics. Given the powerful logic of events, it would work against the Bolsheviks, if the leaders of the Russian Revolution were not the experienced, clear-sighted tacticians that they are.

Naturally, Paul Levi claims that with the new policy the Russian communists have even conceptually abandoned their goals. The proof of this lies in the above quoted words of Lenin about the utilization of personal interest in order to build a bridge between state capitalism and socialism in the country of small peasants. This kind of condemnation of the Bolshevik malefactors is alarmingly reminiscent of the well-known formulation of the French police genius: "Give me five lines written by someone, and I will take him to the gallows". As if apart from the quoted sentence there weren't words of leading Bolsheviks—and not in the least even those from Lenin himself—that encourage a selfless pursuit of socialist solidarity as a powerful, indispensable force of new and higher social life. As though the Russian Revolution were not there before us, an expression of the highest idealism, the enthusiasm of millions transformed into action for a greater collective, the boundless commitment of individuals to a common interest. Neither the Communist Party nor the vast working masses of Soviet Russia viewed their sacrificing solidarity subordinated to this value system and praxis with a nostalgic, 'Once upon a time'. This praxis of solidarity is all the more dynamic the more difficult the tasks which the concession policy poses for the party and the more painfully the sacrifices for this policy are felt by the proletarian masses.

Lenin only said the obvious. The revolutionary, who wants to overthrow the world of capitalism, must be clear about things and also about people as they are. This is the pre-condition for being able to make use of the one as the other to implement his goals. Is it perhaps the fault of Bolshevik tactics that within four years of the Revolution, the war and the civil war, the overwhelming majority of

Russian small peasants have not as yet become fervent communists? Over half a century of 'Marxist theory and practice' of Social Democracy in Germany has not yet managed to bring the proletariat this far. The vestiges of hundreds and thousands of years of social relations in the psyche of people cannot be wiped out overnight by the Revolution.

The Bolsheviks have experienced this most markedly in the sabotage by the intellectuals. The Soviet government had to capitulate in the face of this rebellion of the interest of one social class against the proletarian social order. They could not retain the stipulated equal pay for all socially necessary and useful work and had to concede a privileged status to the intellectuals and the qualified workers. Not with one single syllable did Paul Levi condemn the fact that for the time being the Bolsheviks had to 'discard' their great goal: the elimination of the social contradiction between manual and mental work. On the contrary, he rightly considered it premature and imprudent that immediately after the establishment of the proletarian dictatorship they thought of realising this goal in the manner indicated. The mistake was in 'conceptually' making an assumption about the mentality of 'intellectuals' which, however, could only be the outcome of a development. This concerns the consciousness of the 'intellectuals' with regard to their solidarity with the proletariat in the defeat of capitalism; the knowledge that only their integration in a community of workers freed from exploitation, emancipated and with equal obligations guarantees them freedom of development and influence. In all the phases of the Russian Revolution individual 'intellectuals' have displayed the highest idealism – however, the class as a whole proved itself to be individualistic. To utilize the abilities of the 'intellectuals' in order to build up the communist order the Soviet government was forced to link up with and exploit the 'individual interest' and the economic calculation of this social class. With this, too, it built a bridge intended to lead from capitalism to socialism.

The feelings, thinking and aspirations of the small peasant masses of Soviet Russia are overwhelmingly 'capitalist', not communist. In general, they are dominated by the selfish interest of the individual and not by concern for the good of all, the interest of the entire society. This fact stands clearly and threateningly before the Bolsheviks in the form of many million anti-communist thickheads and many million robust peasant fists that wielding the plough and the sword are an economic and a political power. They cannot be argued away; they have to be taken into account during the economic and social development of Soviet Russia.

As matters stand, the Soviet state cannot escape the need to encourage and exploit the selfish private interest of the Russian small peasant in the reconstruction of the economy and in the increase of their productivity. It is important that the full energy and capability of every individual is mobilized for these goals. Taking the egoism of the peasant into account is only a starting point for the economic foundation of Soviet Russia, nothing more. It is neither the content nor the goal. That is, and remains communism, an economic and social order whose fully developed essence will be the solidarity between all people. This solidarity harmoniously balances the interest of the individual and the interest of the collective. It does not mean denying or neglecting the individual interest, but according due consideration to it and integrating it into the public interest.

Notwithstanding its lofty and ideal substance and goals, scientific socialism, as opposed to Utopianism, has refused to consider human virtues and perfection as 'eternal moral principles' to be the basis of the future higher order. Scientific socialism perceives its fundamental strength in the development of productive forces, in technical perfection, in the nature of the means of production and in work techniques. It is part of its ABC that humans change and develop together with their economic and social conditions, that they are trained at work and through work for life in the community. Together with progress in the social environment the selfish individualist of capitalist times will evolve into a communist, feeling and acting in a spirit of solidarity. In his polemics with Max Steiner, Marx points out that the proletarian revolution was a long and difficult process as it not only had the task of creating new social conditions, but to a greater degree had to shape the people who would have to establish these new conditions. It is a truism that this historical process is a dynamic development not permitting any mechanical division of the objective and subjective forces and in whose course cause will become effect and effect cause in a constantly interconnected movement.

Even the solidarity of the proletariat within itself and its highest form, its solidarity as a class, grow gradually on the harsh ground of proletarian class position in struggle and are simultaneously means, energy, outcome and object of the struggle. In accordance with its historical approach, Marxism has never denied 'exploiting' the still powerful egoistical instincts and characteristics of humans as a means of urging individuals to the highest achievements for the purposes of the emancipation struggle of the proletariat and the realization of communism. And, depending on the personality and the social conditions, either crudely or in refined ways. But regardless of the depths of moral and social existence from which humankind ascends from capitalism to communism, Marxism has always pointed out to the luminous heights of solidarity that have to be attained. All socialist theoreticians, who have worked on the agrarian issue, even the most 'orthodox', agree that 'small peasant egoism' will survive for a long time after the social revolution. It will only gradually be overcome to the extent that education and experiences open the eyes of the peasant to the advantages of socialism. Why then this clamour, if the same also applies to the agrarian policies of the Bolsheviks?

Had not Paul Levi been obsessed with the urge to heap the Bolsheviks with sins 'more numerous than sand in the sea', he would have spared himself the anguished moaning about Lenin's 'counter ideology' statement. In the place of his unfruitful theological text critique made up of quotes, he would have made a fruitful analysis of the social conditions that compelled the concession policy. One really does not have to have Paul Levi's talent and education to understand the differences between Lenin's statements of 1918 and 1921. It should have been Paul Levi's task to examine the great historical contradiction underlying these statements. Only if one were to take this into account, reflect about it and understand it, do the historical circumstances of the Russian Revolution, its character and its course during different periods reveal themselves. The enormous magnitude and the enormous tragedy of the events are laid bare that elevated the Russian Revolution to the most powerful intellectual act of will that history has known till now.

A small minority with bold aspirations and a boundless commitment and who has a clear understanding about the direction and goal of the historical development, cries out with a passionate creative urge into the seething, fermenting, churning chaos of new and old, declining and burgeoning as they undertake to overthrow a world and to build a new one in opposition to the underdeveloped economic and social conditions and also in opposition to the immaturity of the oppressed majority of the people in the country. Will its energy endure to shape people and things until the time an increasing number of awakened people taking their own decisions go from being the kneaded clay of history to becoming its conscious architects, co-creators of the new social life? This is the fateful question before the Russian Revolution. And not just for the Bolsheviks, also not just for Soviet Russia, but for the world proletariat, for humanity.

Underlying the Bolshevik compromise policies since 1921 is the enormous historical contradiction consisting in the fact that the Russian Revolution, thanks to the daring and confident Bolshevik leadership, took on a definite proletarian character and proclaimed spirited proletarian goals despite the backwardness of the social environment. Bolshevik tactics can be understood in their entirety only if one has rightly assessed this contradiction, its harshness and severity, its 'surprises', its tumultuous forward charge and sudden retreat, its great unswerving course towards the goal, despite all occasional aberrations. Anybody raising issues in the manner of Paul Levi regarding 'if and what aberrations and mistakes there are in Russia', was obliged to examine the effect of this contradiction on Bolshevik policies. He should not have been content with looking for the cause of the critical 'deviations' and 'mistakes' solely in the tactics, and to perceive in this tactics nothing but the continuance of old attitudes of the Bolsheviks from the period of emigration. Entangled in the described contradiction, 'organically burdened' with it, as with an inexorable fate, the illuminating and astute characterization by Marx in his "Eighteenth Brumaire," about the nature and course of the proletarian revolution, applies to the greatest extent and perhaps more than at any other time to the Russian Revolution and its Bolshevik policy.

"(...) Proletarian revolutions, like those of the nineteenth century, constantly criticize themselves, constantly interrupt themselves in their own course, return to the apparently accomplished, in order to begin anew; they deride with cruel thoroughness the half-measures, weaknesses, and paltriness of their first attempts, seem to throw down their opponents only so the latter may draw new strength from the earth and rise before them again more gigantic than ever, recoil constantly from the indefinite magnitude of their own goals – until a situation is created which makes all turning back impossible, and the conditions themselves call out: Hic Rhodus, hic salta!"

According to the Marxist concept of history the objective pre-requisite for the communist order is a technically highly developed modern large-scale industry as the determining force of socialism; the subjective pre-requisite is a multitudinous modern proletariat welded together as a class with a clear purpose, who has been tried and trained in economic and political struggle and with a strong fist wrests the leadership of the economy and the state from the bourgeoisie and establishes its dictatorship. In conformity with the economic and social structure of the workers' and peasants' republic, the communist structure of Soviet Russia ought to resemble an inverted pyramid. At the bottom, where the main base should be, a young, little developed, not yet fully established large-scale industry and a young numerically small proletariat. Above them, however, the massive classes of a small peasant and artisan economy – an enormous collection of all possible backward and crude modes of production and correspondingly an overwhelming large group of small peasants that make up at least 80% of the population, and whose huge majority still remains culturally and socially deep in the Middle Ages, in bygone times.

Even the most committed revolutionary could not naively suppose that a few years of proletarian dictatorship could do wonders, bring about an economic development and a change in the consciousness of the many millions of peasants that would have ensured a perfect communist structure. Indeed it is miraculous enough that the pyramid remained standing on its tip whilst civil war and the onslaught of international counter-revolutionaries jolted it. However, in the long run this state was untenable. Only one thing would have been able to avert the collapse of this pyramid balancing on its tip or prevent the crushing and pulverizing of the small base by the overlying cyclopean blocks and that was the strengthening and expansion of the weak, narrow economic and social base from the outside. The rapidly advancing world proletarian revolution would have to compensate internationally for the backwardness of the Russian industry and the weakness of the Russian proletariat. Paul Levi acknowledges all this. Why doesn't he draw the conclusions from this for Bolshevik policies?

After its tumultuous beginning in Russia the world proletarian revolution is progressing in a sluggish, faltering manner. Soviet Russia, the only State where the proletariat has seized power, resembles a lonely island. The economic and political might of capitalism surges against it from all sides, threaten it. And as in the past so perhaps in the future, too, it is also menaced by the military might of capitalism. It was not helped in brotherly solidarity by any proletarian State at a higher economic and cultural stage to develop production in the direction towards communism. Had this happened it would have been in a position to satisfy the needs of the small peasant masses and to convey to them, through experience, the consciousness of their solidarity with the industrial proletariat. On the contrary, what was the bitter experience of the Russian proletariat, who enthusiastically and desperately defended communism? The development of the revolutionary class consciousness of the working class from big capitalist countries, who boasted of a superior culture, was so feeble that on the command of their exploiters and working in their interest these workers first became complicit, were abettors in the attempts to militarily overthrow Soviet Russia, and then they allowed the economic and political blockade.

Soviet Russia was dependent solely on its own strength for the economic construction of the backward and ruined economy. It was supposed to accomplish the titanic task of making up for the omissions of hundreds of years, to make good the crimes of inextricably linked tsarism and capitalism and create something new, path-breaking and exemplary. With one sure jump aimed very high it was supposed to leap over lengthy development periods and development outcomes of enduring strength. However audacious, determined and unswerving the attempt was, this one leap could not achieve it. The historical perspective had made this journey to the goal seem shorter; it could only be achieved in stages, by overcoming very difficult obstacles and lurking dangers. If the revolution was to be carried forward, if the Soviet order was to survive, if the proletariat was to retain political power in order to realize the communist ideal, then the Bolshevik policy had to come to the decision to work out an economic and social *modus vivendi* with the peasantry. From the beginning itself, however, this *modus vivendi* was not only a concession to capitalism; it also included another *modus vivendi* with the real capitalists, nationally and internationally.

(Translated by Madhu Sahni)

VII

Bolshevik Agrarian Policy

Bolshevik agrarian policy as a basic prerequisite of the Russian Revolution / The unfolding of the Russian agrarian revolution / Formation of a large class of middle peasants and the consequences thereof / The pressure to satisfy peasant land hunger / The absence of an advanced technological production system and a modern rural proletariat, and what it means for the agrarian revolution / The initial weakness of the central revolutionary authority and how it affected the agrarian revolution / 'War Communism' and 'commodity shortage' strengthen 'inborn ownership psychology' / Economic and social forces of development directed towards mass industrialisation and communism / Historical difference between French and Russian peasant emancipation / Nationalisation of land, and steps taken towards integration of small farms into the national economy / Contrast between the proletariat and the middle peasantry in Soviet Russia / Growing solidarity between workers and peasants

Paul Levi sees the chief cause behind the Bolshevik policy of concessions within the allegedly faulty agrarian policy of the Bolsheviks ever since they captured power. As a matter of fact, there is an inherent causal relation between the two. The Bolshevik policy of concessions is indeed an outcome of their agrarian policy; but it is not only its outcome. The causal relation between the two policies is in my estimation not as superficial as Paul Levi discovers: as the 'drifting away' of Bolshevik politics from the true path of communism. On the contrary, the root cause common to both policies lies deep within the economy and in the social stratification of Soviet Russia. The agrarian policy of the Bolsheviks was from the very beginning determined by the inescapable necessity of accepting the realities, of facing given historical situations realistically and pragmatically at a time when communism was still unprepared for them – situations which could not be transformed overnight with the help of even the most flawless of legislations and ordinances or by clever administrative measures. It is of no consequence whatsoever if on the one hand recognition is given to the Russian Revolution 'in principle' and it is glorified in rousing tones, but on the other hand the agrarian policy of the Bolsheviks is condemned as a severe mistake. It should be clear to anyone who 'thinks like a Marxist' that under the circumstances which are given and not chosen, the Russian Revolution would simply not have been possible without the agrarian policy pursued by the Bolsheviks. Those who wanted the Russian Revolution to succeed also had to 'swallow' these agrarian policies like a bitter pill. However, those who refused this unpalatable morsel had to refrain from the revolution itself. The reformist socialists are therefore more consistent when they flaunt their 'principles' – like the *petit bourgeois* taking out his best china out of glass cupboards during festivities – and condemn the Russian Revolution 'in principle' because of the Bolshevik agrarian policy. Whether they can be considered to be 'Marxists' is another question altogether. Paul Levi is not a consistent Marxist thinker. When the Russian Revolution broke out, he celebrated it as the "mightiest event of the World War"; for years he remained steadfastly loyal to it, and he claims to be so even today – 'in principle'; but he now condemns, rather late in the day, the agrarian policy of the Revolution pertaining to land as flawed 'Bolshevik policy.'

Anyone who 'thinks like a Marxist' will understand why the agrarian policy of the Russian Revolution necessarily took the present course of development. A new and more advanced form of production will not materialize by administrative decree issued from a bureaucrat's desk. It has to evolve, and its emergence is tied to specific concrete preconditions. In spite of the gigantic and powerful means at its disposal, capitalism during the period of its hegemony has not been able to replace an agrarian economy based on small holdings with a more efficient form of production. It may well have transformed the population of small peasants into the proletariat over large stretches of the country, but it was not in a position to replace the small farm economies through a more advanced form of production. Look at the size and importance of the small peasantry in France, Germany and Italy! We are, of course, fully convinced that socialism and communism are in a position to use much more powerful and productive forces than capitalism to replace the economy based on small farms by a more advanced production method. However, the unfolding of such powers was as yet not possible in Russia. Initially, the revolution here had to be satisfied with paving the way for the desired development of agriculture in the direction of communism. But have the policies of the Bolsheviks not barred this way and diverted the course of development in the opposite direction? The answer to this persistent question is that the capture and assertion of political power by the proletariat is the starting point of the way leading towards communism. The Bolshevik agrarian policy is to be evaluated in the context of this fact.

Those amongst our closest friends and among the socialists, who understood the everlasting value and significance of the Russian October/November Revolution, must have shared the same doubts and concerns regarding the Bolshevik agrarian policy that haunted Rosa Luxemburg. In our assessment, this policy seemed to contradict all the revolutionary actions taken that could have brought about a communist transformation of agriculture – including the peasant economy. There were apprehensions that despite the subjective orientation of Bolshevik agrarian policy, objectively it could lead to counter-revolutionary developments.

These apprehensions appeared to be fully justified during the first phase of the agrarian revolution. The declaration of land as national property was followed by unplanned and haphazard distribution of large agricultural properties among the entire peasantry, which even led to the destruction of large agricultural production units and made rich peasants even richer, turning them—as Comrade Varga has aptly described—into 'anarchists' and not communists. The second phase of the agrarian revolution did little to allay the existing doubts. It brought with it a new system of land distribution through "Committees of the rural poor", which even aspired for the property of big peasants. This new system of distribution was supplemented with an 'extraordinary taxation' in kind by appropriating cattle, machinery etc. belonging to big peasants for the benefit of the 'rural poor'. Distribution took place according to 'souls': each 'soul' received his due share. The result was a socio-economic levelling of all peasants, which was, however, to a great extent restricted locally. This, according to Varga, was because the process was not supported by internal colonisation*; but it may well have been, as I am inclined to think, that the central leadership of the revolution was not strong enough and it did not have a free hand in pushing through economic and social measures in a planned manner all over the gigantic realm. This period concluded with the dissolution of the "Committees of the rural poor" in Central Russia and

---

* Varga: The Agrarian Question in Revolutionary Russia. In: *Rußische Korrespondenz* 1921, Nos. 1 and 3, p. 99. [C.Z.]

with a government decree issuing a moratorium on any further distribution of land for twelve years.

The following period of development was characterized by efforts to integrate individual small farms into the emerging large collective economy and to make the small peasants aware of the relation between them and the working people's state and with the industrial proletariat. This integration was to be realised on the basis of a system of 'quotas'. According to this system, every farming community would have to supply a specified quantity of agricultural produce to the state in exchange for a fixed price payable either in kind in commercial commodities or in money. Even as the supply quota was fixed, additional regulations laid down that the cultivation of the fields and the management of the harvest was to be done according to a specific plan. The small and marginal peasants were to be trained for the nationalized economy under communism by a generous, well-organized, professional and technically proficient, socially engaged awareness programme in order to ensure the implementation of the innovations voluntarily and with understanding. The agrarian policy of Soviet Russia has now arrived at a new stage of development. A system of 'tax in kind' and free trade has emerged in place of the system of 'quotas', which had empowered the state to stake its claim over the entire agrarian produce. On the face of it, this is a step backwards, a concession to private property, to capitalist economy and mentality. Was this regression unavoidable; was it really brought about by the Bolshevik policy alone? Does it imply a sacrifice of communist progress, or should it and can it be of service to it? These are the two questions of far-reaching significance that need to be clarified.

Rosa Luxemburg was able to give her assessment only on the first period of the Bolshevik agrarian policy. The dangers that threatened communist development as a result of the unregulated appropriation and redistribution of large agricultural properties by the small peasants stood out sharply: the danger of technically advanced, rationally organized large agricultural estates regressing into backward small farms; the danger of class antagonism between rich and poor peasants intensifying instead of being resolved through communism, and along with it an intensification of the contradiction between the peasantry and the proletariat; and lastly, as a result of satisfying the peasants' 'hunger for land', an extraordinary growth of a mentality that craves private property, a capitalistic orientation among the majority of the rural population, their shunning of the economy and total retreat from public life, their display of a mindless apathy towards the Soviet Republic and the revolution. The results therefore were as expected: a regression of the material, economic and technical preconditions for the communist restructuring of agriculture; expansion and strengthening of classes obsessed with private property, who resist the implementation of communism with all available means, and who, intoxicated by the smell of the soil of 'their' properties, are ready to forget about the Soviet Republic and deliver it to its enemies without a fight. Rosa Luxemburg reflected upon the consequences of the Bolshevik agrarian policy in the light of the developments in agricultural conditions that had taken place in France since the great revolution.

Paul Levi has been forced to admit that history has allayed one of the fears expressed by Rosa. "The *muzhiks* of Russia did not crawl back behind their big hearths after land redistribution was over, leaving the republic and the revolution high and dry. When the revolution that had given him land was threatened, the Russian peasant stood up to defend it; and no less heroically than the French peasant in 1793. To this extent, he has proven himself to be a useful support to the Soviet Republic." Paul Levi must further concede that history has not confirmed another one of Rosa Luxemburg's critical observations on the consequences of the Bolshevik agrarian policy. This policy did not intensify the contradictions among the peasantry. The initial "chaotic, purely arbitrary nature of land redistribution" did not last. Rosa Luxemburg was no more when the "Committees of the rural poor" undertook a new redistribution of agricultural property, under which many of the big peasants were dispossessed, leading to the rise of a large middle peasantry with more or less equitably distributed property among its members. Nevertheless, this blurring of class contradictions in the countryside still did not have a revolutionary impact; on the contrary, it produced a counter-revolutionary effect. Paul Levi emphasizes correctly that along with Rosa Luxemburg's anxiety, a much hoped for consequence of Bolshevik land distribution has come to naught. The Bolsheviks were convinced that the expected intensification of class contradictions in the countryside would be followed by the intensification of class struggle between rich and poor peasants, which would push masses of poor peasants with little or no land into standing by the side of the industrial proletariat. The Bolsheviks hoped that the elimination of contradictions between peasants and the proletariat would follow from the ensuing revolutionary alliance between these two classes.

The course of the dispossession of rich peasants did not concern itself with these perspectives at all; rather, it went down a different path. What matters and what is characteristic with regard to the agrarian situation in Soviet Russia today is the existence of a substantial middle peasantry. Paul Levi foresees the effects of this change as follows: "If the industrial proletariat expected understanding and support in the countryside three years ago, they would encounter there today among large sections of the homogenized population only the middle peasant with his psychologically ingrained desire to own property—even though he never possessed such property earlier to manifest this mentality—and his religious horror at the thought of anyone laying hands on his recently acquired property, regardless of whether such encroachment takes place at the hands of a Lenin or a Denikin ... the contradiction between the industrial proletariat and the land owners has deepened infinitely, and the common link that bound urban and rural proletarian classes together is now absent. What remains now is, on the one hand, the will to own property, and, on the other, the will to socialism." Invoking Lenin as witness, Paul Levi states that with the emergence of a substantial middle peasantry, a firm and deep foundation has been created, "upon which capitalism can survive and rise up all over again through a renewed and fierce battle against communism. The forms, in which this battle will be fought, are black marketing and speculation." Paul Levi adds: "Black marketing and speculation are troublesome and dangerous weapons in the hands of the peasants, but they are not lethal. The peasantry in Russia – as in all other countries where it is a powerful determining factor – possesses much more dangerous weapons. One of the weapons works like a hammer, the other like a hydraulic press; the former has an immediate shattering effect, the latter crushes slowly but surely. The latter weapon is the dissociation of the peasants and their produce from the market. ... The peasant retracts like a snail into the cottage economy. A State with large industrial cities and an industrial proletariat cannot withstand such pressure over a long period of time. But the hammer that the peasants of Russia hold in their hands is the uprising."

Paul Levi is of the opinion "that there was a possible threat of the use of both these weapons when the Bolsheviks decided to radically restructure their policies in the spring of 1921. ... In the historical context, as a trend, or objectively, the steps taken by the Bolsheviks vis-à-vis the peasants, or rather against them, were not revolutionary; indeed, they were even counter-revolutionary steps taken in order to placate a class that had severed all ties with their comrades-in-arm of 1918, a class that is united, consolidated and determinedly anti-socialist and counter-revolutionary." According to this outlook, the middle peasantry, created by Bolshevik agrarian policy, was powerful and multitudinous enough to enforce, not just the dissociation of agriculture from the national economy based on communism and the return of its capitalistic character. Rather, as an inherent consequence thereof, capitalism in general experienced its resurgence in the Soviet State. The "goal of the Bolsheviks" in 1921 was "to create conditions, under which capitalism could come alive again – if possible, as state capitalism, and if not, then as private capitalism involving the existing types of farmlands, forests and pastures." Evidently, that "curse of every evil deed" has been fulfilled through the Bolshevik agrarian policy as they captured power, so that "propagating still, it brings forth evil". A false step from the very beginning with the 'appeasement' of peasants as its goal, it was destined for capitulation under capitalism.

I suppose that among the leading Bolshevik comrades there were those who had been dealing with the agrarian question thoroughly for years, and who—like the critics of the agrarian policy within their party, including Paul Levi,—were well-versed in the corpus of socialist literature on this subject. This assumption is, of course, neither meant as flattery for one nor as royal affront for the other. It is a simple statement of what is obvious. Given the agrarian character of Russia, the Bolsheviks were compelled to devote special attention to the agrarian question. Had they resorted to 'doctrinarism' and tried to avoid dealing with this issue, then they would have been stopped short by fierce and fundamental confrontations with the other socialist and revolutionary parties, especially with the Social Revolutionaries. Why then, despite all this, did the Bolsheviks introduce, after seizing power and taking over the state, an agrarian policy that could pose a serious threat to communism, and which carried within itself the possible outcomes described earlier? Why did they not take immediate steps to curb the ransacking of large agricultural properties, to expand large agricultural estates, to integrate the fragmented and economically inefficient small holdings into rationally organized larger units, to hinder the emergence and spread of a middle peasantry? Why was the Bolshevik agrarian policy restricted initially to mainly satisfying the Russian peasants' 'appetite for land'? Or, to be precise, why was it restricted to giving the peasants a free hand in satisfying their own 'land hunger' in a 'chaotic and purely arbitrary manner?'

The Bolshevik agrarian policy did in fact sweep aside the most astute and fundamental argumentations by the best socialist theoreticians regarding how the proletariat should deal with the nationalisation of agriculture after the seizure of power and resolve agrarian issues. The policy allowed the illiterate *muzhiks* with their antediluvian ideas and techniques of farming to 'philosophize with a hammer' instead. When the Bolsheviks captured power, history demanded from them not theories but action: the gigantic task of a proletarian revolution. But a revolution cannot be 'made' on the basis of the most perfect of prescriptions and out of thin air. Action is its mandate: quick and decisive action. Initially, Bolshevik politics was primarily determined by the historical necessity of ensuring the victory of the proletarian revolution, its continuation and progress. The assertion of political power was essential for this. Agrarian policies of the party had to be subordinated to this aim.

The structure of Russian society ruled out the possibility of a social revolution as the exclusive work of the proletariat. With peasants comprising approximately 80 per cent of the population, it would be impossible to bring about a revolution *without*, let alone *against* them. The revolution could only be the collective action of the proletariat and the peasantry, where the proletariat, as the historically most powerful and most advanced dominant class, would continue to determine its course and targets. But how can one persuade the peasants to commit themselves to the red banner of proletarian revolution? History had already given a reply to this question well before the Bolsheviks, as representatives of the proletariat, boldly grasped the helm of the state. "Peace and land" were the two inseparable revolutionary demands of the peasants. The *muzhiks'* call for peace was at the end of it all the call of the soil: agricultural land could no longer do without the attention of tillers, sowers and reapers. The land issue was hence the only concrete and crystallizing factor that could awaken irresistible revolutionary impulses in the minds of the peasants and spur the peasant masses on into action.

History, however, had taught the Bolsheviks something else too. The peasants demanded from the revolution not promises, principles and programmes but tangible action and land that produced food. One of the main reasons for the fall of the Kerinsky government was its failure to come up with a practical solution for agricultural problems. I would like to believe that the ruling Mensheviks and the Social Revolutionaries had addressed these with scientific rigour and enthusiasm to work out a solid and unimpeachable programme. But peasants—including the Russian *muzhiks*—are first and foremost believers in *realpolitik* or, if you will, they are 'crude materialists' who as a rule give precedence to what they 'have' over what they 'could have had'. In the summer of 1917 the peasant masses regarded the ownership of land, of which they had been dreaming and from which they hoped to produce food with the sweat of their brow, as undoubtedly more valuable than the Kerensky government's vision of great transitions in the future leading to greater productivity and less hardship under a rationally organized economic system.

The *muzhiks'* unsatisfied 'hunger for land' was a determining factor that helped the urban industrial proletariat to break the hegemony of 'democracy'. At the same time it was a shield against the military dictatorship of the 'Whites'. It prevented Russian Vendees from sending armies of Chouans to the tsarist generals who were planning to wipe out the revolutionary urban proletariat in bloody skirmishes. But how indeed were the peasants supposed to fight for the defenders of the 'masters' who denied them land and bread? Thus, the peasants turned out to be a revolutionary force on two fronts. The Soviet elections and the decisions taken by the Soviets confirmed that they had drawn their conclusions from the prevailing circumstances. Together, the *muzhiks* and the proletarians handed over political power to the Bolsheviks as the party embodying the inviolable oath of initiating agrarian reforms. The Bolshevik motto "All power to the Soviets" inherently implied the demands of giving factories to the workers and land to the peasants. The Bolsheviks were morally bound to honour the faith reposed in them by the rural population. It was the most elementary of necessities for the survival of the revolution: the co-operative alliance between the proletariat and the *muzhiks* had to remain intact. The price to be paid for the fastest possible realization of these tasks was to give land to the peasants. All agricultural land was declared as national property and made available for utilization to those who tilled it.

All attempts to 'expropriate' millions of small peasants would have been impossible and sheer madness. Even the most intransigent socialist opponents of the Bolshevik agrarian policy have admitted this. And yet, why were no long-term steps taken at all and implemented with iron-willed determination? They would surely have led to the predominance of large agricultural farms in a very short time, bringing about co-operative unity in farming, and eventually leading to the integration of small land holdings into the national economy. Taking such steps would have been easy – but on paper; and eventually their implementation too would have been easy – but again on paper. They would, however, have been impossible to put into practice. The implementation of these steps would have incurred the wrath of the *muzhiks* and would have turned them into bitter opponents without steering agrarian production relations decisively in the direction of communism.

Russian agriculture is not yet advanced and 'industrialized' enough to have the character of a large modern, rationalized industry. The method of production on large agricultural properties was still characterized by feudalism, and land owners who practised modern farming methods were by and large a rare occurrence. Large agricultural enterprises could be found in significant numbers only in Poland, in regions near the Baltic Sea, and in some parts of Ukraine. The character of agriculture was thus determined by small farms, whose backwardness has repeatedly been referred to before. When the Bolsheviks came to power, the number of large farms was minuscule to the point of being non-existent. Those that had begun to develop under tsarism were mostly situated in isolated areas. As a result, agriculture in Soviet Russia lacked a modern technical production apparatus – including good quality seeds and seed shops, high grade breeding cattle etc. – in order to bring about a revolution in production quickly. A weak and dilapidated industry, burdened with the immediate and immense task of arming the Red Army, was not in a position to address this deficiency. Despite all their enthusiasm for communism, it was not possible for the industrial workers to conjure up steam ploughs, sowing, mowing and threshing machines etc. out of the blue. They were in fact unable to supply in sufficient numbers even the most basic and conventional tools required by *muzhiks* for their work. The blockade imposed on the Workers' and Peasants' State by the capitalists hindered the import of means and materials of production from abroad. The situation in Russian agriculture being what it was, Bolshevik agrarian policy could not fall back on a professional and socially trained rural workforce which could carry forward the new and higher 'form of economy'. It is true that there were millions of 'rural poor'; however, apart from the few regions in the pre-revolutionary empire named earlier, there was no modern rural proletariat to speak of, which could have come forward as a revolutionary force in society and a revolutionizing force in the economy.

Last but not least, the character and progress of Bolshevik agrarian policy in its initial stages can also be attributed to the substantial weakness of the central revolutionary leadership during those days. As the know-alls secretly know all too well, this weakness was not a result of a lack of historical insight, or a lack of sophisticated revolutionary formulas and of steely resoluteness on the part of the Bolshevik leadership. It was an outcome of the weakness of a class as a whole, of the proletariat, the most important motive force behind the revolution and the sturdiest support base of the central leadership. This weakness was compounded by the underdeveloped and largely destroyed transport options in the enormous country and by as yet insufficient and sometimes non-existent communication between large urban centres of the revolution and provincial towns. "The heavens are high and the councils of people's commissars far away," said the *muzhiks* as they 'divided up' this or that large agricultural estate aimlessly, laying waste not only extensive tracts of mechanically tilled fertile land, but also driving away cattle and carrying away tools and implements. Due to the initial weakness of the revolutionary central authority, even the nationalisation of industry was preceded by a period in which the proletariat began to 'expropriate the expropriators' by occupying factories in a 'chaotic and purely arbitrary' manner.

Under the given circumstances, the beginning of the Russian agrarian revolution was 'the work of the peasants themselves' not in a deeply historical sense, but in a rather mundane and literal one. In contradiction to every theory and programme, it started with a prelude that seemed to be a replica of the great French Revolution. The *muzhiks* completely destroyed feudal properties that had the potential to give birth to a young and large-scale capitalistic enterprise.

Bolshevik agrarian policy could neither have hindered these developments nor should they have tried doing so. It had to be concerned with freeing space for building a new society and with giving a free hand to the revolution. It had to restrict itself for the time being to removing legal and political barriers protecting the old order that needed to be pulled down; and it had to capture and safeguard for the new order what could still be captured and salvaged from the wild and elemental storm unleashed by the forces rebelling against the old order.

As the Bolshevik agrarian policy further unfolded with all its consequences, were the satiation of the *muzhiks'* 'hunger for land' and the growth of the middle peasantry the sole reasons for the irresistible manifestation of the 'age-old inborn ownership psychology' as its inevitable fate, thus forcing the ruling Bolsheviks to enter into a pact with capitalism? I beg to differ. Looking at things in this light is as good as applying a bit of Marxist make-up on the point of view of Bible-believers: if God had not planted the tree of knowledge in the Garden of Eden, then humanity would not have been so full of faults, and my friend August Wilhelm Schulze would not have turned out to be the old sinner that he is! It is indisputable that the newly acquired ownership of land provided a basis on which the anti-communist or, perhaps more accurately, the non-communist instincts and values of peasants could proliferate abundantly under the first intoxicating effects of gratification. That this was to a large extent really the case was, however, also determined by other factors.

Communism came to the *muzhiks* in the form of 'War Communism', which took away from them the fruits of their labour without gratifying their need for industrial commodities in exchange. The villages experienced "solidarity with the industrial proletariat" in the form of Collection Commissions which took away grain, butter, slaughter animals etc., and in the form of empty or inadequately stocked distribution centres for consumer products. These experiences were not exactly suited to fill the peasants with a burning enthusiasm for communism. In spite of it, they endured the situation patiently, sacrificed, renounced and fought for the Soviet Republic, whenever and as long as it was threatened by the forces of counter-revolution. They defended what was 'their' farmland within the republic. After defending it heroically with their blood, they believed they had secured it for themselves once and for all, and after going back to their daily chores, they started becoming stubborn and rebellious against the new system. Profiteering and black-marketing acquired monstrous proportions in the countryside – not only because the 'old and inherent ownership psychology' goaded them into secretly selling and hoarding riches, but rather it was because day-to-day needs required the purchase of essential commodities which could not be procured through normal means. Eventually the peasants forced the Soviet Government to supply through capitalistic means what communism was as yet unable to provide.

Undoubtedly, it was more—or perhaps as much—the unbearable daily shortages that were behind this regressive tendency as the conscious and obstinate anti-communist mindset and hostile antagonism towards the industrial proletariat. The peasants' ungratified 'hunger for commodities' drove them in a reactionary direction, just as the 'hunger for land' had steered them earlier in a revolutionary direction. The weakness and backwardness of the industry and the economy in Soviet Russia—their effects compounded by the blockade, war and civil war—are in the annals of history the 'big culprits' who pushed the peasants back into capitalist production. If one does not lose sight of this fact, then a different and more hopeful developmental prospect opens up beside the bleak view sketched by Paul Levi for the future of communism in Soviet Russia. The reconstruction and growth of agriculture and industry in the Soviet Republic will lay a solid foundation inch by inch, on which the *muzhiks'* individualistic fanaticism for private property will be defeated with the help of the experience of solidarity within the greater community, and where the antagonism between peasants and the industrial proletariat will be eliminated.

The much maligned Bolshevik agrarian policy has tried to direct the people and their material conditions towards this goal. Admittedly, the official Soviet farming enterprises, the co-operative agricultural production units and 'Red Communes', the free communist settlements of like-minded people, are all like little islands in an ocean of a small farm economy. Under pressure from the overall economic conditions, they were unable to develop rapidly or strongly enough to exercise a definite influence on the transformation of Soviet Russian agriculture into a large-scale industry. This as well as other branches of the Soviet economy suffer from the general infirmity of the production ventures of the Workers' and Peasants' State, that is, from lack of organisation and work discipline, and a crippling bureaucratic system. Quite a few 'communes' have collapsed or are wasting away pathetically. Among all other types of new large-scale agricultural ventures, the development of the 'communes' is said to have been the least favourable. The reason is probably that for the most part these were established with much enthusiasm for communism, but with little technical expertise, experience and practical sense. Nevertheless, the large-scale and cooperative agricultural ventures have proven to be sturdy supports for state-regulated production in the villages; they have shown that regardless of all the difficulties there is a healthy start to their development into technically advanced model national ventures. Already these large farms have not been without influence on the production techniques and the social outlook of neighbouring *muzhiks*.

Extensive education and field work by the Soviet government and its various agencies have had a successful effect in two ways. To say that the Soviet government is unparalleled in history for having compressed within a few years the work of centuries accomplished in other countries in other times is not just flowery rhetoric but a simple fact. Propaganda tableaus crisscrossed the far-flung country carrying exemplary agricultural exhibitions; experts competent in theory and trained in the practical field explained the illustrative material, conducted classes etc. The number of evening schools, schools for further education, courses for literacy and for specialized subjects and similar institutions was remarkably large. The 'Red Army' itself has been a massive educational institution along with being an efficient defence organisation, as it sent thousands of peasants back to the countryside enriched with knowledge and awakened social commitment. Professional knowledge of a higher calibre, as also the fertile seeds of social solidarity were disseminated amongst the rural population in far away provinces and the remotest villages. These seeds, too, did not necessarily always fall on infertile ground.

Memories of the old village parish communities have not been totally erased in the minds of the *muzhiks*, and a vague communistic feeling, sustained by naïve religiosity and faith in the Bible, slumbers in the subconscious of many. Traces of propaganda by the *Narodniki* (populists) and Social Revolutionaries of different periods and persuasions have definitely not yet blown away everywhere. The voice of the greatest revolutionary artist of our time, of the fierce opponent of private property and capitalism, the voice of

Tolstoy has penetrated deep into peasant villages thanks to zealous followers and 'simple pilgrims'. The Russian peasants' willingness to form *artels*, co-operative associations based on particular trades, is still very much alive. Thus the ground has already been cleared for the emergence of co-operative and public ventures, and for the formation of a consciousness of solidarity among the peasant masses to rise up against the spirit of capitalism.

Food shortage and the struggle for survival have led to the formation of family co-operatives and neighbourhood co-operatives in some villages for the procurement and proper use of bare necessities, for collective tilling of land with shared draught animals etc. Peasants in provinces unaffected by droughts and failed harvests have shown generosity and solidarity towards their brothers in the deprived areas. "As a true Communist, one only has to speak to them simply and from the heart," said a reliable source with immense experience as a 'collector in rural areas'. Peasants and peasant women in several provinces have already secured over 50 per cent of the running costs of schools and educational institutions in their villages with voluntary payment of taxes in kind, thus making the budgetary burden of the central authorities lighter. It is noteworthy that peasant women in particular have stood up so emphatically for this regulation concerning children. I would not dare to assert that such an issue-specific vote among the peasant populations of Germany or France would have thrown up a similar result. Nobody will look at such phenomena as proof of how strong the urge for communism is among the peasants of Soviet Russia. Nevertheless, they are like bits of straw floating in the air that indicate where the wind is blowing from and where it is going.

While observing the changes taking place in agriculture in Soviet Russia, the superficial similarity with peasant emancipation in France automatically comes to the fore. However, the fundamental historical difference between the proletarian revolution here and the bourgeois revolution yonder forbids messianic prophecies about further developments in the Soviet Republic based on this similarity. The aim of the great French Revolution was the emancipation of the bourgeoisie by establishing equal rights of movable bourgeois property and immovable feudal landed property. The hideously grinning face of capitalism peered from behind the shimmering veil of equality, liberty and brotherhood. Universal human rights as innate natural rights began and ended with the rights and privileges of property ownership. The individual was dissociated from old social ties and left to fend for himself. The atmosphere in society was filled with the aura of the concepts of ownership and property.

The aim of the proletarian revolution in Soviet Russia is the emancipation of the proletariat, the last exploited class in society, through the establishment of communism. The elimination of private ownership of the means of production will liberate flesh and blood human beings from the enslaving and withering force of morbid private property. The simple garments of the working people will clothe strong and beautiful human beings in their all-round harmonious development. Collective life is the right and duty of every individual. The concepts of work and solidarity will pervade the social environment. The longer the peasantry of Soviet Russia resists this influence the less they will be able to do it. The new communist order will overcome the old capitalistic one because visible and invisible waves of development will flow towards the peasants from the social environment of the liberation of the proletariat.

The Bolsheviks have not abandoned the fundamental tenets of communist agrarian policy for their ‘new policies’. Land, the most important resource in agrarian production, has not become private property; it remains a property of the state and of the public. The peasant only has the right to make use of the resource as an individual and to individual appropriation of the produce after deduction of the taxes paid in kind. However, it is not only this contribution that reminds him of his dependence on the state and the ties that bind him to the greater community. Universal labour duty – working on land alone will entail the right to make use of it – and the right of intervention in agricultural production invested with the state represented by various Soviet agencies for this purpose have probably had a much stronger impact in this regard. Thanks to this right, the state can exert its influence on the land use pattern, mode of cultivation, extent of land earmarked for sowing, the choice of cereals or root crop to be cultivated and so on. All this is achieved mostly with the help of field work and educational and advisory missions, but these measures can also be enforced.

These measures alone will not help Bolshevik agrarian policy to establish communism in the countryside; however, they can prepare the way for it. The policy familiarizes the peasant population with the commonality of purpose behind planned economy and production and which, as an expression of the solidarity of interests, transcends the confines of districts and provinces, and extends to the larger national community. It is as such a product of a proletarian revolution, because unlike a bourgeois revolution it cannot be restricted to organising the political hegemony of an upcoming class; it must rather accomplish the infinitely more difficult and fundamental task of organising the production of the entire society. The bourgeois revolution and the bourgeoisie left this task to individual capitalists, and today more and more wealth flows from their hands into those of syndicates and trusts rather than to the society as a whole, because that would include the exploited have-nots engaged in production.

What has been achieved in Soviet Russia under the leadership of the Bolsheviks towards reorganising agriculture appears insignificant if measured against the set targets, but substantial, if measured against the given condition of the economy as a whole and of agriculture in particular. It embodies the gigantic outcome of willpower, dedication and insight. The process of transition was bound to bring forth the most contradictory results, some brought about by the resistance of the powerful old order, others by the upcoming but still weak new world. The revolution had shattered the old production relations in the countryside before the new production relations had formed, before there was even time to put them in place, when the divide between the two was still tremendously wide, and when other more concrete realities very different from the thin paper partition in the form of a written title deed separated them from each other. After the war and the severe shortages, which also affected the *muzhiks*, were over, the Bolsheviks were forced to retreat from implementing their policies for the time being and to refrain from continuing with those economic innovations that were undertaken prematurely and which could not be sustained due to developments in the economy.

Paul Levi has treated Bolshevik agrarian policy as a 'thing in and for itself' without inquiring into the historical basis, upon which it must be established. In his assessment of the policy he has made a direct connection between its beginning stages and its latest status; everything else that lies in between is Hecuba to him. He has admitted only those phenomena into his field of observation which point towards the resurgence and flourishing of capitalism, leaving out the germination and flowering of a new order developing towards communism. I believe the following expositions can clarify the inadequacy and futility of such a treatment of one of the most difficult problems of the proletarian revolution. A critique based on it is bound to remain purely negative. Paul Levi has in fact not provided a single perspective that could show the way to the communist transformation of agriculture in Soviet Russia free from all the 'aberrations' and 'failings' of the Bolshevik agrarian policy. Towards the end of his Introduction to ardently call for 'democracy' as a panacea means very little. At the end of his critique there is only yawning nothingness.

Understandably, at present everything in sharp contradiction with the aspirations of the Russian Revolution and its first reaching-for-the-stars steps press themselves to the fore. The contrast is too glaring and too painful. Russian comrades themselves have thrown light upon these developments because they must identify them clearly in order to learn how to deal with them. However, if one has any intention of forming a judgment about the agrarian revolution in Soviet Russia and about the Bolshevik agrarian policy, then it is not enough to merely observe these identified phenomena and their proliferation in order to draw general conclusions. With its dense cluster of roots deep inside the earth, a massive ancient tree can easily sprout lush green shoots, because nourishment flows to them through thousands of hidden capillaries. How slowly a tree grows by comparison from a seed! And yet, those lush green branches, lacking the strength to grow into a trunk, can only form bushy clusters, whereas next to them the weak and unassuming little sapling will grow into a mighty tree in the years to come, and its powerful trunk will bear the spreading stems and branches with lush foliage. The November Revolution has felled the tree of capitalism in Russia, but its roots are still buried deep in the economy, and branch after branch keeps growing from them. The young tree of communism is growing slowly, very slowly, even as the roots of the felled giant deprive it of nourishment. Should this discourage us? Are we justified in concluding from what is after all the law of development that the gardener tending and looking after the sapling is worthless? That he does not know how to take good care?

Only after a comprehensive examination of the total economy of Soviet Russia can it be said about the Bolshevik agrarian policy: "Weighed and found wanting", or "Successful!" An investigation of this sort would no doubt be an urgent and extremely rewarding task not only with regard to understanding the Russian Revolution and the policies of its most distinguished leaders, but also in the interest of future proletarian revolutions in other countries. On the basis of such an investigation alone will it be revealed what aspects of the Bolshevik agrarian revolution are rooted in specifically Russian conditions and which ones are defective and, therefore, cannot lay claim to the validity of the general norms of the proletarian revolution. It will also even be found that problems of utmost difficulty come up, which the working class in every country must tackle when it comes to power. The task that lies ahead as a result awaits resolution. It cannot be tackled incidentally in between and on the side of day-to-day political struggles, because it demands a thorough processing of multi-layered source materials as also an in-depth on-the-spot study of economic and social relations and their effects on people, who are both objects and subjects of these. This task cannot be brought any closer to its successful conclusion if somebody wrathfully tears through the garden of the *Russische Korrespondenz* and various other brochures and if, instead of gleaning lessons from the rich inventory of data and research material contained in them, he merely plucks out quotation blossoms that especially flatter his critical eye.

The 'new policy' of the Bolsheviks is a compromise and not bankruptcy. The type of capitalism that Lenin wants to lead the partially antediluvian Russian economy into is not the capitalism of the highly developed exploitative and enslaving German economy, under which Stinnes tries to subjugate the German proletariat. The two are not—as Paul Levi seems to fear—the complementary left and right boots forming a pair. Capitalism in Soviet Russia is a transitory phase, where it is supposed to assist in the progress towards communism. Capitalism in the West is a permanent system meant to block the path of communism. Resurgent capitalism that is trying to become profitable on Soviet Russian soil cannot develop into the 'usual type of agricultural, forest and pastoral capitalism'. The 'state capitalism' of the Workers' and Peasants' Republic will be quite different from the 'state capitalism' of a bourgeois democracy. The organized political power of the proletariat represented in the state occupies a vital position between one type of capitalism here and another over there, determining its vitality and purpose. The same word will cover social matters of various types; old concepts will acquire new and transformed meanings. Paul Levi is right in saying,

"There are not only measurements and numbers in things; the spirit is there too." The spirit of the proletariat trying to escape from the clutches of capitalism and aspiring towards consummate humanity can achieve these goals only if it overcomes capitalism completely inch by inch and frees every class in society from its spell. This is the spirit and the will power of the proletariat, led by a class-based party that wields political power, a party that is conscious of the productive value of its power and of its responsibilities.

Some things cannot be obliterated from the social evolution taking place in Soviet Russia, and that includes not only the resurgence of capitalism, but also the fact that the proletarian revolution has forcefully steered this evolution on to new paths, and that proletarian power has been guiding it throughout on these paths and maintaining the course. Therefore, I feel there is no basis in Paul Levi's prediction pronounced with apodictic certainty about an unfolding contradiction between the proletariat and the peasantry, which would intensify into the bitterest class struggle and shatter today's Soviet ethos. The realization of this possibility requires only one precondition: the emergence of a class of rich land owners and of their counterpart, the agrarian proletariat. This would lead to the manifestation of class contradiction in the countryside in all its sharpness between capital and labour, between exploiters and the exploited. This would, however, also necessarily lead to the rise of a modern agrarian proletariat, who would inevitably be forced to stand by the industrial proletariat. But apart from that, Bolshevik economic policy as a whole is definitely moving in the direction of letting the state take over large-scale production in the most important sectors of the economy; only under very exceptional and strictly delineated provisos does it hand over management to co-operatives – and even to individual or collective capitalist ventures. The road towards large-scale industrialisation of agriculture taken by this policy passes through the Soviet economy, the co-operatives and the 'communes'. As far as I can judge, there is as yet no indication that it will choose to breed a class of rich peasants.

Although the middle peasantry created by the agrarian revolution in Soviet Russia is based on small-scale capitalist production, the contradiction between it and the industrial proletariat is not the same as the one between the industrial proletariat and the bourgeoisie. Generally speaking, the Russian middle peasant has no more land at his disposal than what he can till together with his family members. He does not employ wage labour from outside; neither does he appropriate surplus value produced by others. The contradiction between him and the industrial proletariat is not so much in the sphere of production as in that of circulation and trade. The relationship between them is that of sellers and buyers of products, of course with their roles reversed. In their mutual business they only deal with what Marx termed 'commodities'; that is, they deal in agricultural and industrial products, and not in the ultimate 'commodity of commodities': human labour. The peasant seeks profit and not the right to exploit humans or to appropriate surplus value that the proletariat produces for him.

He will try to sell his agricultural produce at the highest possible price and buy industrial products as cheaply as possible. However, he will also learn that prices must have parity, that there are limits to how 'expensive' and 'cheap' things can be. The price of his produce must match the purchasing power of the proletariat, and the cheapness of industrially produced goods must not endanger the very existence of the producer – this must become a cultural value in the Republic of Soviets. The middle peasant of Soviet Russia has therefore no immediate interest in exploiting and suppressing the industrial proletariat. As an independent producer—not being a proprietor—the peasant feels and is closer to him than to the big capitalists who amass wealth without putting in labour and by pocketing surplus value produced by others.

The economic foundation of the relationship between the middle peasant and the proletariat is enveloped by a new social atmosphere that values labour and solidarity, and which came up – as has been stressed already – together with the proletarian revolution. Soviet government and Soviet power do not solely stand for peasant power; they represent first and foremost the power of workers. With the development of the economy and industry, the political organisation of labour power will increasingly gain in strength and significance in order to influence and shape economic and social matters – even in the countryside! Only when Soviet Russian industry raises itself from its present state of devastation and paralysis and begins to flourish can agriculture experience a healthy development and achieve a higher rate of growth. The *muzhik*, aided by his outdated and fragmented mode of small-scale production, can carry on with his existence through thick and thin as his forefathers had done;

however, he will be unable to aspire to a more developed form of social life through increased productivity in his work.

The more rationally organized agricultural production is, the more culturally rich the life of the peasants becomes, the stronger and closer will their relation be with industry and the proletariat. Under the present blissful state following the satiation of 'land hunger' and under the effect of the abnormal situation, the *muzhik* may not be fully and clearly aware of the commonality of interest shared by him and the industrial proletariat. It will change when the pulse of economic life in Soviet Russia begins to beat regularly and with vitality, when modern industry is in a position to supply more, much more of the most important things to the peasants for their production. The inevitable 'industrialisation' of agriculture will inseparably unite peasants and the proletariat as creative, productive forces, and will help diminish and overcome – not without conflicts to be sure – the contradiction between country and city, until it disappears completely under fully evolved communism. In this regard, the electrification of the economy planned and initiated by the Soviet government is the best and most generous agrarian programme and the best instance of agrarian policy.

The contradiction prevailing in the development of Soviet Russia now—and likely to prevail in the near future as well—is definitely not a contradiction between peasantry and the industrial proletariat. It is the much more powerful, far deeper and all-encompassing contradiction between capitalism and labour, between the proletariat and the bourgeoisie. And by bourgeoisie we, of course, mean the powerful international bourgeoisie and not the Russian big capitalists only, who are by and large quite inconsequential. The relative power and strength of these two mortal enemies could hardly be more unequal than they are. The Russian proletariat upholds and defends with utmost heroism and unshakable dedication the Soviet Republic, the first and only great and consequential position of political authority that the gathering storm of world revolution has given to the proletarians of the world. They, however, have not yet unified themselves into a single indomitable power capable of repulsing the advance of the world bourgeoisie against the Workers' and Peasants' State, a power that would be capable of turning around to launch an attack on capitalism. Soviet Russia is still bearing the entire burden of this struggle alone. It has been forced to give concessions to the small capitalists at home and the big capitalists from abroad. But the power of the idea of freedom and justice—which acquired a living and concrete form among its worker and the peasant population—has so far sustained its strength, so that it has been able to assert its key position until now for the victory of communism. Heavy industries in core production sectors are still firmly in the hands of the Soviet state. A bitter and heated battle is being fought relentlessly for their control, in which the enemies of the Russian proletariat are not the middle peasantry but the international cliques of exploitative industrial and financial capitalists with the political backing of their respective states.

After the military defeat of the 'Whites', this battle is being fought today not on battlefields with weapons; it is continuing with 'peaceful means' no less dangerous at congresses and conferences of capitalist governments, in the chambers of banking, trading and industrial associations, and in fact at any place where the world bourgeoisie hatches plans and takes steps to transform Soviet Russia into a colonial goldmine for international exploitation. It is likely to be fought in the coming days itself on the ground of the Workers' and Peasants' State and within its economy if the desires and ambitions of the world bourgeoisie were to be fulfilled. On the one side capitalism, on the other communism; private property on one side and state and collective property on the other – this will be the battle cry, under which the battle will be fought for Soviet Russia's heavy industry, indeed for the very existence of Soviet Russia! The Soviet system is unlikely to survive the capitalist recapture of heavy industry; at any rate, its backbone would be broken.

In the relentless struggle of the Soviet Republic against the world bourgeoisie, the *muzhiks* will fight side by side with the proletariat as during the bloody battles against Yudenich and Wrangel. They know that the fall of the Soviet power would lead to their own fall. They know that if today battles are being fought for the control of factories, in which the proletariat is forging his liberty, tomorrow battles will be fought for his fields, which he cultivates with hard labour. The contradiction between the peasantry and the proletariat will recede into the background in the face of the historical struggle between the Soviet state, the vanguard of the international proletariat, and the international bourgeoisie.

No one will contest that along with the trends in development shown here there will be others, in which the 'ownership psychology' of the Russian middle peasant will triumph. As in the spring of

1921, situations are likely to develop in the future when a gaping divide will separate the mutually contradictory demands of the peasantry and the proletariat. The same considerations will necessarily be a determining factor now for the decisions of the leading party of the Russian proletariat as was the case during the critical situation earlier. The organized political power of the proletariat in the form of the Soviet state will have to be asserted even at the cost of making painful sacrifices, because this dictatorship is and shall remain the *sine qua non* of 'nationalisation' by the proletariat, of transforming the capitalist system into a communist one.

In its attempts to reach this goal, the Bolshevik Soviet government was confronted with an emergency in 1921 and, as Paul Levi put it derisively, it had to decide in favour of the 'larger battalion' of peasants. The larger battalions will however not continue to be the stronger ones forever. This is ensured by developments that are shifting critical social power towards the progressive economic forces, wherever they are active. Hence, the problem of the mutually contradictory interests of both classes united under Soviet authority will in no case continue to demand a solution under the same conditions as before when the situation necessitated concessions. Despite the acutest sufferings of the Russian proletariat today, history will unambiguously and indelibly record the 'new Bolshevik policy' as justified. Its vision is directed towards the future.

(Translated by Romit Roy)

VIII

Difficulties and Dangers of the Bolshevik Policy of Concessions

Persistence of class antagonism between capitalists and the proletariat within the workers' State / Soviet leadership as guide to the trade unions and for labour legislation / The Soviet state as employer / Significance of the appropriation of political power by the class-based party of the proletariat for the further development towards communism

The concessions given by the Bolsheviks to peasants—including artisans and small-scale industry—are a counterpart to those given to modern-day capitalists, particularly to those from overseas. The said concessions are widely known, as also the conditions under which granting them became necessary. The reformist socialists regard the Bolshevist policy of concessions as a solemn recognition of capitalism – as if dealing with contingent issues implied recognizing them as sacrosanct and inviolable! If that were the case, then we would have 'recognized' capitalism in all capitalist states – for after all we live under it, and we fight against it. But is the situation quite the same in Soviet Russia? The revolution here had clearly overcome capitalism, with which the ruling Bolsheviks have now signed a pact – in fact, they have had to sign a pact. This is true, but only apparently so. The political leaders of the Russian proletariat were unable to bring about a more advanced communist form of economy in a single stroke. They had to be satisfied with supporting and accelerating with utmost vigour its rise and development. Political power in Germany passed into the hands of the proletariat in 1918. In spite of this, we have been witnessing endless concessions for the capitalists; we find vestiges of feudalism lingering in economic, political and social relations even today. A battle must be waged decisively against monarchism which is threatening the republic. Do these things imply a sworn 'recognition' of capitalism, of feudalism, and of their 'privileges' for all eternity?

Paul Levi foresees only one outcome of the policy of concessions: crippling of proletarian class struggle and bankruptcy of the Bolshevik Party. Lenin wrote: "The concessionaire is a capitalist. He runs his business in a capitalist way for the sake of making profit." Based on this statement, Paul Levi comes to the following conclusions:

"What is the task of the trade unions? Is it their task to say: 'Work for the capitalist; he will make big profits; but thanks to these big profits the base will be built upon which one day our government will be able to establish communism?' Or should they be telling the workers: 'Don't work for the capitalist and his profit; bring down his profit; capitalism is hell'? They can say either this or that. In the earlier case they would be acting as recruiting agents of capitalism; in the latter instance there will be a conflict with the concessionaire, and the concessionaire will cry out for help to those who granted him the concession. And then?

"No, it is necessary to boldly face the facts: there are two classes in Russia, and they are mutually irreconcilable. The first entails the agrarian class and, for the time being still resting on its shoulders, the classes of industrial and mercantile capitalists. The other is the proletarian class. As anywhere else in the world, there is in Russia little scope of an armistice and reconciliation in the class struggle immanent to society, and a party that tries to reconcile nevertheless – a party that tries on the one hand to render unto capitalists the things that belong to capitalists, and on the other hand to give unto the proletariat the things that are theirs – such a party would be the first to be crushed in this struggle. The Bolsheviks have undertaken the task of yielding to the capitalists for the time being in order to rescue the proletariat in future."

Who would then deny the immense difficulties and dangers that hover around the Bolshevik policy of concessions? Difficulties and dangers for the party itself, for the proletariat – and not just the Russian proletariat, but the entire proletariat of the world, to whom the Russian Revolution shows the way like a towering column of fire – and for communism. The policy of concessions is indeed a crushing burden of responsibility for the Bolsheviks. But does it point solely towards that single miserable prospect as shown by Paul Levi? I do not think so. I believe I have refuted in the preceding discussions the paranoid notion that like St. Christopher the Russian peasantry would carry the child of modern capitalism across the raging river of the proletarian revolution in the Soviet Republic. But as far as the irreconcilable class contradictions between the proletariat and capitalists are concerned, they will have very different consequences in the Workers' and Peasants' State as compared to what is taken for granted in Paul Levi's seemingly radical but actually rather simplistic formulation of 'either-or'.

To be sure, English, German or American capitalists are not acquiring concessions from the Soviet state only to fill their hearts with the uplifting feeling of participating in the reconstruction of the Russian economy and hence helping the world economy. They would rather cross themselves at the thought of laying the economic foundation of communism. They seek profit, the fattest profit possible under the most favourable circumstances. The capitalist must also be able to accumulate surplus value – not because he feels that he has been called upon to be the 'bearer of progress', to carry production to the next higher level, and hence to promote culture; he would rather want to ensure his prospects of higher levels of profit in the future. However, if an entrepreneur from any one of the capitalist 'fatherlands' wants to go digging for treasure on Russian soil, he would have to sign a pact with the devil – with the Bolshevist government. And this government is not going to hand over the proletariat to him for ruthless and crushing exploitation in order to make profits. The predatory greed of capitalism will be under stringent regulation thanks to the Soviet state's laws protecting workers' rights, and even the entrepreneur will have to submit to these laws.

There is no doubt that the capitalist will try everything to circumvent the laws, to look for loopholes in the restrictions. The Soviet state agencies and the trade unions will be there to prevent him from practising the tricks of his trade. The trade unions will have to continue being the executors in the most intense proletarian class struggle not only for the implementation of the laws protecting workers' rights but also for other proletarian demands. They can do this with far greater efficacy than the trade unions in capitalist countries. In cases of conflict with the entrepreneurs, the might of the Workers' and Peasants' State will be behind them, and although this state has been temporarily obliged to enter into a pact with capitalism, it is fundamentally different from a bourgeois state; it is a political organisation for the emancipation of labour and not for the protection of profits and of capitalistic forces of exploitation. That is also the reason why the state is entitled to give the capitalists access to the natural resources of the country for appropriate utilization, not however for devastating plunder. The inheritance of the proletariat must be preserved. With far greater authority than any ruling bourgeois democracy, the Soviet Republic commands the capitalists that in order to enhance their profits they have to economically exploit raw materials, rationalize the organisation of factories, and perfect the means of production and the production processes. It is a well-known fact that unrestrained and reckless exploitation of the proletariat and the progressive development of the production apparatus are inversely proportional factors. While protecting the workers, Soviet Russia will goad the capitalists to economic progress with the barb of 'self-interest.'

No Bolshevik – however convinced he may be by the government and its policy of concessions – would contradict Paul Levi's elementary wisdom that even the greatest achievements of excellent labour protection legislation are in no way comparable to the total emancipation of the proletariat from the oppressive drudgery of capitalism. However, even Paul Levi must admit that these achievements have a higher significance as they alleviate the harsh lot of the proletarian class, which should not be disdained. He will have to concede that these achievements will raise the work-efficiency as well as the fighting spirit and battle-worthiness of the workers to higher levels. Where the economic base is capitalistic by nature its achievements will not be surrounded with the gentle zephyr of an unlikely harmony of the classes. Rather, the savage storms of class struggle will blow ceaselessly, forcing the proletariat to come face to face with the capitalists in every factory to fight the battle to the end. In all these instances, the pertinent question is whether the proletariat is fighting in a bourgeois state which tries to suppress its struggles either with naked violence or with clandestine tricks; or whether it is fighting under the Soviet state which ensures favourable conditions to carry the struggle forward. Paul Levi's threatening challenge of "Either-Or" and his loudly rhetorical question "And then?" are based on straightforward but unsound assumptions. The Russian trade unions in alliance with the Soviets will sweep aside such doubtful speculations by preparing the workers with knowledge and organisation for the fiercest class struggle to bring down the curtain on capitalistic economy.

The given historical conditions, in which the policy of concessions is rooted, confront the ruling Bolsheviks with conflicts that have deeper implications and are much more difficult than merely choosing between the rights of the proletariat and the demands of the capitalists. The Soviet state has turned into an entrepreneurial venture on a grand scale. It will have to organize, administer and head large industries in the most important branches of the economy. It will have to do this in such a way as to turn around capitalistic profit-making entrepreneurship into a communist need-based economy. But even the Workers' State must consider the generation of surplus value by its workers. It must establish production units that are not just models of technological and social progress; they must also combine the highest levels of productivity with the most civilized working conditions. The Soviet state must fund its budget out of the revenue it earns even as it supports the most generous social causes, ensures savings for the purpose of running a more advanced and socially responsible economy, and creates a life of freedom and dignity for all. It must take in its stride the competition and enmity of capitalists both within and beyond its borders. It must satisfy all these demands as part of the massive task entrusted to it by the proletarian revolution: to organize a national economy on a new communist base.

To carry out these mammoth tasks, the Soviet Russian government has at its disposal an inefficient and shattered production apparatus, immense hindrances in the path of its administrative functioning compounded by devastations in the global economic conditions, eight years of war, the civil war itself, a decimated and inexperienced proletarian workforce steeped in the traditional production practices left over from a pre-capitalistic order and hence incapable of rising overnight to the challenges of integrating into large modern mechanized industries. It is not to be forgotten that the proletariat of the old capitalist countries has had to pass through ruthless schooling under capitalism for decades or even centuries to arrive at its present level of work-discipline and capacity for intensive labour. This schooling began with the torturous workhouse legislation in England. Entire generations have had to suffer body and soul, indeed have perished under it, which even today continues with its 'upbringing' by wielding the whip of starvation. Despite this, the workers of Western Europe have lost many of their productive virtues in the aftermath of the war.

It goes without saying that the Soviet Republic of 'socialist Tartars' will be incapable of educating the proletarian masses for the new modes of production with the 'humane' methods in the manner of an exploitative capitalist economy. These masses have, after the miseries of the imperialist war, heroically endured almost four years of unspeakable hardship and countless sacrifices fighting for their emancipation; hunger and deprivation have torn them apart, and their vitality has decreased greatly. Neither can 'democratization' to the greatest possible extent nor the most rigid 'party discipline' help the Bolsheviks at the helm to overnight raise a workforce from the dust of the earth that is endowed with the organisational skills and leadership qualities needed for unleashing material and human forces of production in the nationalized factories. In addition to all this, each new day brings with it new problems that cry out for a solution – problems in the realm of the proletarian revolution caused by conflicts between the old but now dissolved social and production relations and the new ones gradually taking shape; problems in the relationship between the enterprise-level bureaucrats and workers, between manual and intellectual labour, and so on.

This cursorily sketched state of affairs is ripe, all too ripe for situations, in which the Soviet government and its agencies meant to represent the long-term interests of the proletariat as a class could clash with the wishes, demands and interests of individual workers or particular workers' groups. These circumstances necessitate comprehensive and energetic activity by the trade unions in every sphere. In the fight against the capitalists and as instruments of proletarian struggle, trade unions need the support of the Soviet state. The latter too can ill afford to do without the support of the trade unions as instruments in the processes of organising and managing nationalized production, economic reconstruction, transformation and education of the working masses professionally as well as socially. What 'Soviet Russia' achieves as 'entrepreneur', as economic organizer, how it thereby resolves still existing contradictions, will have considerable influence on the pattern of working conditions in the capitalistic enterprises that receive concessions or are on lease. The appropriateness of her own performance as such will increase her control over them. It is therefore striking that not even in passing has Paul Levi touched upon the burden of tasks that the proletarian revolution has brought with it in this regard, and how the Bolsheviks intend to cope with them. The congresses of the party and the Soviets, the meetings and consultations among the state agencies of the Soviets, and a copious body of literature are proof of the tremendous importance that is attached to this particular area of their activities. This is most vividly apparent in the unsparing criticism of their own performance and achievements. The economic tasks translate into problems of Bolshevik politics, of the Bolshevik party. The proper understanding of these requires as a precondition the tackling of the former.

But let pass over from what Paul Levi is silent about to what he does expound: although he does not say it in so many words, one can hear clearly enough the underlying tone of his critique that Bolshevik politics not only grants concessions to capitalism but ultimately has itself turned capitalist and bourgeois, or opportunistic through and through – which is one and the same thing. Thus, having said 'A' for concessions, the Bolsheviks would inevitably have to say 'B' and stand by the capitalists in the struggle between the latter and the proletariat; then, to gloss over the betrayal of the workers, would follow 'C' as preaching reconciliation between the classes; and, unable to stop, the Bolsheviks would recite from 'A' to 'Z' all the letters of the alphabet of opportunistic and counter-revolutionary politics. "The party is a part of social existence; and if the party has been practising the politics of concession even for a period of five years, it would reflect the spirit of such politics, and not that of the revolution."

Paul Levi has lost sight not only of the historic causes behind the new Bolshevik policies but also of their unshakable resolve to remain true to their great historic mission. He insinuates that for the Bolsheviks the means to an end has become the end in itself: the appropriation of political power. However, in cases such as these, ends and means cannot be separated easily. The perpetuation and progress of the proletarian revolution in Soviet Russia is at stake, and it is indeed dependent upon the appropriation of political power by the class-based party of the proletariat. Capturing political power and the establishment of the dictatorship of the proletariat is only the beginning of the revolution. It is a decisive victory, but not the final one against capitalism. Such a victory will be won only when the economic foundation walls of the communist order have been erected so high and so sturdily that all the battering and storming by the forces of capitalism will not be able to breach them and bring them down. What is required for the formation of such an order is not a plan that displays great wisdom and elegance but the possession of political power and the will to use it with utmost energy in the service of communism. Germany and Soviet Russia are classic and historic textbook examples.

In Germany, the objective conditions are ripe for the proletarian revolution, and the proletariat is mature enough to take over national production; but by contrast there is immaturity in the revolutionary will to act, to capture political power and to use it ruthlessly.

When, after the military capitulation of German imperialism, political power passed into the hands of the proletariat, they threw it away into the lap of the bourgeoisie. And what was the result of such foolishness? Nationalisation commissions toiling away for three years to dispel apprehensions and fears about the nationalisation of the economy; detailed plans for nationalizing industries deemed "most ripe for nationalisation", such that they would be agreeable even for canny capitalists; the possibility knocking at the door that the Imperial Railways and the postal system could be taken over by Hugo Stinnes; the eight-hour work-day and the right to strike in extreme danger.

In Russia, there is by contrast extreme tension between the factors of economic development, social structure and the material preconditions for 'nationalisation'; negligible training among the numerically small industrial proletariat for modern large-scale industrial production; but on the other hand: maturity and eagerness on the part of the proletariat to offer sacrifices for this historic mission, to capture state authority and establish its dictatorship which they are ready to assert and protect unwaveringly under the leadership of the party that represents their class with determination and loyalty towards their aims and aspirations. The result? Transformation of land and all its natural resources into social property; despite concessions nationalisation of large-scale industries; monopoly over foreign trade; a comprehensive legislation for the protection of workers; the trade unions blossoming towards greater power. Are all these bare facts not enough to convince Paul Levi that "Paris is well worth a Mass"?

Indeed, the Soviet leadership signed a pact with capitalism in the sphere of economics not for reasons of mutual reconciliation, but only in order to strengthen itself further for a resounding victory against capitalism. The latter is assuredly not going to lord it over Soviet Russia, but instead be her servant and helper. Nevertheless, a question of world-historical consequence rises up to confront the young Republic of Soviets: will the daring feat of containing the growth of capitalism succeed on Russian soil so that it paves the way for communism instead of obstructing it? Will it be possible to separate the progressive cultural elements of capitalism from its reactionary, anti-cultural aspect? Will the Bolsheviks not end up sharing the fate of Goethe's "Sorcerer's Apprentice", who was unable to rid himself of the spirits he had invoked? As long as the answers to these questions depend on the pulsating historic developments in Soviet Russia, there can only be affirmation for the proletarian revolutionary forces, provided the political leadership of the Russian proletariat is made secure, allowed to strengthen itself, and grows. This leadership is embodied in the revolutionary class-based party of the proletariat, in the party of the Bolsheviks. A widespread and fundamental basis is provided for it by the Soviets. Together they constitute a single historical entity, a glorious and sacred entity of the proletarian revolution.

(Translated by Romit Roy)

IX

Soviet Power, Proletarian Class Rule and Party Dictatorship

Does the proletarian system of government guarantee proletarian class rule? / The relation between the revolutionary proletarian class party and the masses as a decisive factor of the content of the proletarian system of government / The contrast between the Jacobin-Blanquist centralisation of the dictatorship from above and the revolutionary self-centralisation by the most active masses / The supposed 'mechanisation' of the lives of the party and masses due to excessive centralisation of the system of organisation by the Bolsheviks and its devastating consequences / The Kronstadt mutiny of 1921 – no evidence of the Soviet government having lost its proletarian class base / The relationship between the Russian industrial proletariat and the Bolshevik party / The epic historical mission of the revolutionary proletariat and its leading class party / Reasons for the distance between the Bolshevik party and a section of the industrial proletariat

Paul Levi is of the opinion that this existence is torn apart and going up in smoke on the ruins of the former proud unity, indeed that it is already extinguished. He rates the value of the Soviet power so low that he thinks its maintenance is paid for much too dearly by the price of the 'new policy'. In his opinion, the tactics of the Bolsheviks have rendered the system of workers' councils of Russia an empty phrase, so that its historical sense for the proletariat has fully disappeared and does not now signify anything. His verdict takes up Lenin's polemics against Kautsky about the proletarian dictatorship, and the political and historical difference between the form of government and the form of state. Paul Levi agrees with Lenin's view that the form of government is of secondary importance. "Monarchy or republic, they are nothing but different disguises for the same essence, the dictatorship of the bourgeoisie. The form of the state is another matter altogether. The task of the revolution is to smash the bourgeois state machine to pieces and to replace the bourgeois form of state by the proletarian form of state."

Paul Levi processes this thought and, with logical consequence, brings up the question: "Does that form of a proletarian state exist which by its mere existence as form secures the rule of the proletariat or is a change under the cover of the proletarian form of state, too, possible so that no more proletarian forces but other forces become decisive?" Paul Levi is right to answer this question in the negative, and from this negation he concludes that it may be true that the Soviet system is the most favourable form for the proletariat, but as a mere form it does not guarantee that this rule actually exists. The proletarian form of state just as the bourgeois form of state is compatible with different forms of government. Under the cover of the proletarian Soviet state, too, it would be possible that political, historical changes take place by which the real exercise of political power would be wrested from the proletariat's hands. Even under the Soviet system it would be possible that the dictatorship of the bourgeoisie, of the peasants or the dictatorship of a party, too, of a party bureaucracy, of a single person will rise up above the proletariat.

The logical consistency of this theorem, as an abstraction, cannot be doubted. It is a truism that no form of social organisation, no form of state is a socially decisive power by means of its 'mere formal existence'; that each such form gets life and value, becomes its real nature only through its political, historical content. The revolutionary significance of the Soviet system depends on the socially radical use the proletariat makes and must make of it as an inexorable law of history. Paul Levi's argumentation will stay as undisputed as the syllogism: "All people are mortal. Lenin and Trotsky are people. Thus Lenin and Trotsky are mortal." For Paul Levi, however, the crux is not the shadowy figure of theoretical abstraction. The theoretical abstraction is the tautened bowstring with which the bowman launches the poisoned arrow of his assessment of Bolshevik policy. This policy resulted, according to Paul Levi, in the fact that, under the cover of the Soviet system, the proletariat was downgraded from a dictating to a 'dictated' class. As a consequence of this policy, the rule of the Bolsheviks themselves as revolutionary class party of the proletariat is up in the air. This party can continue to maintain itself only as the tyranny of an unfit and partially corrupt party bureaucracy by using aimless and senseless terror and by renouncing its fundamental ideal: communism.

In Paul Levi's opinion, the Bolsheviks have, thanks to their agrarian policy, "lost their former support within the peasantry, that of the poor peasants; they all had become middle peasants and opponents of every communist policy". But they "also lost support among the proletariat, as it emerges from the debates at their Tenth Party Congress". Already in February 1921, they were "without class base and lasted thanks to the power of their organisation, a power which cannot be maintained for a longer time". This situation forced them to surrender to capitalism. Beside the agrarian policy, the fundamental attitude of the Bolsheviks to the problem of the relation between revolutionary party and proletarian masses is, according to Paul Levi, responsible for this "objectively counter-revolutionary" development. This attitude is, in his opinion, still the same as it "was, almost twenty years ago, a purely literary controversy between Lenin and Rosa Luxemburg which, at that time, appeared in the modest garb of a dispute about the form of organisation and has today to be examined in a context of great significance for world history".

At that time, Rosa Luxemburg opposed to Lenin's opinion that "the revolutionary social democrat was nothing but a Jacobin associated in an inseparable manner with the organisation of the proletariat so far as it is conscious of its class". According to her, the tightest centralisation of the organisation, from the viewpoint of the formal tasks of a revolutionary proletarian class party, appeared *a priori* as an imperative condition for its fighting fitness and energy. But far more important than the formal requirements of the fighting organisation would be the specific historical conditions of the proletarian class struggle. "The socialist movement, in the history of class societies, is the first movement which, in all its aspects and throughout its course, aims at the organisation and independent direct action of the masses." The given historical conditions of the proletarian struggle for emancipation exclude the simple transfer of Jacobin-Blanquist centralism to the organisation of socialist parties. They entail "a complete reassessment of the ideas of organisation; there comes up a totally new content for the concept of centralism, a totally new view of the mutual relation of organisation and the struggle ...

"The conditions of social democratic action are fundamentally different (from the conditions of 'conspiratorial centralism'). This action emerges historically out of elementary class struggle. Doing so, it moves within the dialectical contradiction that here the proletarian army recruits itself in the course of the fight only and attains clarity about the tasks of the fight, too, in the course of fight itself. Clarification and struggle here are neither different nor chronologically separated moments as they are in a Blanquist movement; rather they are different aspects of the same process. On the one hand, there exist—except for the general principles of the struggle—no ready, fixed in advance, detailed fighting tactics in which the social democratic members could be drilled. On the other hand, the struggle process that creates the organisation also produces a constant fluctuation of the sphere of influence of social democracy. ... It (social democratic centralism) can be nothing but the imperious collective will of the enlightened and fighting vanguard of the working class in relation to its individual groups. One can say it is the 'self-centralisation' of the leading stratum of the proletariat, its majority rule within its own party organisation."

Paul Levi uses Rosa Luxemburg's general fundamental attitude to the problem of organisation of 1904 in a schematic and mechanical manner as a yardstick for Bolshevik policy from the proletarian revolution onward. He neglects the "specific historical conditions of proletarian struggle" in Russia and their concrete effects upon organisation and policy of the Bolsheviks. Doing so, he commits the same mistake criticized by Rosa Luxemburg in Lenin's point of view. As if hypnotised, he stares at a caricature of the Bolshevik party and its policy, which he himself has especially created *ad usum delphine* of his critique. Of course, it is easy to dismiss such a caricature playfully off the cuff and to call out to the shuddering international proletariat: "Throw the monster to the wolves!" The core of Paul Levi's explanation is that the Bolsheviks, overdoing and permanently freezing the concept of centralised organisation, have developed into a party which is not rooted in the masses in a most lively interaction with them. They do not maintain the masses in revolutionary activity in its highest historical sense; instead of that disregarding them they rule and govern through their bureaucracy. Neither their organisation nor their policy embodies the concentrated will or actions of the proletarian masses. The Bolsheviks make a distinction between three tiers of the supporters of the revolutionary movement: "(i) the mass of the exploited and oppressed people, i.e. the mass of the industrial proletariat and the peasants (of that time, in 1919). (ii) The avant-garde of the mass of the exploited and oppressed people, i.e., the urban industrial proletariat. (iii) The vanguard of the industrial proletariat, i.e., the communists."

"Each of the three tiers has its special sphere of tasks and it is an essential task to maintain the connection between these three spheres ... 1. The task of the vanguard, i.e., of the communists, consists in proving themselves to be the most reliable leaders of the proletariat by being disciplined and goal oriented. 2. The task of the avant-garde, that is, of the industrial proletariat, consists in technically starting up, maintaining and controlling the machinery of the proletarian state ... 3. The task of the wide masses of the oppressed people consists in being brought in for... 'participation in the administration,' or in learning by experience to recognize the disciplined and decisive avant-garde (vanguard of the proletariat) to be their reliable leaders"*.

The instrument of connection between the three tiers of the supporters of the revolution and the three spheres of tasks should be and had been the Soviets. They had "to awaken the broad masses and to take them forward to historical creativity". However, "the Soviets have played out this role; the Soviets have collapsed, they have collapsed because of the fact that the classes which were formerly interlinked by them, the workers and the peasants, have no common cause any more ... The organisational base of the dictatorship is becoming narrower".

Moreover: "For the Bolsheviks, the proletarian revolution is a process taking place within the system of vanguard, avant-garde and the masses." The higher sphere has an effect on the lower one by "mechanical means" only. Nothing is more significant than this: in spring 1921, when the Bolsheviks lost the connection with the proletarian masses, which earlier had been established by the soviet system, they deliberated about a form of organisation and found that now the trade unions could be the 'lever' by which the non-party masses must be brought in. They did not understand that the proletarian revolution, too, is a part of the live process of development of the whole without "walls and partitions", where "neither levers nor oxygen masks can replace the rule of nature". Surely, for the development of humanity, "the great struggle to be fought out by the individual, by the sexes, by the estates, by the classes is the form of development" and the "most lively struggle is the most lively form of development". But for the petty-minded Bolsheviks, the police officer and the executioner replace the proud, bold, revolutionary

---

* Levi emphasizes here that Lenin's wording, important for him, about the tasks of the broad masses is "questionably inconsistent." [C.Z.]

fighter who, even in civil war, engages with the opponent "in a free play of forces". Police force and terror in order to eliminate the bourgeoisie; they must be eliminated, but it must be "the result of the social regrouping, which is implied by revolution". Police force and terror in order to overcome the reformist socialists by "banishing them from the ground as parties, as trends," who can only be overcome internally by the revolutionaries "if these fight freely against the mistakes". In a word: the revolution as mechanics, as mechanical coercion, that is, according to Paul Levi, the decisive, historical credo, the conviction of the Bolsheviks.

And what are the fruits of this credo which he saw maturing after the Bolshevik policy had beaten 'democracy' to death? "The Soviets were dead ... they were ash, burnt out. And the trade unions shall serve as a stopgap replacement as they are the only organisation in which wider masses of 'non-party masses' are present. Non-party? Could a reproach be more severe than this that within such a proletariat, which had been a shining example for the proletarians since 1905 and would be so for all time, after four years of proletarian rule the vast mass of people are 'non-party'? Have they indeed become uninterested? Are they sitting on the side, indifferent and bowing their heads while their lives which they had so often put at risk are at stake? Have they become indifferent or do they not want to say what they think? Do they mind their tongues or do they loathe the revolution so becoming 'non-party'? Is not each one of them a living reproach? Whatever it may be! The Russian Revolution and its leading party have not been able to connect the masses with the destiny of the revolution. They are standing aside and are not in the rows of the fighters. Public life is dead. The spirit of democracy, which alone constitutes the breath of the masses, has passed away. A tightly centralised party, a brilliant Central Committee, a bad bureaucracy hovers somewhere above the water. But down below everything is disorderly and desolate. And so, the forward thrust of the peasantry did not meet with a strong, lively, active, enthusiastic proletariat. It met a vanguard which had no majority behind it. Thus the fate of the vanguard was predestined."

The dictatorship of the proletariat "is only then conquered state power when and as long as it is backed up by the will, the strength, the enthusiasm, the confidence in victory of the proletarian class. It is both the state and the form of the state, moreover the one expressed through the other. It is both the core and the shell, and where the core and the shell are wasting away, there the 'dictatorship of the proletariat' is no more." Paul Levi believes that "the revivifying breath of such confidence in victory and the will of the proletarian class would teach how to overcome many of the obstacles which caused such bleeding wounds to the Russian Revolution. For, ultimately the life of a great nation does not consist only of mechanically calculated arithmetical values and forces." The proletarian revolution needs confidence in victory and the enduring enthusiastic will of the exploited and oppressed masses. That is the 'authority', that is 'the terror of the revolution', before which the enemies shiver. "Where, however, this powerful class force dies out, the substitutes—concession at the one, organisation at the other front, police measures at both fronts—must in the long run fail."

With reference to Rosa Luxemburg's critique of 1918, I have already in the above taken a good look at that fundamental attitude to the problems brought up in the course of the revolution, which is meant to support and to cover Paul Levi's own assessment of the Bolsheviks' policy. Therefore, I confine myself to throwing light on the value, the qualification of such assessment itself with reference to some striking cases. According to this prosecutor and judge of the Bolsheviks' policy, the Kronstadt rising in 1921 is a conclusive evidence for his assertion that a deep rift began opening up between the Bolsheviks and the proletarian masses. He writes about it: "It is an extremely naive story of the historical facts some 'experts' peddle around who make the Kronstadt rising out to be the put-up job of a couple of tsarist officers with the aid of French francs or that of a couple of 'Mensheviks'. It may be that some tsarist generals operated behind the Kronstadt mariners – we do not know. It may be that 'Menshevik slogans' played a role during the Kronstadt rising – we do not know. With certainty, however, we know that neither the tsarist generals nor French francs nor the Menshevik slogans are a sufficient explanation for the fact that it was possible that the **most loyal sons of the revolution**[*], the erstwhile most devoted supporters of the Bolsheviks, the elite of the revolutionary fighters proven in hundreds of battles, revolted against those to whom they had up to then been attached. This fact can only be explained by a deep crisis within the proletariat itself, by a severe conflict having come

[*] Emphasized in the original text [C.Z.].

into being between the avant-garde and the vanguard, perhaps within the vanguard itself."

The given account is 'truth and fiction,' as probably every autobiography is, and the 'Introduction' to the posthumously published pamphlet is certainly, unconsciously and unintentionally, a bit of autobiography. This account is extraordinarily characteristic of the way Paul Levi writes history and pronounces judgment. There exists documentary proof that French francs, tsarist officers and Social Revolutionaries as well as 'Menshevik' slogans had a large share in the Kronstadt rising. Nevertheless, Paul Levi does not know if it is true. The doubting Thomas, however, becomes a quickly faithful person as soon as he is able to put his critical fingers in wounds allegedly hit by the Russian Revolution. Above all, he knows "one thing with certainty" – that "the most loyal sons of the revolution, the most devoted supporters of the Bolsheviks," were the insurgents. He remains silent about the slogans of the rebels – abolition of quotas, free trade, and 'democracy' – slogans which suggest that it was not "the most loyal sons of the revolution" who had rebelled. He remains silent about the fact that the Kronstadt marine troops, the most prominent supporters of the revolt, had changed in their social composition. They no more consisted of the "most loyal sons of the revolution," who had fearlessly pushed through the first victorious battles of the proletariat in Petersburg. Those heroes had bled to death on all fronts, on all battlefields in the passionate struggle for freedom. As reliable revolutionary elite, they still were ready for active service as leaders in the 'Red Army.' Most of them were recruited from among the metal workers and other urban proletarians of the Baltic territories of revolutionary Russia. As a result of secession by the marginal Baltic States, the Soviet government was forced into bringing in the sons of peasants from the banks of the river Don for service as 'seaworthy' marine soldiers. Corresponding to the changed social background was a changed social attitude. Thus the Kronstadt rising was intrinsically a reflection or, more correctly spoken, an offshoot of the peasant riots and peasant revolts that were imminent or had already erupted in several provinces of southern Russia. The slogans of the Kronstadt rebels are clear clues, being the demands of the peasants who rebelled against 'War Communism'.

In my opinion, Radek has exposed this in a very convincing manner in the same number of the *Russische Korrespondenz* referred to by Paul Levi in connection with this problem. It is hardly thinkable that Paul Levi did not read just this particular article. Surely, he had the right to reject Radek's allegation or to question it with the same casual irony as the extremely "naive stories about the historical facts told by a couple of experts in Germany". But in the face of the significance he gives to the Kronstadt events, he should not have kept silent about Radek's explanation without further ado in order to compose his touching poetical verse about the spontaneously revolting "most loyal sons of the revolution" for the "extremely naive stories about the historical facts told by a couple of experts in Germany," by whom he is regarded as an irrefutable authority. Besides, it seems reasonable to suppose that the composition, the character, of the Kronstadt civil population, too, had changed. The large-scale manufacturing industry—especially the metalworking industry—which had taken an important upward trend before the war in the Petersburg district mainly depended on imports from foreign countries in order to be supplied with coal, ores and semi-finished products. As a result of the war and of the blockade, importation collapsed almost completely and it is indeed an "extremely naive story of the historical facts" told by anti-Bolshevik incorrigible liars who make the revolution and especially the Bolsheviks responsible for that collapse. The civil war and its effects, by cordoning off the Petersburg district from the Ural Mountains and from southern Russia, intensified the collapse, a situation which, together with the shortage of food, led to the migration of many industrial proletarians from there. One can well suppose that the declining movement in Kronstadt, too, provoked a stepping back of the industrial proletariat behind the petty bourgeois element. This circumstance, too, must have contributed to the creation of a favourable ground for a mutiny in Kronstadt. By the way, the geographic location of the place, its strategic importance is suggestive of the fact that the "extremely naive story about the historical facts" of "a couple of tsarist officers with the aid of French francs" was certainly not at all so "extremely naive" as Paul Levi alleges it.

In any case, in the Kronstadt rising, influences and objectives of the most different kinds and tendency became inextricably mixed, which initially coalesced into one point: on the intention to get rid, cost what it may, of the Bolshevik government as being the main obstacle for the realization of the separate aims of the individual groups of rebels.

Whether they rebelled in the name of tsarism or 'West European civilization' or 'democracy', the different banners concealed the same obvious commodity or contraband – the rule of the bourgeoisie, the restoration of capitalism as sovereign ruler because, in the current historical hour, 'democracy', in the form ecstatically idolised and extolled by the Mensheviks who style themselves as Marxists and by the Social Revolutionaries, is not accosting the regime of the State of workers and peasants as a bloodless abstraction but as the dictatorship of the bourgeois class, in garments ready for the campaign, with swords drawn against the proletarian revolution. This is how the tragic Kronstadt events are to be pictured; not bathed in the glorious purely romantic rays of rebellious yearning for freedom against the Bolsheviks' tyrannical power and against the 'blunders' and 'aberrations' of their politics, leading away from the path of communism. These events bear the assault-helmet of counter-revolution. The way things were these events cannot be explained simply and unambiguously "by a deep crisis within the proletariat itself, with a severe conflict that has arisen between the 'vanguard' and the 'avant-garde', perhaps even within the vanguard". One fact clearly reveals this: The victory of the Soviet government over the rebels was the result not only of the military performance of the 'Red Army' but equally of the attitude of the proletariat—foremost of the Petersburg proletariat.

This fact is characteristic of the relationship between the 'vanguard' and the avant-garde' of the Russian Revolution, between the Communist Party and the industrial proletariat. Who would deny the fact that among the proletarian masses there existed great turmoil and deep discontent in the winter of 1920/1921 and in spring 1921? And that too not only in minor, remote industrial centres but also in the big hubs of the proletarian revolution that had withstood many a stormy attack, in 'red' St. Petersburg, in 'red' Moscow. The Bolsheviks would be the last to deny this. During those dreadful, fateful months the assemblies of the workers as well as the meetings of the urban Soviets and their organs resonated with disturbing complaints, sharp criticisms and the most urgent demands of the worker masses. The programmes of the Communist Party were dominated by debates about the causes and the significance of the spreading political unrest, but above all about the means of mitigating the abject poverty, of clearing away obvious, avoidable social evils, about informing the ignorant and supporting the vacillating and despairing people by showing superior judgement and an energetic will. In short: about winning and strengthening the confidence of the non-communist industrial proletarians in the Soviet government and their Party.

Undoubtedly, this trust—the firm basis of the Bolshevik power—the most precious thing the proletarian masses are able to give, was not yet gained to the necessary extent or it had been shaken. For the Communist Party, screening its politics and its relationship with the producing masses, especially with the industrial proletariat, by merciless self-criticism was a vital matter, a condition of its historical right to exist. The result, passing from the realm of insight into the realm of practice, of action, was: the 'politics of concessions' and deepened, energetic efforts to minimise the distance between the Party and the non-communist proletarians and to establish the closest possible relations between the communists and these proletarians in all sectors, above all in the trade unions, as a precondition that these instinctive rebels against capitalism became conscious fighters against it and architects of communism.

Between July and October 1917, the masses of the Russian industrial proletariat had gathered around the Bolsheviks in an unstoppable and rapid manner. They were driven in that direction by the straight betrayal of the proletarian interests by the "one and only, pure democracy" of the Kerensky government, a government adorned with Mensheviks, too, as captives and servants of bourgeois politics. This betrayal lent irresistible charm to the slogan "All power to the Soviets," which included the aim: all factories, the entire industry to the proletarians, extermination of sweating, enslaving capitalism; freedom and abundance due to the fruits and wreaths bestowed by communism. Under the leadership of the upright, confidently advancing Bolsheviks, the proletarian masses had experienced the beginning of fulfilling their yearning; but not just that: they had brought it into being themselves by the fact that the fervour of their hearts and the forceful, seething thoughts had armed their fists for the revolutionary fight. The Bolsheviks steadfastly pointed to the lofty goal. Should not, under their experienced leadership, the following masses of the working people attain it through the same bold, glorious stormy attack as they had conquered state power? That was the hope; that was the rock-solid belief of the widest masses of the industrial proletariat who did not master communism with pondering reason but instinctively with burning hearts grasped it to be their salvation. Confidence in the leaders outstripped their comprehension of communism and especially the circumstances, and let the idea become a reality as an outcome of mass action.

Happy to behold they began the steep climb to the gleaming heights of communism together with the Bolsheviks. Year after year, they loyally and fearlessly followed their leadership through the dreadful bloody dangers of the civil war and the war at the fronts; full of self-denial they withstood the hardest deprivations, famines and heavy frost; strong in their belief they wrung, day after day, new performances of work out of their dwindling, fading forces. They were hungry and exhausted, many hundred thousands, who, for more than one year, sacrificed their leisure hours of Saturdays and Sundays to community service for free, on a voluntary basis. The proletarian masses, who strived upwards to communism, bravely withstood the big disappointments, as they had need and danger. What they had hoped for with religious force and enthusiasm remained unfulfilled – they did not see a Soviet banner of the victorious proletariat in any other State of the world. "Was such a faith ever seen in old Israel?" Did the workers of other countries, who make a great show of their superiority over the Russian illiterates, ever activate the same heroism and courage of martyrs in the struggle for their own liberation?

Feeling and mood had welded the 'vanguard' and 'avant-garde' of the Russian Revolution firmly together in the thrill of self-defence, the imposed defensive struggles for Soviet Russia's existence. The inevitability of the privations and harshness of 'War Communism' was comprehended by the non-communist industrial proletarians too. The peace treaty broke up or loosened the iron ring with which they had been held together with the minority of people who were trained in questions of communism. Now, the consciousness of the great historical class interest and class work was darkened by the special interests of groups and individuals among the non-communist workers. Communism did not begin as a permanent Sunday and holiday as they had naively thought. It began externally as a dark, dull working day, full of tribulation, distress and sorrow. The non-communist masses did not as yet sense the inner light and warmth, the historical magnitude of the new presenting itself in its workman's garbs.

Lenin and Trotsky, too, were not in a position to repeat Christ's miracle related in the Bible: to satiate four thousand hungry people with the aid of two loaves of bread and two fishes after which basketfuls of residuals still remained to be collected. It was not possible for the Communist Party and the Soviet Government to wring – out of the weak, backward, decomposed economy – such results which would have secured for the populace a better life or which would have at least ensured the previous frugal fare. The orders of economic authorities, the measures taken by organizers and managers of industrial enterprises in order to increase work productivity using the methods and discipline of modern large-scale industry were felt to be hard by large sections of the working class. Their feelings and habits were still rooted in the leisurely routine of the pre-capitalist era; they did not understand the difference between extreme exertion for the common weal and the most intensive exploitation for the sake of capitalist profit. The masses of the industrial proletariat who had to perform more and better services for Soviet Russia's maintenance and its communist construction had lived, too, for seven years under the scalding heat of war and revolution; they were chronically undernourished, strained, worn out, worried; they were stirred up by extraordinary events, jolted out of the habitual routine of innumerable generations, extremely daring but full of expectation, too.

Is it surprising that, within the industrial proletariat, the 'fellow travellers' of communism separated themselves from the 'firm believers' when the relative peace was not followed by the awaited necessary disappearance of their hardship? The former did not see what the latter realized: the fact that, in the beginning, the communist construction of the Soviet Republic (a republic governed by workers' councils) was inevitably not just a struggle, a passionate struggle, with the diverse obstacles raised up due to the conditions of the shattered economy and with the convoluted problems resulting from the effects of the proletarian revolution, but also a bitter, tenacious fight against the open and hidden enemies, the remnants and the defenders of the old economic order in the social institutions and in the psyche of millions of people. But like the conquest of state power the fight and struggle for the building up of communism had to be the work of the proletariat itself as a class. Even the most brilliant leaders could not release the class from such work. The 'fellow travellers' of communism were disappointed that the leading Bolsheviks did not release the proletariat from its historical task, that they did not build up the communist system for and instead of the proletariat. They grumbled, they were angry with the Bolsheviks, and small groups of them began a 'mutiny' against them.

It is an indisputable and undisputed fact that mistakes in the economic organisation and administration and some of the measures increased the difficulties of the situation, and with that the discontent within the industrial proletariat. The Bolsheviks are excellent revolutionary fighters and politicians but they are not such good economists and administrators. As leaders of a proletarian revolution they have to master an unending harder task in comparison with the great revolutionaries of the bourgeois class in former periods. These had only to organize the political power in the state according to the necessities of their own class. Organising the social economy continued to be a private matter of the individual capitalists, who were 'sovereigns in their own homes'. Anarchy was and is the characteristic feature of social production under a bourgeois government. The proletarian subversion goes far beyond the aim of bourgeois revolutions. It goes into the depths of the society; it radically changes the economy so that, with the last exploited and enslaved class, "all human beings born equal will become a noble species". Therefore, the revolutionary proletariat cannot restrict itself to "hammering the old rotten thing, the state, into something new." It has to restructure the entire social economy in a communist way. All economic entities have to be made into communist organisations and incorporated in the common macro economy. The social system of communist production has to overcome the anarchy of its capitalist forerunner. A historic mission of gigantic dimensions!

In order to fulfil it, the leading party of the Russian proletariat does not have at its disposal the same body of technical knowledge and practical experience as it has of the revolutionary struggle. There are neither positive nor negative examples in history they could learn from. The Paris Commune of 1871 had a very brief existence under essentially different historical circumstances so that it could not leave a great example behind for the communist creation of Soviet Russia. The Bolsheviks had to rely on themselves in order to creatively regulate the chaotic economy.

To be sure: they have among them economists with extensive and profound education, who have an excellent theoretical mastery of the production problems; they have scholars, engineers and technicians, experienced practical men whose abilities and knowledge can strongly promote the communist construction of the economy. Many non-communist intellectuals and tsarist civil servants cooperate with them according to their former fields of activity, but not always with a pure attitude and clean hands. How few, however, are the constructive forces compared with the gigantic work to be done and the cumulative and enormous difficulties of its execution! Extensive and brilliant plans were made in order to set up and enhance the economy in the direction of communism; production programmes were exemplarily devised for the individual industrial sectors, economic fields etc.; there were ingeniously designed distribution mechanisms. However, much of all this remained 'futuristic', much of it was poorly, even inadequately, executed.

The underlying reason for the above is not just the historical lack of maturity, already emphasized, of the objective and subjective conditions of the proletarian revolution and of the communist system. It would be a cowardly self-deception not to recognize that it is also partly caused by the practical weakness, lack of education and experience of the leading party of the revolution for the economic and administrative tasks. Not all those appointed to such tasks were, in their abilities and character, exceptional and dedicated. Enthusiasm for communism could not replace a dispassionate perspective on economic and social realities; revolutionary military prowess is no substitute for a professional and technical training. Where the abilities and power of economic organisation and leadership were absent there often came up an unthinking, mechanical, paralyzing bureaucracy. Corrupt self-interest dominated over the sense of social duty in the case of some administrators and leaders.

None other than the leading Bolsheviks themselves have mercilessly and truthfully brought into the open and castigated the shortcomings and the deplorable state of the revolutionary and transitional economy. With as much zealousness as persistence they strive to overcome such shortcomings, for they clearly recognize the fact that the radical change of the social economy is the problem, the central problem, of the proletarian revolution. One could mount up a big collection of quotations of error admissions and improvement proposals. Let me only remind you about Lenin's sharp, unsparing views expressed in several Party congresses. It seems that such very instructive and stimulating remarks did not make any impression upon Paul Levi. Apart from the Bolshevik agrarian policy, which he has subjected in its entirety to a petty-minded critique, Paul Levi hardly hints at the significant complex of questions in this context. With his damnation of the entire Bolshevik policy, he also cannot explain the crucial causes of the 'tension' between 'vanguard' and 'avant-garde'. But the 'democracy' that he appeals to as the *deus ex machina*, which will rescue communism from its deadly embrace by Bolshevism, does not open up or, at best, presents only a very nebulous perspective regarding how to avoid or minimise the 'distance' between the Communist Party and the proletarian masses, as it became evident in spring 1921.

When, in those days, a "crisis was emerging" among the industrial proletariat and there was danger of big peasant revolts spreading out, Bolshevik policy could less than before permit itself the luxury of experimenting with Menshevik and Social Revolutionary political ideas and formulas. Stained with the weaknesses and crimes committed by the Kerensky government, the Mensheviks and Social Revolutionaries had become discredited among the working masses and had demonstrated their incapacity. Making pacts with them and their propaganda would have increased political unrest and insecurity among the proletariat, the forces of which had to be gathered in a unified will to endure and engage in self-sacrificing activity.

Making such pacts was not necessary, too, for securing a wide field of successful activities for people who were willing to help the Soviet power in the construction of higher economic and social forms on the basis of the Soviet system. If, because of narrow-minded fanatical dogmatism, the Bolsheviks had failed to recognize the benefits of welcoming the co-operation of the lively, competent forces of the country, iron necessity would have compelled them to do so. The necessity is present in the extent and the variety of the economic and social tasks, which are constantly growing with the Soviet system, and in the small group of trained, technically efficient people amidst most patent illiteracy. In the years 1920 and 1921 certainly far more non-communists of all political hues than communists were engaged in social institutions, schools and educational institutes, in economic and administrative departments. Especially in the industrial enterprises, the direction and administration was very often in the hands of former executives and owners. It is an undisputed fact that in many cases the non-communists have abused their responsible positions for the 'sabotage' of the new system.

To be sure: not always "the right man came into the right position". Excesses of bureaucracy and party life as well as individual influence had the effect that many people of outstanding merit, many competent persons wasted away in the shadow, while incapable careerists swung upwards. Everywhere human beings are fallible, among communists, too, but cases of such nature cannot be booked onto the debit page regarding the fundamental character of Bolshevik policy – this is shown by the conditions in countries of the 'most perfect democracy', too. It was caused not by the policy but by the psychology or by the political attitude of several non-communist but worthy persons that they, disgruntled and disappointed, turned away, not understanding that the need of the moment for the Soviet government was to act and not to philosophise or discuss.

How would a proclamation of 'democracy' have altered the facts that were striking bleeding wounds in the masses of Soviet Russia's working people? The global bourgeoisie would not at all have responded with suspending the blockade and boycott while, in its opinion, 'civilization' is defiled and annihilated by the negation of any poser's and adventurer's right to press out gold from the bodies and souls of poor people. The global bourgeois would suddenly have discovered as true what they till then had disputed as 'rabble-rousing slogans': the fact that without economic liberty and power 'democracy' cannot be realized in society. Besides, the magic charm of 'democracy' would have satisfied the longings of little circles of advocates of parliamentarianism but would not overnight have given the masses the Christmas present of an economy which could satiate the hungry stomachs of millions of people.

The troubled proletarians, living in want, however, were 'grossly materially' minded. They did not dream of 'the pretty eyes' of the political formulas of bourgeois democracy. In the cold, dark flats where they suffered hunger and cold, in the enterprises where they toiled and painfully yielded output, their longings were focused on such prosaic things as potatoes, bread, flour and cabbage, as clothes and shoes, as warmth and light. It was not that they were roused by reading Heinrich Heine's poems; the 'logic of soup' and ‘reasons of dumplings’ were more important for them than the Menshevik and Social Revolutionary proclamations of redemption. In no way was it due to dissatisfaction with the alleged wrong line of Bolshevik policy that sections of the proletarian ‘avant-garde’ of revolution, of the vanguard, began to get alienated. As far as poverty of the economy was not the reason, it was deficiencies, errors, irregularities in the distribution of the scarce necessities of life and in administration. The vacillating and wavering people again solidly gathered around the Soviet power when it succeeded—in spite of the enormous difficulties created by the bitterly experienced sloppiness and injustice of authorities—in checking such irregularities, but above all when a somewhat more substantial supply provisions and their better distribution were secured for the industrial population. And today, when the hazardous ‘concession policy’ has been affecting the lifestyle of the Russian proletariat since the last one year, the ‘avant-garde’ is standing by its ‘vanguard’ with unshakeable confidence.

This relation suggests a historical comparison – of course *mutatis mutandis.* February 1848, Paris: Hungry for bread and freedom as well as for social justice, agitated by vague socialist ideals, the revolutionary proletariat shattered the throne of the business-minded bourgeois king Louis Philippe. By doing so, it hopes to have shattered the rule of the exploiting capitalists, too, whom this king, in the correct knowledge of his function, had invited to “Enrich yourselves!” In a mixture of naive confidence and nascent doubt, the proletariat leaves to bourgeois republicans and reformers the new order and thereby its own destiny. It draws up a bill for three months of its hunger and poverty. These three months suffice to teach the Paris workers that they have cut off the shimmering crown only, but not the head of the awful monster which tears them limb to limb. In the June battle, six thousand proud rebels underwrite with their blood that the pact between the treacherous bourgeois windbags of revolution and the proletarian fighters of revolution, the pact between the bourgeoisie and the working class, has been torn to pieces.

Soviet Russia 1917 to 1922: Almost five years of proletarian revolution. For the young Russian proletariat, it was almost five years of indescribable, exhausting suffering and heroic fights. In spite of it all, the alliance between it and its leading class party is firm and strong. Indeed, it is a “very simple tale of history” to explain this fact by a "national Russian character" or by the "dullness of the masses" or even by the "Bolshevik tyranny and reign of terror". Against the famine of millions, against the revolting will of the entire, united class, in whose hands history gave the strongest, forward driving power in Soviet Russia, too, bayonets and machine guns are helpless. Especially in a country of revolution and in an era of revolution.

The situation in spring 1921 induced the Bolsheviks to analyse the relation between 'vanguard' and 'avant-garde' also from the point of view of the other side. They did not only ask: how do the proletarian masses relate to us? But also: how do we relate to the proletarian masses? Further above, we have heard how deeply distressing, how wretched the answer was according to Paul Levi. Allegedly, it was not only the observation but even the open acknowledgement of the Party's incapacity to include the proletariat in all its various layers, to hold it and to fill it with a communist spirit, and to let the full sum of its historical power of action become a vibrant, liberating act. Within the party, the letter had killed the spirit; the rigid organisational method had strangled dynamic, contradictory historical life. How could the Party give the proletariat that what had been lost by the Party? The Communist Party had separated from the masses and, blindly complacent, had retreated into its shell. With democracy trampled down outside the Party the best historical life within the Party had died, a life which must flow back and forth between the Party and the masses in a continuous alternating current. The quotations with which Paul Levi supports his view are genuine, but the spirit with which they have been selected and compiled, and in which they have been interpreted, is false.

Why then at the moment of the 1921 crisis a distance became evident between the Party and a part of the non-communist proletariat? Was it because the Bolsheviks had been left behind by the advancing masses in the struggle for communism? The contrary is true. The Bolshevik policy had run to the target so bravely and with such intensity that only the elite of the proletarian avant-garde had the stamina to follow them. Seen from the outside, the entire proletariat had marched with the Bolsheviks, a solid, united 'power house' of the revolution. Only they were not yet able to attain political and social, historical maturity in order to be internally insolubly affiliated with the Bolsheviks, and that means with communism itself, because the Bolsheviks are the most passionate and most conscious champions of communism. This is not an indication of the weakness of the proletarian masses or of Bolshevik policy.

After having assumed political power, the Bolsheviks as the revolutionary class party of the proletariat had not only to organize government and economy on a new basis but also to radically transform the entire social superstructure according to the goal of communism. There was no field of social life where they had not to destroy and to build, to shove aside what was dying and to secure strong growth for what was sprouting. I want to pick out some tasks: Social security for people in need had to be put on a different basis and to be extended; in reality, it had to be created anew, in the spirit of full fraternity, as social obligation and individual entitlement.

The woman had to be integrated in the radically changing system as a member of society with equal economic, political and social rights and duties. The educational right of the child had to be secured. Political and civil laws had to be infused with a new spirit through new norms. The most important, fundamental task was that of organising popular education and culture in their widest and deepest sense and rendering them effective as creative forces of innovation.

The communist building of Soviet Russia with the variety and juxtaposition of requirements is a titanic task which cannot be performed by one party alone, even if such a party were the acme of political wisdom and power. It will be the work of millions of people who come together as a class with their historical aspirations and actions, year after year. Fully grasping this, the Bolsheviks tackled this work passionately and with a strong hand as if it could be or even must be the result of their own lifetime itself. And they let their burning desire and their irresistible energy flow into the proletarian 'avant-garde', into the widest masses of working people whom they invited to do the building work. The Bolsheviks had to do so. In this great historical moment it had to be the work of the masses in order to give the base and the superstructure of the Soviet republic its decisive character, its clear destiny.

The masses of working people followed this invitation with wonderful, matchless élan. Living in want, bleeding from their lesions, they started the communist building work with dedication, enthusiasm, wild energy, and with strong faith – the marvellous assets of a young and fresh race, which had not become arrogant, tired and cynical by an old civilization, and the marvellous assets of a young and fresh class, which is striving up to the light of culture without capitalism having pressed the marrow out of its bones for generations. In the urban and rural Soviets, in the trade unions and co-operatives, in the Soviet organs and social institutions, in the courses for illiterates and evening art performances – what a rich, generous life! What an awakening, stirring and moving, what a groping of ways to somewhere, what a testing of yearning forces, what a developing and performing of hardly guessed abilities! The intoxicating, bracing breath of a great historical day of creation stormed through Soviet Russia, not the work of a single one who, in a commanding manner, called out: "Come into being!" but the work of millions who sensed and understood themselves in their humanity and fervently cheered: "We are!"

Should it be astonishing that the Communist Party overestimated the degree of maturity of the proletarian masses in the face of this excellent development? This development was the lifelong work to which the best in their ranks, thousands and tens of thousands of people had given, and continue to give their lifeblood day after day and which has become history. The Party felt so firmly connected to the proletariat, so united with the proletariat that it identified its own being with the being of the awakening masses. The 1921 crisis resulted in disillusionment and showed, at the least, that not all who stood with their feet with the proletarian 'avant-garde' of the revolution were with their hearts and minds totally devoted to communism and capable of coping with their part of the tasks. The Bolsheviks, however, were not an association of scholars who would be satisfied by historically explaining the distance between themselves and the non-communist masses or by making philosophical comments about it. They were politicians spurred on by thirst for action who must be active by intrinsic necessity, who wanted to clear up the conflict. The crucial point of their debates about the situation was, therefore, not the question: when and how the proletarian masses will come to us? But the other question: how shall we come to the proletarian masses in the quickest and most successful way?

The latter question was posed in the Party discussions and at the Tenth Party Congress of the Bolsheviks with such sharpness and answered with such deeply radical self-criticism as is usually characteristic of our Russian friends' struggles to comprehend issues.

All this in an atmosphere of hot party-political polemics and aimed at the specific, concrete goal of the day. Under such circumstances the sharp turn of phrase by the best of leaders is to be taken with the necessary grain of salt. Therefore, it is a blunder of Paul Levi's when he accepts the words regarding "lack of oxygen" and of the new "oxygen cylinder" of the trade unions used by Zinoviev at the Eleventh Congress of the Bolsheviks as being an exhaustive characterisation of the Communist Party and its relationship to the masses. His mockery is rather shabby when he claims that the Bolsheviks, after having mechanised and destroyed the life of the Soviets by their mindless dogmatism, were not capable of finding anything better than a new mechanical link with the masses, a new form of organisation, the trade unions.

Object of the debates was not the spirit which would connect the 'vanguard' and 'avant-garde' with the masses, and become the most vibrant life and activity of a whole, of an irresistible united power. It was a matter of the means by which the spirit could enter the proletariat in order to become the focused will and conscious action of the class. How? Had the organisational form for the Bolsheviks become from an instrument with a purpose into the most holy end in itself, a self-operating wonderful machine, which would raise the proletariat to the heights of historical action ability thanks to its immanent mechanical forces? But is not the history of their party a convincing proof of their seeking and trying to subordinate the best organisational form as a servant and tool of the most purposeful and strong-willed revolutionary spirit and of making a maximum of revolutionary insight and energy of the proletarian masses themselves effective and decisive?

These poor wretches did not at all need to discover the trade unions as agents between Party and proletarian masses only after the alleged bankruptcy of their policy in the Soviets. A long time back, prior to the 1921 crisis, they had evaluated the trade unions according to their great historical importance for the proletarian struggle for emancipation. It is, however, not difficult to comprehend and is related to the weak development of these organisations under the tsarist regime that in the first period of the establishment of the proletarian dictatorship they withdrew behind the Soviets. However, as the tasks of proletariat increased—beside smashing and clearing away the old regime, building the new regime, especially organising the economy—all the more evident became the importance of the trade unions as the education and development organs of the revolutionary working class. The closest connection and mutual interpenetration of the lives of the Party and trade unions for realising the ideals of the communist revolution is strived for with increasing clarity and energy. And precisely that Bolshevik Party Congress—of whose meaningful work Paul Levi reports nothing but the despicable attempt to maintain a sinking ship over water—occupied itself with the tasks of trade unions in passionate, serious debates.* The role of the trade unions in the implementation of the proletarian revolution is steadily increasing and will be of indispensable value when, in factories and workshops, Soviet Russia will fight with capitalism to which it had temporarily to grant concessions. Not in fight against the Soviets but in co-operation with them, the trade unions will defend and continue the beginnings of the building of communist society.

(Translator wishes to remain anonymous)

---

* For the study of this question it is urgently recommended to see: "*Russische Korrespondenz" ("Russian Correspondence')*, 1921, issues 3, 4 and 5. [C.Z.]

X

Increasing Development of the Soviets and their Firm Alliance with the Industrial Proletariat and its Class-based Party

Growing electoral participation in All-Russian Soviet Congresses, District and Provincial Conferences; growing party membership; profession, educational qualification and gender of the elected representatives / Party membership and professions of the members of the Soviet Executive Committees / Function of the Soviets as expression of the will of the masses and their actions under the leadership of the Bolshevik Party / The Bolshevik Party as a conscious expression of the will, activity and progress of the proletariat

The claim that the Soviets have exhausted their role in the proletarian revolution in Russia is a piece of idle gossip. They are, in fact, still in the early stages of their development, and as such they are in form and substance the most complete manifestation of social democracy founded upon collective social labour. For this reason they shall continue to be the forum, where the industrial proletariat and the peasants of the Russian Soviet Republic represent their historic class interests and aspirations. Surely, in spite of the deafening clash of opinions and interests and transcending all diverse contingent issues, a single great purpose unites all productive people: the emancipation of labour with the help of communism. Nine-tenth of the entire agrarian population of Soviet Russia is engaged in labour, and its existence is thus increasingly and inseparably becoming one with the proletariat; agrarian workers must therefore look ahead and face their communist future.

The development of the Soviets has been on an ascending track. They have increasingly become a mobilizing force for large urban and rural populations while acting as a centre of gravity, wherein the political and social lives of the masses converge, and from where they aspire towards ever expanding horizons. There is statistical evidence for this that simultaneously throws light on the outward party political development.* 35,625,000 voters elected their

* Uranovsky: The Soviets and their Development between 1917 and 1920. *Russische Korrespondenz*, (*Russian Correspondence*) 1921, issues. 1 and 2. [C.Z.]

representatives at the Fifth All-Russian Soviet Congress of 4 July 1918; but at the Sixth Congress of 6 September that same year around 59,300,000 voters—in other words the greater half of the entire population of the Soviet Union—participated. The number of voters at the subsequent All-Russian Soviet Congresses is said to have been even bigger. At the Fourth All-Russian Soviet Congress 69 out of every 100 representatives were Communists, 20 out of 100 were 'Left Social Revolutionaries', and one was 'independent'. By the Fifth Congress the number of representatives of the 'Left Social Revolutionaries' rose to 32 out of 100, whereas the Communists fell to 60; the position of the 'Independents' remained unchanged at one. A markedly different picture emerges in the pattern of representation during the Sixth Congress, 90 per cent of which was made up of Communists; the 'Left Social Revolutionaries' now comprised only one per cent, and the numerical strength of the 'Independents' fell to one out of every 300. The 'Left Social Revolutionaries' had become a minority on the verge of extinction. It was a result of the endless assassinations and conspiracies they had been hatching to overthrow the Soviet government. These activities had an effect not only on the voting population, which turned away from the party, but also on the government which was forced to make use of its authority derived from the dictatorship of the proletariat to take steps against the 'Left Social Revolutionaries' in order to defend the very existence of Soviet Russia.

A total of 103201 workers and peasants participated in the District Conferences of the Soviets between 1 January 1918 and 1 January 1920. During the first half of 1918, the Communists averaged 42 out of 100 delegates and the 'Independents' numbered 38. In the second half of 1919, the 'Independents' saw their average increase to 45 per cent and the Communists to 49 per cent of all representatives. Workers and peasants delegated a total of 15029 representatives to the 74 Provincial Conferences of Soviets in the same two-year period. Out of 100 delegates, the Communists comprised on an average 53, non-Communists 33, and the 'Independents' 14 delegates at such conferences during the first half of 1918. In the second half of 1919, the composition of delegates was as follows: 74 per cent Communists and 22 per cent 'Independents'. The remaining delegates at the District and Provincial Conferences of Soviets were from various non-Communist parties.

According to the data given here, a distinct pattern of development common to the two types of conferences is discernible. Both Communist and 'Independent' delegates have grown in number. This, of course, indicates that the representatives of non-Communist parties at the Soviet conferences have become fewer in number; in fact they have very nearly disappeared, ceding ground mainly to the 'Independents' at the District Conferences, but at the Provincial Conferences chiefly to the Communists. This difference reflects the social stratification of the electorate. The District Conferences are primarily assemblies of peasants who as a class have only just embarked upon the process of 'politicization', and whose propensity it is to wait and watch cautiously before forming a judgment about the political parties, but who as 'Independents' tend to 'sympathize' with the Communists. The Provincial Conferences are, however, overwhelmingly made up of the industrial proletariat who due to the prevailing conditions of their class can be guided much faster in the direction of communism, and who are, therefore, more readily accessible for social agitation. The available aggregates over a two-year period at the Provincial Conferences of Ivanovo-Vosnesensk confirm this analysis. The number of Communist delegates rose from 55 per cent to 88 per cent from the first half of 1918 to the end of the second half of 1919; however, the representation of the 'Independents' came down from 26 to 11 per cent. Daily newspapers provide the following data regarding the composition of the Soviet Congresses in the first half of 1921: among the delegates of the Provincial Conferences 74.7 per cent were Communists and 25.3 per cent were 'Independents'; in the District Congresses, however, 41.5 per cent were Communists, 58.3 per cent were 'Independents' and 0.2 per cent were members of other parties. These numbers confirm the above conclusions. They also make it clear that the composition of the conferences is the result of development and a manifestation of the prevailing conditions, and not an outcome of pressure from outside. The number of Communist representatives at the Provincial Conferences has hardly grown; in fact their numbers at the District Conferences have even come down, but the number of 'Independents' has increased sharply. It is obvious that the composition of the Soviet Congresses in those months reflects the prevailing conditions of those times.

Of particular significance for the existence and functioning of the Soviets is the composition of the congresses on the basis of the profession of the delegates. The Soviet Congresses of the first half of 1921 show a predominance of peasants. They constituted almost two-thirds of the total number of delegates at the District Congresses, and over one-third at the Provincial Congresses. At the Provincial Congresses, 35.9 out of 100 representatives were peasants, 31.2 workers, 23 government employees and 9.9 from various other professions like doctors, teachers etc. At the District Congresses, there were out of 100 delegates 63.2 peasants, 14.4 workers, 16.2 government employees and 6.2 other professionals. 79 per cent of the delegates to Provincial Congresses and 80.8 per cent of them at the District Congresses had enjoyed 'school education'; 20.3 and 16.5 per cent respectively had received 'continuous higher schooling'; the rate of illiteracy among the representatives of Provincial Congresses was 0.7 per cent, and among those at District Congresses 2.7 per cent. Women made up 4.4 out of 100 delegates at Provincial Congresses and only 2.2 out of 100 at the District Congresses. These figures are self-explanatory, and they indicate a process that has only just begun.

The lively cross-section of the population seen at the Soviets is also visible in the composition of their Executive Committees. The following table from 1921 with regard to this aspect provides the relevant figures. The percentages of the members in the Executive Committees are:

	Urban Soviets	Provincial Soviets	District Soviets
Workers	43.9	35.4	27.2
Peasants	10.7	15.4	29.5
Govt. Employees	26.8	29.3	24.5
Doctors	2.4	1.1	1.1
Jurists	---	0.9	0.1
Teachers	3.9	8.7	7.1
Technicians	2.0	2.8	1.3
Students	4.9	3.7	3.8
Others	5.4	2.7	5.4

Workers and peasants together make up more than half of the membership of the Urban, Provincial and District Soviets. Due attention should be given to the sizeable percentage of workers, whose numbers come close to those of the peasants not only in the Urban Soviets, but also in the Provincial ones and even in the purely rural District Soviets. Government officials make up close to one-fourth of all members—or even a little more than that—in the Executive Committees of all the different Soviets. “Bureaucratization, with all its accompanying evils, is threatening the autonomy of the Soviets that represent collective life in society – just as we had prophesied!” anxious souls will insist. I am, however, inclined to think that this outcome can be explained on the basis of the relationships presented here earlier, and not by assuming an alleged ‘petrifaction’ of the Bolshevik Party. The Executive Committees cannot do without the co-operation of an experienced and professionally trained administrative staff. In any case, the numerical strength of workers and peasants in the Committees is substantial enough to counter any threat of bureaucratization, and they will be all the more successful in this venture, the faster their own training in this area progresses. Their contact with the productive masses is guaranteed and kept alive in the Soviet system, which will ensure that they themselves do not fall prey to a crippling, deadening bureaucratic mindset.

I was, unfortunately, unable to find among the data available to me any more detailed information regarding the development of the Soviets. Based on occasional publications in daily newspapers about the election results of the Soviets and about the composition of Soviet conferences and Soviet organs, it may be concluded that the development has continued more or less on the same path. Workers and peasants are increasingly participating in the work of the Executive Committees. Participation during elections to the Soviets is growing steadily in cities as well as in the countryside; peasants by and large delegate power to the ‘Independents’, the industrial proletariat is represented as a class ‘in the Communist Party’. The last elections in 1921 to the Soviets of the large municipality of Moscow have demonstrated all this graphically. When the elections were due, memories of last winter’s terrible scarcity and the political ‘crisis’ still haunted the proletariat. The immediate consequences of the ‘new policy’ were felt and threw up questions of far-reaching significance for the working and living conditions of the proletariat. Animated and heated discussions took place at the assemblies in factories and districts. Communist politics as a whole, the economic and social measures taken by the government and the local Soviets, the stance of the party’s wings etc. were subjected to thorough and even scathing criticism. However, overt and covert Mensheviks and other non-Communists were unable to make use of this fire to cook their respective parties' trifling broths. Resolutions moved by them did not even get the number of votes critics had anticipated. Electoral participation was stronger than ever before, and Communists triumphed brilliantly. Under the circumstances there could not have been any question of a *corriger la fortune* by the Bolshevik Soviet leadership. The Bolsheviks were not in a position to influence the will of the masses either with promises or with threats. The results of the elections were a manifestation of the trust that the proletarian masses had invested in the Communist Party and its policies.

The outward development of the Soviets is, however, not a standard of measurement for the quality of life and values within. Nevertheless, it is still possible to conclude from the growing participation of the proletariat and peasant population during Soviet elections that there is an increasing interest among the masses in the formation of collective social life; that they are increasingly making use of what Lenin in his argument against Kautsky formulated as "better opportunities for managing and running the state". And that, indeed, is a sign and an assurance of healthy internal development. Voting and being voted to the Soviets encompass the most active and continual, personal as well as objective relationship between voters and the elected, the former keeping the latter under stringent control. The robust participation during elections indicates the people's will to power and social transformation; it counters stagnation and rigidity in social life in the Soviets. It expands the spheres of mutual influence involving hundreds of thousands, even millions of new participants in this historic action.

The Soviets must prove their worth each day with their actions, and by working towards building a new political and social order like a house that radiates brightness and warmth for all working people. This endeavour can be sustained and intensified only if the Soviets are not merely totally subservient to the will of the masses; they must indeed embody in their deeds and actions the labour and accomplishments of the masses. However imperfect and flawed the work of the Soviets may still be, as it is bound to be, it has nevertheless received a historic mandate crystallized in mass action. Its value has been understood and accepted, and it has come to be a vital force for the existence of Soviet Russia during all these years of the bitterest of struggles. The growing enthusiasm for elections among the working population in Soviet Russia—without the blessings of bourgeois 'democracy'—is in sharp contrast to the rapid spread of electoral fatigue and lack of interest in parliamentary politics in those countries, which have been enjoying the much acclaimed benefits of 'democracy'. This contrast has a clear and historical significance. On the one hand, it is a manifestation of the vital and productive life of the masses liberated by the revolution; on the other hand, it is indicative of the enslavement and crippling of the masses and their activities under the mediatory system of bourgeois society. If anyone wishes to experience this contrast between historical death and historical vitality in flesh and blood examples, then one has only to sit through a session of any one of the parliaments in Western Europe—if it does not happen to be a stage-show of a 'great day' for the politically uninitiated and deficient—and a Soviet conference, where hundreds or even thousands of workers and peasants strive with a commitment bordering on religious fervour to understand and bring about something new, something that hitherto had hardly existed for them.

With his masterfully amplified forensic eloquence Paul Levi casts the gravest aspersions on the Bolshevik Party because of the very presence of 'Independents' in Soviet Russia. How much more outraged and resounding would his rhetoric be if there were to be no more 'Independents' in Soviet Russia! From the heights of his weighty, historical, and objective outlook Paul Levi would have to admit this as proof of the use of methods of force and violence to suppress the stirrings of collective social life, to turn it into an automaton. But then, while pronouncing his judgment on the Bolshevik Party, he plummets from heavenly heights down to the rather mundane earth of subjective feelings. He forgets during the fall that what he preached so urgently to the Bolshevik Party as being superfluous is valid not only for the historic coming of age of the proletarian masses but also for the maturity of the Bolshevik Party: that this growing maturity is life itself, and thought and action – an organic process of development and not a mechanical one.

The reference to Lenin's depiction of the three stages of revolutionaries and their spheres of activities is a schematic representation, a conceptual abstraction to help understand revolutionary life – nothing more. It is not revolutionary life itself and is not meant to be understood as the law concerning revolutionary life either for the Bolshevik Party or for the proletarian masses and their relationship to each other. Lenin is definitely not 'of the same mould' as the fool who thought historical processes could be caught in a schematic representation and distilled by means of clever organisational moves, which could then be kept ready, bottled and corked, for use at every stage and for every purpose in life. The schematic representation is the equivalent of what the party stands for with its presence and influence among the working masses: it is like the sturdy skeleton of a body with moving muscles, a beating heart and tingling nerves, a person who is energy, feelings, intellect, movement and action. It is not supposed to keep the party in 'heroic isolation' by separating it from the mass of workers, whom it must empower and prepare for action. This schematic representation should instead make it easier for the party to connect with the masses. The work and struggle of each day will not tolerate such a sharp separation of the 'vanguard' from the 'advance guard' and the 'masses'; they will break down any entrenched barrier between them. Work and struggle bring about constant change and expansion in the spheres of influence of a revolutionary workers' party. Paul Levi alleges, however, that, like cattle on a barren heath, the Bolsheviks are going round in circles under the spell of Lenin's schematic representation. If that were the case, how could they have become the revolutionary class-based party of the Russian proletariat? How could they have laid the foundation of a new state and a new society? How were they able to defend until now the Soviet Republic against an entire antagonistic world? This herculean task, under which the Bolsheviks are now basking in glory, could not have been the work of the party alone; it would have to be mass action, the action of an entire class.

The Bolshevik party and the Russian proletariat have risen to historic greatness together and with each other's help. They were not separate historical entities that came together to form a whole; their heartfelt unity is an organic formative process rooted in the soil of proletarian class struggle, nurtured by the fiery lifeblood of revolution, drawing power from and kept alive by their daily labour and battles, driven forward towards a higher form of humanity that is communism. The party thus stands not beside or above the proletarian masses of Soviet Russia, but in their midst; its progress is simultaneously the progress of the masses. Its existence has become the life and progress of the class, of the Russian proletariat, without for an instant ceasing to be the most conscious, clear-sighted and bold expression of the will and vitality of the proletariat. It thrives in the warm beat of the hearts and fists of nameless and unknown millions scripting their own emancipation from bondage, and metamorphosing from patiently sighing cross-bearers of capitalism into defiant fighters against it and into robust builders of communism. It is historical action driven and borne by the power of countless millions; even the 'errors' and 'deviations' of revolutionary life are more fruitful for the exploited and downtrodden than the meticulous inaction and procrastination in the name of 'democracy' found in the reformist corners of the world.

Paul Levi sees only terrifying signs of devastation and death in Bolshevik ideology and in the politics of the Communist Party, in the Soviets and in the trade unions of the Soviet Republic. These are, in fact, phantom projections of his changed political convictions; the blazing flame of revolutionary communism within him has gone out; it is dead and gone. His critique of Bolshevik politics—not of any particular errors and weaknesses, but of the fundamental principle and its grand historic trajectory—is tantamount to a rejection of the Russian Revolution. "Men make their own history, but they do not make it as they please; they do not make it under self-selected circumstances, but under circumstances existing already, given and transmitted from the past. The tradition of all dead generations weighs like a nightmare on the brains of the living." Thus begins Marx's *Eighteenth Brumaire*.

The Bolsheviks carry the burden of historical legacies of countless bygone generations. If they could indeed freely write their own history and "under self-selected circumstances", then they would certainly have chosen to "create" the revolution in the manner of a lyrical poem sitting in a garden pavilion, delighting the soul and the senses with the fragrant blooms of democracy, secure in the knowledge that – thanks to an excellent education and to lessons of wisdom – not a single syllable would be out of place to violate "the laws of the art of poetry" laid down by cliquish poetasters and critics. History, however, was never so benevolent as to grant them this freedom. Instead, it let the Bolsheviks "carry the burden of guilt" during the great historic hour and "left them to suffer the pain" of shouldering the responsibility. It gave them only one choice: either to refrain from leading the revolution for which the exploited masses called out to them, or to carry out the revolution "the way they were forced to do" – economically and socially unprepared for communism, braving the conflagrations of proletarian dictatorship, under civil war and terror.

The tragedy of the Bolsheviks is that they have to carry on with the revolution "out of conditions ... they find close at hand". They will be forever glorified for having done it nevertheless. When the masses of revolutionary factory workers, peasants and soldiers wrested total power for the Soviets in October 1917 and handed it over in all good faith to the Bolsheviks, the latter knew only too well what this was all about. Once the revolution had started to flow, its waves would continue to break – even without the Bolsheviks and over their heads, devouring the inactive in its path, only to gather sand and seep into the lowlands of bourgeois reformism and entrenched bourgeois class dominance. Or they themselves would have to take over the leadership of the revolution in order to preserve its proletarian aspirations and intentions, and to drive it forward towards this goal. The decision that they took contained within it the appropriate political tactics; and that too was a product of historical necessity and not taken "out of conditions chosen by them".

(Translated by Romit Roy)

XI

The Significance of the Russian Revolution for the World Proletariat

The repudiation of Bolshevik politics with its great universal approach is a cover for abandoning the proletarian revolution itself / The myth of the 'mechanical' transfer of Bolshevist politics to countries with other historical conditions / The lessons and the example of the Russian Revolution for the world proletariat / The safeguarding of the Russian Revolution through the proclamation of its proletarian character and its approach to the world revolution / Soviet Russia as the first great state, which advocates the abolition of private property and the right of common property / The duty of the international proletariat towards Soviet Russia

The Mensheviks and their West European siblings are in their own way consistent when they view the proletarian revolution, which is being accomplished as a firm, inevitable historical law, as "too early", and a "historical misunderstanding," a "historical mistake" etc. for Russia because of its tactics. They firmly believe that the overthrow should have been a bourgeois one, which would have first created by "democratic" means the preconditions for a slowly and carefully prepared "definitely successful" proletarian revolution. These superior masters of history repudiate that they have renounced the revolution. They are ready to "have" one "when the time is opportune", which only they would be able to feel through its pulse, and when the revolution remains a "pleasant" one that the "right thinking" bourgeoisie need not dread. A revolution which is as unblemished as Walter von der Vogelweide regards Empress Irene: "Rose without a thorn, dove without guile!" With such an understanding they push the proletarian revolution to the never-never land and displace it from the realm of class struggles into that of morality.

Paul Levi did not express in his 'Introduction' that he shares this understanding – only his outlook towards Bolshevik politics leads inevitably to it. This outlook starts with Rosa Luxemburg and ends with Hilferding, Stampfer and Kautsky. The real Foreword of the posthumously published pamphlet was the founding of that caricature of a proletarian mass party which called itself "Kommunistische Arbeitsgemeinschaft", (Communist Working Collective).

Paul Levi's Afterword to it began with a call: "To the revolutionary workers of Germany",* which justifies joining the Independent Social Democrats in this way: "... we have never disputed that the Independent Social Democratic Party remained true to the principles of Marxism in the long years of war as well as after the war." A sentence during which the writer clearly seems to have forgotten the founding of the Spartacus League and the KPD (Communist Party of Germany) by Rosa Luxemburg with his outstanding participation. The Afterword ended with the defection to the Independent Social Democrats. Paul Levi would perhaps deny to the communists that his Marxism and communism have vanished. As a well-read man he would explain to them with help of Victor Hugo: "Me, a renegade! What are you thinking of? Then the whole of nature is a renegade, since it never ceases to evolve." Nobody would want to curb Paul Levi's right to develop backwards. However, he does not have the right to use Rosa Luxemburg – that brilliant and true revolutionary. Looking towards her, he should not talk about his path as "our path."

Rosa Luxemburg would never ever have walked this path with Paul Levi. Her clear historical understanding and revolutionary spirit would have prevented her from joining the ranks of revolutionary philistines and revolutionary Pharisees – those who pray every day in the name of 'socialism': "We thank you God, that we are not like the Bolshevik robbers, murderers and tax collectors; instead by relinquishing the capture of power and socialisation we have kept ourselves worthy and well-suited for the collaboration with Lloyd George and Poincaré, with Morgan and Stinnes." In this historic moment Rosa Luxemburg would indignantly reject the 'Marxist' hawking and spitting "critical distancing from the Bolsheviks" as dissociating oneself from the lone proletarian state which the world revolution has created in its first stormy attempt, in fact, as a desertion from the world proletarian revolutionary camp itself. She would scourge the large number of reformist talks raining down about the Bolshevik attempt at wanting to impose socialism through unsuitable means at an unsuitable time and on an unsuitable object, and that international socialism must stand as the only great hope for the future of the weary and the burdened and should not sully

* *Freiheit,* no. 141, morning edition, Friday, 24 March, 1922. [C.Z.]

itself through solidarity with this attempt, as being a self-deception and deception of the masses.

As if socialism could ever triumph without revolution and the revolution would be possible without violence and hardship, without commotion and confusion, without long agonising searching, groping and collecting of experience by the proletarian masses and their leaders, as if the revolution were possible as a consistently implemented plan and not as a historical becoming, whose classical social completion does not happen at the outset. Are the workers' leaders, in fact, so poor in spirit and knowledge that they would fail to indicate to the salvation seeking masses the historical differences between the received and passed down conditions for the proletarian revolution in Russia and in those countries where the soil is already thoroughly prepared for communism by capitalism? That they would fail to demonstrate the significance of this fact for the proletarian struggle for freedom to the millions, who are crying out in these countries for bread and for their children's right to food and education; those millions who work as human beings but who also want to enjoy the fruits of their labour as human beings? The reformist socialists – whether they brag about their reformism or shamefacedly seek to conceal it – insist on the constraints of the 'historical situation'; they claim for themselves the right to betray along with the revolutionary struggle the revolutionary aim of the proletariat as well. Yet what is right for the clever reformist socialists is clearly not acceptable to the reckless Bolsheviks. Compelled by the 'historical situation' these obdurate outlaws insist on carrying out the revolution in the way "it must be carried out".

Within the historical justification of Bolshevik politics with its general universal approach exists at the same time its limitation. The Russian Revolution has progressed so far and worked out the essential features of the struggle of the classes for socialism and communism so clearly that civil war, dictatorship of the proletariat and the Soviet system are evaluated as historical, international phenomena and forms of the proletarian revolution. However, its implementation would undoubtedly be very varied. It depends on the big complex of diverse and intermingled circumstances, which existing simultaneously in individual countries clash with one other and achieve utmost historical activity when the hammer blow of revolution destroys the obsolete social norms and ties. Finally, it would be determined by the degree of maturity of the capitalist economy for communism and by the balance of power between the conflicting classes.

That is why this hue and cry that the world must be protected from the mechanical transfer of Bolshevist methods is senseless. Its purpose is clear. What one wants to banish is Soviet Russia's spirit of proletarian revolution, which is moving about amidst the proletarians of all countries and is a terrifying spectre for the world bourgeoisie and all those who hate or fear the proletarian revolution, this historic becoming active of the exploited and oppressed masses. With this revolutionary spirit the unfulfilled longing of innumerable generations has risen, generations whose existence was throughout their lives reduced to nothing but a pale, sad shadow of strong and splendid humankind under the enslaving force of property, and who had thus declined into becoming a shadow of their ancestors. With the revolutionary spirit rises the dirge of the countless millions of fellow human beings whom the might of property pushes into the deepest recesses of misery because the owners not only want to extract the customary capitalist toll from the workers, but also the fantastic treasures which are necessary to wipe out the criminal work of destruction of the imperialist war and boost the crumbling national and international economy.

This revolutionary spirit must actively, effectively intervene in history, must 'make' history the way it has done in Russia, embodied in the will of millions of proletarians and poor peasants, a will which finds its conscious, purposeful manifestation as a deed in the party of Bolsheviks and their politics. This revolutionary spirit would also be irresistible and victorious in other countries, when its actions carry the characteristic traits of the Russian Revolution, of Bolshevik politics, i.e. fidelity to the goal, bold decisiveness and sheer dedication. There it would follow the path shown by history, the path it pursued in Russia and which it continues to follow. However valuable all the historical knowledge that the Russian Revolution has brought to the international proletariat, its most valuable gift is the living example, born anew every day in tribulation and misery, at work and struggle. The great example of the prevalence and working of that revolutionary spirit has united the working masses and their class party into an active entity and empowered it for every sacrifice, for the mightiest heroism.

With this spirit, inspired and borne by it, Bolshevik politics has created the Russian Soviet state, defends and maintains it, completes its achievement of rugged excellence against which the forces of the world bourgeoisie are up in arms and which gets vituperated, ridiculed and reviled by dwarves. But does not the ear of the world proletariat also resound with the accusation that the Bolsheviks have betrayed this achievement through a pact with capitalism after they sacrificed the demands of a genuine 'socialist politics' only for the sake of this very achievement? Don't the doubts arise: Why did communism aim for revolution, when the time for its realization was not ripe objectively and subjectively? Why lead the proletariat to the struggle for eradication of capitalism, inspire it with the belief in its liberation through communism, when grim necessity compels the restoration of capitalism in the country, and to tolerate that millions and millions toil for its profit? Would not the "outcome of the revolution, compromise with capitalism" have been possible to achieve without the terrible struggles and sacrifices of these years, on the path of 'democracy', thanks to an amicable collaboration of proletariat and bourgeoisie, in other words: through resumption of coalition politics, through realization of the Menshevik watchwords of a purely bourgeois revolution, which would have brought 'democracy' and social reforms?

Whatever is said on these questions by the successful social democratic pragmatic politicians, by the profound inventors of magical socialist recipes for a painless and splendid revolution, by the democratically and ethically perfumed masters of ceremonies for good, impeccable manners of history does sound so very 'reasonable' and superior. However, it is historically trivial and wrong.

Only by breaking out of the narrow framework of bourgeois revolution the Bolsheviks led the revolution into the wide historical battlefield of struggle for the emancipation of all workers and enslaved people through communism, that they showed the highest goal to the largest masses, not as a comforting hope for the future but as an immediate and practical task of the day demanding toil and sacrifice; only through this has the Russian Revolution let millions of minds, hearts, hands become productive, has attained the historic greatness, the blazing radiance, the fervent glow, the strong, deep breath, in short the characteristic traits of a new, active, higher human life. And only through this could it become the inspirer and admonisher for those disinherited and trampled upon from the banks of Thames to those of the Ganges and Mississippi, from the factories of Barcelona, Turin, North France and the Rhineland to the sites of capitalist exploitation in Tokyo and New York. Does anyone seriously believe that the vast masses of Russian workers and peasants would have suffered and struggled year after year for anything less than the Soviet system— for the social mess of pottage on the democratic platter—happy and proud in the awareness of living and dying for a great goal?

Despite the historically given circumstances not being ripe for communism, the Bolsheviks could, in fact, they had to set it as the goal for the revolution – and not simply because the mass of the Russian proletariat had become mature enough in its intention to enforce communism through struggle. No, it was also because the Bolsheviks as believers in international socialism, as Marxists, were convinced about the approach and development of the proletarian revolution as world revolution. On Russian soil, under the most adverse conditions, it had soared daringly defiant and undeterred on its first flight. Here it had encountered least resistance from hostile forces, here the keenness of human gumption had surpassed the development of objective conditions and wanted to be its creator and master in freedom. Should not the class, which is historically destined for the overthrow of capitalism, be ready for this deed of regenerating social life in the countries of advanced and highly advanced capitalist economic development?

The Bolsheviks answered this question in the affirmative, and they had to learn through their bitter experience – it seems to me the most painful experience of their hard years of struggle – that in the countries of advanced capitalist 'culture', the maturity of the will of the proletariat for communism can slowly and laboriously hobble miles behind the economic ripeness. They thought that they discerned definite signs of revolutionary ripeness in the proletarian classes of all the countries. It was, however, the passionate beating of their own revolutionary heart, the commanding voice of their own resolute will, which seemed to them to resound from outside. Thus the Bolsheviks were wrong in their conjecture that the world revolution would move forward at a much faster pace than has been, in fact, the case since then. This miscalculation alone has been more fruitful and productive—nationally and internationally—than all the warnings that the proletariat should not take a risk because maybe it might not yet win. These warnings are correct and they seem to work out exactly. Nevertheless, historically speaking, they represent a great miscalculation for the exploited since their result is less than naught, ending as they do in the consolidation of the sovereign power of the bourgeoisie. On the other side, the revolutionary zeal and force of the Russian proletariat got newly ignited in the most desperate moments through the Bolshevik 'miscalculation', and the glow of the belief and will out of which it is born blazes gloriously in the soul of millions of the non-Russian proletariat, a vigorous force of revolutionary development.

It is a historical law that a class which rises to freedom and power does not reach its goal in one attempt, that it is pushed back again and again behind this goal, behind the starting point of a far-reaching struggle. If carried out in bourgeois fashion and with bourgeois slogans, as the Mensheviks considered to be the need of the hour, the revolution in Russia would not even have been in a position to quickly and thoroughly raze the position of power of feudal society. When the revolutionary proletarians and soldiers seized power under the leadership of Bolsheviks in Petersburg and Moscow and raised the banner of the Soviet star, 'pure democracy' faced the threat of succumbing to military dictatorship, of getting devoured by the tsarist counter-revolution. Only because the Bolsheviks immediately gave the revolution the titanic magnitude and titanic goal of proletarian revolution could the forces of the masses be unleashed and become historically effective. In a ridiculously short time span they have achieved more for change in the society constructively and destructively than all that the bourgeois revolutions could do in the course of centuries.

As thoroughly as in Russia, where all the ties, all the privileged positions, all the remnants of feudal society have been cleared away in every reach of social life by the proletarian revolution, no bourgeois revolution in any country in West Europe has achieved this. All the nations of bourgeois democracy—not barring the republics overseas—are still stuffed with ancestral lumber from the feudal society. The iron broom of the proletarian revolution has swept Soviet Russia clean of the same and has brought in air and light for development and growth of seeds and saplings of new relationships between human beings. As bearer and executor of proletarian revolution Bolshevik politics deliberately did more than that. It literally built from scratch social forces and social institutions which are the creators and creations of new social existence, creators and creations pulsating with the comradely spirit of supreme unfolding of vigour and fulfilment for all, in fraternal solidarity with everybody.

The mortal enemies of the Bolsheviks must bear witness to their historic work. It has been declared in the "Programme of Right Social Revolutionaries": the legacy of the Bolsheviks must be seen as a reality, every single root of which has so deeply penetrated the ground, that to pull it out would tantamount to propagation of chaos and economic breakdown.* Indeed! If Bolshevik Soviet power were to collapse today, the mark of the years of its rule—of which each day was a day of consuming turbulence of work and struggle—would not go away. These days of work and struggle would not merely glow immortally in history. They would remain indestructibly alive in social institutions and entities, whose characteristics got redefined by the strong fist of the proletarian revolution and in millions of souls, in whom the liberating breath of those days of work and struggle would continue to act. After these years of Bolshevik power and politics never would a Russia emerge which would even faintly resemble the ideal of a backward-looking admirer of the tsarist system, but also not a Russia which would realize the yearnings of the world bourgeoisie, which while claiming to look forward towards the golden treasures of democracy, however, also gazes backwards at the vanishing splendour of boundless, perpetually exploitative and hegemonic power. For Soviet Russia, the state of the working people is still alive and, despite their policy of concessions, the Bolsheviks will be able to put to good use its power to further the goals of the proletarian revolution.

To be sure, the absolute 'purists,' who want to wage the revolutionary struggle only at the 'right time,' and the aesthetes of the proletarian struggle for emancipation lament and say that since 1917 the Bolsheviks are destroying with their own hands the monumental achievement of the proletarian revolution. Would it not have been worthier for the greatness of this achievement and the unswerving resolve and devotion of all those who executed it to thwart the historically hostile forces in a tumultuous battle with the slogan "all or nothing" than by using the clever strategy of beating an orderly retreat? What a magnificent end to a magnificent aspiration! To bury the revolutionary action of the Bolsheviks under the rubble of their

* Cited by Zinoviev at the Eighth All-Russia Congress of Soviets in Moscow in December 1920, in a lecture on "Expansion of the Soviets and Bureaucratism", *Russische Korrespondenz* (*Russian Correspondence*), 1921, issues I and II, p. 34.

achievement would be nice—and easy. Greatly and infinitely more difficult it is to preserve their revolutionary deed, goal and achievement of exhilarating stress and struggle in the mundane, cold, grey routine of a pact with capitalism and a tenacious struggle with it in the ordinariness of tenancy agreement, concessions etc.

The Genoa Conference was the flaming beacon over the globe that this pact hardly means a truce with capitalism, let alone peace. Like in Brest-Litovsk, here too the two waves of historically old and new have collided with each other. The sordid haggling of the international bourgeoisie and their respective governments over sources of petroleum, over the distribution of war booty, died down; the cunning intrigue between English and French imperialism became irrelevant, as with Soviet Russia's delegation the proletarian revolution stepped in front of this international united front for the suppression and plunder of the workers by proclaiming the historical right of common property as opposed to the might of private property. The importance of this great historic moment and Soviet Russia's position, as poor yet unconquered and determined to fight, was thrown into sharp relief by the dead silence of the international proletariat, which was not even bold enough to defend its right to bread in the face of capitalist rapacity and was silent in all languages about its revolutionary birth right to freedom.

The Bolsheviks consider with a cool gaze the gravity of the burden and the responsibility of their pact with capitalism. Teeth tightly clenched, every muscle and nerve tightened in steely determination, they venture to take the burden and responsibility upon themselves. They are forced to do it; history has led them to their Gethsemane and does not let this cup of bitter wine pass them by. As a revolutionary workers' party, as the conscious will and the conscious might of the Russian proletariat, the communists are the only party, which is able to retain and employ Soviet power, the revolutionary instrument of the revolutionary goal, hampered by world capitalism but not vanquished by it. Severe difficulties piled up in front of the Russian working class, in front of its party when it captured power and established its dictatorship. To assert proletarian power and dictatorship in the years since then unheard of sacrifices had to be made and dangers without precedent had to be defied. The most difficult and most dangerous part of the struggle for establishing communism in Soviet Russia demanding maximum sacrifice begins only now, where capitalism has to be fought, shoulder to shoulder, every day, every hour, not merely "in every hammering workshop and every hut harbouring grief", but in the soul of every worker, on whom "the tradition of all dead generations weighs like a nightmare".

The grave historic hour of the Russian Revolution should not find the international proletariat to be an insignificant group any longer. It must finally stand determinedly at the side of Soviet Russia. In moral solidarity – to strengthen and to inspire the forces that the revolution has historically called to life with their most active self-help; in economic solidarity – to promote the establishment and expansion of the Soviet economy oriented toward communism; in political solidarity – to defeat the cravings of the international bourgeoisie and their governments for exploitation and domination. Every concession that capitalism wrests from Soviet Russia must burn in the soul of the international proletariat like one's own defeat, indeed as one's own fault. The Russian proletariat, covered in wounds and exhausted, has till now done its revolutionary duty, and continues to do it heroically and self-denyingly. It is high time for the international proletariat to finally do its duty. Does it really prefer to destroy itself and die historically, and millions of its kind also physically and morally, instead of fighting?

Confronting the situation head on, the revolutionary working class party of Bolsheviks should not let anything get in the way of its ideological and organisational unity. In it the revolutionary class life of the Russian proletariat has consolidated into a historic motive force. The revolutionary working class party of the Bolsheviks must adhere to the general line of its politics. Being bound to history it will lead to the historic goal. Bolshevik politics is the first attempt on the highest world-historical scale to conduct 'Marxist politics', to raise social life and its development from being the play of blind, anarchically operating forces to become the work of science and conscious will. With this attempt on a grand scale the strong voice of the proletarian revolution drowns out the chorus of opponents, the clatter of the arms of the enemies. Demanding struggle now and in future it cries out to the Party the great Florentine poet's lofty words with which Marx has prefaced the first volume of his "Capital": *Segui il tuo corso e lascia dir le genti.* (Follow your own course, and let the people talk!)

(Translated by Namita Khare)

List of Journals and Newspapers

Berliner Lokalanzeiger	*Berlin Local Advertiser*
Berliner Tagesblatt	*The Berlin Daily*
Deutsche Tageszeitung	*The German Daily*
Freiheit	*Freedom*
Freisinnige Zeitung	*Liberal newspaper*
Germania	*Germania*
Iskra	*Spark*
Kreuzzeitung	conservative Christian newspaper
Lokalanzeiger	*Local Advertiser*
Mitteilungsblatt	*Bulletin*
Morgenpost	*Morning Post*
Neue Rheinische Zeitung	*New Rhenish newspaper*
Neue Zeit	*New Times*
Rote Fahne	*Red Flag*
Russische Korrespondenz	*Russian Correspondence*
Tägliche Rundschau	*Daily Review*
Unser Weg	*Our Path*
Volkszeitung	*People's newspaper*
Vorwärts	*Forward*
Vossische Zeitung	*Vossisch newspaper*

Political Parties

KPD	Kommunistische Partei Deutschlands (Communist Party of Germany)
PPS	Partei Polnischer Sozialisten (Polish Socialist Party)
SPD	Sozialdemokratische Partei Detuschlands (Social Democratic Party of Germany)
USPD	Unabhängige Sozialdemokratische Partei Deutschlands (Independent Social Democratic Party of Germany)

35195386R00125

Printed in Great Britain
by Amazon